NEW YORK UNIVERSITY SERIES IN
EDUCATION AND SOCIALIZATION IN AMERICAN HISTORY

THE REVOLUTIONARY COLLEGE
American Presbyterian Higher Education, 1707–1837
Howard Miller

THE CLASSLESS PROFESSION
American Schoolmen of the Nineteenth Century
Paul H. Mattingly

COLLEGIATE WOMEN
Domesticity and Career in Turn-of-the-Century America
Roberta Frankfort

SCHOOLED LAWYERS
A Study in the Clash of Professional Cultures
William R. Johnson

The publication of this work has been aided by a grant
from the Andrew W. Mellon Foundation

A University of Wisconsin Law Student, circa 1900. (*State Historical Society of Wisconsin.*)

SCHOOLED LAWYERS:
A STUDY IN THE CLASH
OF PROFESSIONAL
CULTURES

by

William R. Johnson

New York : NEW YORK UNIVERSITY PRESS : 1978

Library of Congress Cataloging in Publication Data

Johnson, William R   1943-
    Schooled lawyers.

    (New York University series in education and
socialization in American history)
    Includes bibliographical references and index.
    1.   Law—Study and teaching—United States—History.
2.   Law schools—United States—History.   I.   Title.
II.   Series: New York University. New York University series in education and socialization in American
history.
KF272.J6   340'.07'1173   77-82753
ISBN 0-8147-4159-2

Manufactured in the United States of America

For my Parents and
my Grandmother
and to the
Memory of my Grandfather

Contents

Acknowledgments

Over the years that I have been struggling to form this material into a book, I have incurred enormous debts. My most profound obligation, which I am glad to have a public forum to acknowledge, is to my wife Lynn, who has supported me and my work in ways that only she and I can understand. While I hope I can find ways to diminish my debt to her, I know that I can never repay it fully.

Support of a different though no less necessary kind came from the institutional environments in which this study was conceived and refined: the Educational Policy Studies Department at the University of Wisconsin, Madison; and the Division of Education at the University of Maryland Baltimore County. People, of course, created the congenial and stimulating atmosphere in those institutions. At Wisconsin, Jurgen Herbst and Carl Kaestle gave substantial and helpful critiques at important stages of this history; and Merle Borrowman, whose idea this study was, constantly gave me advice and encouragement in the early years of my graduate study that went far beyond any traditional expectations. He has continued to offer important support at crucial junctures in my work. At the University of Maryland Baltimore County, Saied Jacob, Richard Neville, Homer Schamp, Cy Witte and Charles Woolston created an atmosphere of intellectual excitement and conviviality which did much to nurture not only this study, but me as well. At Maryland, too, I am grateful to William G. Rothstein who, even as he often disagreed with my interpretations, continued to educate me both about professions and about writing.

Institutional and personal backing has been crucial in other ways. The University of Wisconsin Law School provided generous financial support during the first two years of research and writing; and the University of Maryland Baltimore County awarded me a summer research grant to continue my research and a small stipend to assist with the expense of typing the final manuscript. Dr. Frank Cook, Director of the University of Wisconsin Memorial Library archives, and Mr. Paul Gratke, Director of the Marquette University archives, were unfailingly helpful in responding to my various requests for assistance. Dean Robert F. Boden of the Marquette University Law School made my research in Milwaukee both pleasant and profitable. I also want to acknowledge the help of my research assistant, Karen Robinson, and to express my appreciation to Mary Lee Baysinger, Connie Englehart, and Cheryl Phillips for typing the various drafts of the manuscript.

A special place in this acknowledgment must be reserved for two people who have offered constructive criticism and encouragement over the longest period. Professor Willard Hurst of the University of Wisconsin Law School always was willing to offer helpful advice even when the manuscript perhaps showed little promise. His critiques have amounted to an informal tutorial in legal history which surely has saved me from errors of fact and interpretation. Finally, while I take full responsibility for what I have written, Paul Mattingly, Professor of Educational History at New York University, contributed more than anyone else to this study. Not only did he offer continual support and encouragement, but he also asked questions that I found difficult and sometimes impossible to answer. In the struggle to confront the questions he posed, the book has benefited immeasurably.

Introduction

This is a study of the development of legal education, the legal profession and higher education in America from the early nineteenth century into the third decade of the twentieth century. In its broadest contours the book traces a familiar story: the decline of the apprenticeship arrangement in the late nineteenth century and the subsequent rise of the law school as the central institutional pathway into the legal profession. While the broad outlines of that development are well known, the factors underlying this important shift remain remarkably obscure. And our understanding of this critical event remains cloudy because most historians have viewed the emergence of the twentieth-century university-sponsored law schools as a logical, almost preordained event. Therefore, researchers so far have focused their energies upon understanding the internal institutional development of important and prestigious individual law schools; and their interpretations have stressed the contributions that such schools and their prominent professors and deans have made to our present-day notions of what constitutes proper legal training. At their worst, such histories are entirely celebratory; at their best, these histories continue to analyze the past largely through the lens of present professional concerns and assumptions.

With that in mind, this study attempts to meet the past on its own terms by analyzing the relationships among the varied set of institutional arrangements that have existed at different times to prepare students for a career in law. In attempting to explain why the university model of legal training eventually emerged from a cluster of training arrangements as the dominant force in American legal education, the book focuses on two closely related themes: the development of the American legal profession and the growth of the American university. This concentration on the concerns of professionals and academics is not merely background to the main story. Instead, changes in the nature and conditions of legal practice combined with shifts in the intellectual outlook of academics to cause fundamental alterations in modes of professional training. The present contours of legal education, this study argues, are not so much the product of systematic and sustained discussion of how best to teach young men and women legal techniques and professional values but instead are the result of piecemeal adjustment to changing academic and professional concerns.

American institutions of higher learning had a more decisive impact than did the legal profession on the eventual configuration of the twentieth-century law school. Academics, concerned with the protection of the liberal arts college and, later, with the elaboration of the ideal of the American university, succeeded, first, in establishing a tradition of college-sponsored professional training and, second, in implanting in the minds of professionals the notion that law must be studied as a science. In the late eighteenth and early nineteenth centuries men had justified the study of law in the colleges because it formed part of a gentleman's liberal education. Beginning in the antebellum period, however, college men gradually established a pattern, eventually to become a tradition, of college-sponsored professional training in the law. These men did so either by attaching existing private law schools to the liberal arts college or by establishing new law schools modeled upon the proprietary schools. Collegiate support of professional training, they believed, might offer a vivid rebuttal to critics who argued that the traditional liberal arts curriculum did not provide a practical kind of education. Additionally, though much more circumspectly, college men suggested that a law school loosely affiliated with the college would align the interests of a powerful professional group on the side of the liberal arts. As a result of this strategy devised by college men to defend the liberal arts from attack and to broaden the base of college support, there emerged in America a tradition of college-sponsored professional training in the law.

As some colleges were transformed into universities in the late nineteenth century, they had a second decisive impact on the eventual form of the twentieth-century law school. For most of the nineteenth century college-sponsored law schools languished on the fringes of the academic community. As colleges became universities, however, they rediscovered their professional schools and made them a more integral part of the institution. Law schools, as a consequence, were expected to conform to the values of the university community. The resulting commitment to objective scientific study and research radically changed the nature of the law faculty and the nature of the curriculum at the most prestigious university law schools. Led by Harvard in the 1870s, career law professors replaced active practitioners on the faculty; and the case method of instruction, in which students learned the techniques of legal reasoning rather than the principles of law, replaced the traditional combination of textbooks, lectures and recitation in the curriculum. Slowly, and at times in the face of opposition from practitioners, the model of legal education promoted by the universities and their law schools came to dominate professional preparation until, by 1930, that model represented the standard against which all other law schools were measured.

The legal profession did not take the initiative in sponsoring or shaping law schools because for most of the nineteenth century the law school, whether proprietary or attached to a college, played no significant role in the process of professional preparation and certification. Students picked up professional knowledge, techniques and values through the apprenticeship experience (which centered upon but was not identical with study in an attorney's office); practitioners maintained professional discipline through the "convivial" life of the judicial circuit. In that context, the nineteenth-century law school was designed only to give students a logically arranged and highly abstract overview of legal principles, knowledge that they already had been exposed to under different circumstances. What to the modern eye appears to be an institution with remarkably indifferent, even irresponsible, academic standards was, in reality, a quite sensibly organized school with limited yet well-defined responsibilities. For most of the nineteenth century, lawyers and law students were content that it should remain that way.

After about 1870, however, the legal profession began to attach greater importance to school-centered legal training. Lawyers did so in response to two important shifts in the nature of professional life. The breakdown of the judicial circuit as a device for maintaining professional solidarity and discipline was one important change. As the more prominent and successful lawyers left the itinerant life of the circuit and established a legal practice in a limited geographic area, the opportunities for professional companionship and therefore the voluntary imposition of group standards began to disappear. As a result, lawyers began to form bar associations in an effort to regulate professional conduct more formally, and they began to establish more stringent admission requirements, both in the statutes and in the law schools, in an effort to regulate entry into the profession.

Second, the nature of legal practice itself began to change after about 1870. Prominent lawyers who had established reputations as courtroom advocates on the judicial circuit began to shift the focus of their legal practice to serve corporate and business interests more exclusively. Because enormous sums of money often were at stake and because the consequences of courtroom defeat therefore became much more serious, lawyers began to cultivate a different set of legal skills. Office counseling, designed to arrange a client's affairs so as to prevent later court challenge, became of greater importance than courtroom advocacy designed to extricate a client from an immediate crisis. This shift from advocacy to counseling led to a greater emphasis upon technical mastery of the law; and, in the long run, it contributed to the importance of law schools where sophisticated technical abilities could be taught more systematically and more efficiently.

Although lawyers after 1870 began to see the need for a more prominent role for law schools in legal education, they did not enthusiastically embrace the highly theoretical, academically selective law school promoted by the universities. Instead, lawyers attempted to adjust to the shifting conditions of professional life by restoring the harmonious relationship between theoretical instruction in the law school and practical instruction in the law office characteristic of early nineteenth-century professional preparation. Out of their efforts emerged an image of the law school as the ideal law office. Practitioners, not career law professors, staffed the faculty, and the curriculum combined both theoretical and practice courses. In essence, the law school, conceived of as an ideal law office, represented an attempt to preserve traditional professional values. Eminent practitioners serving on the law faculty would continue to select those young men judged worthy of becoming lawyers and these same practitioners would gradually introduce their protégés to the knowledge and norms of professional life. As practitioners looked to the past, however, they were unable to anticipate the future, and, as a new set of professional problems emerged in the first three decades of the twentieth century, practitioners abandoned the image of the law school as the ideal law office.

Practitioners gradually accepted the type of academically selective law school promoted by the universities in an attempt both to "cleanse" the bar of immigrant lawyers who, they believed, engaged in unethical practices and in an attempt to control economic competition within the profession. For elite members of the bar located in metropolitan areas the most disturbing development of the early twentieth century was the sudden influx of lawyers of foreign background into the legal profession. Leaders of the metropolitan bar charged that immigrants, poorly trained and without the incalculable moral advantages of birth and nurture in America, viewed law only as a business, not as a noble profession. Openly advertising for business and creating unnecessary litigation, these lawyers threatened to undermine the code of professional ethics and, more important, the fundamental values of American life. In an effort to preserve professional values from what they believed to be the eroding influence of foreigners, then, the leaders of the metropolitan bar became the first group of practitioners to support higher academic standards governing admission to the legal profession.

Country practitioners, however, simply because they numerically dominated state bar associations and hence could better influence state legislatures, had a more decisive influence in the movement toward more stringent academic standards governing admission to the law schools and, ultimately, the legal profession itself. After 1920 lawyers from the smaller towns and cities also began to press for higher bar admission standards not, as the leaders of the metropolitan bar had done, for a combination of economic and ethical reasons but instead for much more narrowly economic reasons. Country practitioners began to believe that their profession had become overcrowded and therefore that access to the profession must be restricted in order to protect lawyers from competition. Higher academic requirements would erect the necessary barrier. By 1930, then, practitioners both in metropolitan areas and in the countryside had struck an alliance with law professors in support of the academically restrictive model of legal education that the university law schools had developed.

Underlying the alliance between practitioners and schoolmen was a profound shift in the conception of the professional lawyer. Two images of the professional competed for supremacy between the years 1870 and 1930. One image, promoted by the older generation of law teachers (themselves usually active practitioners), viewed the lawyer essentially as a conscious maker of law who, in the search for justice, could not be fettered by a mindless search for precedents. Prior judicial decisions, representing the wisdom of the ages, might provide useful guidelines or suggestive examples, but they could not be used to avoid individual moral responsibility for the outcome of the legal process. The second image of the professional, developed initially by the first generation of career law professors, viewed the lawyer essentially as a scientist whose research revealed the legal principles embedded in the record of appealed cases. The scientific lawyer, using the law library as his laboratory, attempted to render justice objective and permanent. The search for permanence and objectivity through science proved elusive, but the assumption that law was a science gradually came to pervade the consciousness of practitioners as well as professors. Although science was often confused with technique, the vision of the legal expert as the professional emerged triumphant between 1900 and 1930; that vision, in turn, led to the assumption that the law was a private profession, the intellectual and economic boundaries of which had to be protected from the encroachments of outsiders. After 1930 the American legal profession viewed law as a technical field of expertise which not only was far too difficult for laymen to master but also was far too complex for them even to understand. That, ultimately, is the overarching theme of this book.

Since this study is intended to be of more than local interest, the heavy reliance upon Wisconsin materials to support the basic arguments should be discussed. The detailed use of evidence from a single state obviously limits the certainty of the generalizations drawn. Although I have made an effort to indicate where the Wisconsin experience differed and where it corresponded to trends in other parts of the country, the arguments set forth in this book clearly will have to be tested against evidence gathered in other states and regions. At present that task would be immensely difficult because the existing secondary literature makes virtually no attempt to explore the relationships among professional development, professional education and the history of American higher education.

Thus, the intensive analysis of a limited body of evidence does have distinct and, at this stage of our knowledge, absolutely essential advantages. One important advantage is that this study can concentrate on the detailed process of historical development in a way that a more broadly based survey simply could not do. The intensive study of the process of historical change, moreover, can focus our attention on the historical questions debated rather than focus exclusively on the answers that emerged from those debates; it can direct our attention to the alternatives set forth as much as on the precise direction in which development eventually proceeded. As this should suggest, the Wisconsin experience must be seen as unique in many of its particulars; equally important, however, that experience cannot be dismissed as idiosyncratic, either in the general problems that confronted men in Wisconsin or in the underlying social, professional and academic conditions that contributed to the formation of those problems. Hopefully, then, this study will serve to frame questions that can guide additional research in profitable directions.

The analysis of the Wisconsin experience provides an even more important benefit: It begins to construct a desperately needed regional perspective in the historiography of the law and of the legal profession now dominated by a focus on the eastern United States. The need for a regional perspective is not merely a matter of providing a broader view of legal history that recognizes the variety and diversity of the American experience. More fundamentally, as I argue in Chapter 7, a regional (and eventually comparative) perspective is the first step necessary in the construction of an interpretive framework for understanding the more general development of American legal institutions. The historical development of the law and of the legal profession obviously proceeded at a different pace in the various sections of the country. The timing of those developments was determined to a large extent by local economic, social and intellectual life. But the historical development of legal institutions and ideas has not been only a product of local conditions and needs. Institutions and ideas have developed also through a process of imitation. (The case method, developed in the eastern university law schools and then adopted by many of the law schools in the Midwest, is perhaps the best example.) Reform by imitation, however, sometimes created situations where local circumstances did not yet support the imported reforms. Because the imported reforms were nurtured by and were the products of a different set of professional values, the opportunity exists in such cases to observe and analyze the clash of professional cultures.

The Wisconsin experience, then, becomes a study of professional cultures in conflict. When the Harvard case method of legal instruction was introduced into Wisconsin in the 1890s, it represented the invasion from the east of an image of the lawyer as primarily an office counselor. The lawyer was viewed as an objective scientist who merely discovered legal rules through the careful analysis of statutory regulations and especially common-law precedent. As a result, the role of the lawyer became one of guiding clients through the existing thicket of legal rules rather than raising substantive questions about the rules themselves. The still dominant professional culture in Wisconsin, however, revered the lawyer as an advocate. Operating more in the courtroom than the office, advocates eschewed legal technicality and were impatient with narrow legal logic. They used their skilled personal and professional judgment to articulate basic social and moral values as they made, not simply discovered, legal rules. Of course, lawyers always had combined the roles of counselor and advocate in their work, but the conception of the professional as a scientific expert threatened to tip the balance entirely toward the image of the lawyer as counselor.

In the early years of the twentieth century many lawyers argued that the emergence of the lawyer as technical legal expert was historically inevitable. They believed that the more complicated economic, political and social relations of twentieth-century life demanded a corresponding technical complexity within the law. This study, however, argues that the two images of the lawyer as advocate and as counselor represent continuing tensions in the law. The rise to prominence of the "scientific" counselor, the technical legal expert, far from being an inevitable response to social and economic complexity, represented the legacy of the link established in the nineteenth century between American law schools and the American university. Better educated lawyers, judges, and law-trained public officials certainly were needed to help identify and articulate values and choices in the twentieth century; the university law schools, with their stress on a value-neutral science of law, however, did not provide lawyers with the knowledge and skills necessary to define and shape broad questions of public policy. Instead universities schooled lawyers in the techniques and methods necessary to manipulate the existing legal system.

SCHOOLED LAWYERS: A STUDY IN THE CLASH OF PROFESSIONAL CULTURES

CHAPTER ONE

The Antebellum College and Professional Studies: A Strategic Alliance

In the years between 1820 and 1860 friends of the American liberal arts college, often men on the administration or faculty with some legal background themselves, were largely responsible for the emergence of college-sponsored law schools. These men attempted to bring law schools into the institutional orbit of the antebellum college in order to create a strategic alliance with a powerful professional group. The support of the legal profession for the college-sponsored law school, they hoped, would strengthen the central college itself by enlarging the number of influential people who would defend and support the liberal arts. Although their aim was to protect the liberal arts college from its attackers, their effect was to establish in America a tradition of college-sponsored legal training.

A Strategic and Uneasy Alliance

College men embraced professional studies gingerly, even reluctantly. What these men suggested was a limited and rather uneasy alliance with certain professions, not a wholesale commitment to professional or technical training. Such a commitment had potential advantages, but it also carried certain risks. And nowhere was that struggle to articulate the place of professional schools in American higher education better revealed than in Wisconsin during the 1850s. In 1857 the

1

chancellor of the University of Wisconsin, John Lathrop, reported to the legislature on the advantages of a university-sponsored law school and in so doing he indicated how tentative must be the alliance between the liberal arts and professional studies.

Lathrop began his report by asserting that "it is undoubtedly true that the main design of the University land grant was: to provide for the youth of Wisconsin an institution of general liberal education." Professional education, he admitted, "obviously stands on different ground. It may be considered more distinctly in the light of an individual investment, and, like other investments, may be safely left, in an intelligent community, to individual enterprise,—the precise expected return being, in all cases, personal wealth and distinction." Because professional schools could be expected to benefit mainly the individual rather than society, "care should be exercised, [so] that the burden of their support should not be so far assumed by the [state] treasury as to prevent the full development of the *main design* of the University, as a school of general scientific and philosophical education for the youth of Wisconsin."

Having assured the legislators (and quite possibly the Board of Regents and himself) of his commitment to liberal education, Lathrop went on to argue that nevertheless "it is . . . for the mutual advantage of all, that the professional schools should be gathered around the school of general liberal education. This combination presents the distinct idea of an American University—more hopeful, doubtless, than any of the various original forms of the University of the old world." Such an arrangement would have a salutary effect on the professional schools because the "presence of the central school, of general intellectual culture, tends to liberalize the professions, by saving them from the narrow and bigoted views naturally generated in isolated and specific technical schools, and by inducing a more catholic appreciation of other portions of the social economy." [1] Equally important, professional schools sponsored by a university would further the goals of the liberal arts college in two important ways.

Here, however, Lathrop became much more circumspect. He first suggested that "the presence of the professional schools does not debase pure science, but exalts it by the constant suggestion of its beneficient social uses." Without elaborating on that theme, Lathrop went on to suggest that by sponsoring professional schools "a more potent influence and a better assurance of success is thus secured to the parent school, than can be derived from any other quarter." [2] Stated more bluntly—which Lathrop never did—his argument for the inclusion of professional schools in a state university was as follows: First, the presence of professional schools could be used to defend the university against the charge that it did not offer practical training (in Lathrop's vague phrase, the professional schools would suggest the "beneficient social uses" of "pure science"). Second, the existence of professional schools in the university community would align the interests of powerful groups, like lawyers and doctors, on the side of the school as a whole.

It is not hard to see why Lathrop so carefully crafted his statement in support of professional education. Addressing a legislature that had been attacking the University of Wisconsin for its elitism and for its impractical curriculum (the charges were closely related because many legislators believed that a classical course of study was a luxury that only the elite could afford), Lathrop linked his defense of the liberal arts with an attack on the professions and their "narrow and bigoted views." That strategy was nicely designed to conceal the underlying purpose of Lathrop's position, which was to suggest that the University strike a strategic alliance with the professions. Yet Lathrop's statement was not simply, and perhaps not even consciously, that of a political strategist. It also revealed a genuine ambivalence toward the presence of professional schools within the university. After emphasizing that the liberal arts must remain the central mission of a university, Lathrop indicated that the learned professions of law and medicine posed the least threat to that commitment. "Whether we desire it or not," he remarked somewhat defensively, "it is still true that a more liberal style of general culture is demanded in these professions than in the others." [3] And legal training, even more than medical training, might be granted a place in the university because of its historic association with the liberal arts. The problem that confronted Lathrop, however, was that nowhere in America in the 1850s did existing law schools (there were in 1850 fifteen college-sponsored schools and perhaps an equal number of private schools) provide a congenial environment for the study of law as a part of a liberal education. Although proposals for such a conception of legal study had been common in the years between 1775 and 1820, the actual development of law schools themselves, even those connected to colleges, had been along narrow technical lines. Thus Lathrop proposed his strategic alliance tentatively because he was treading on unfamiliar and shifting ground.

Liberal and Technical Training in the Law

In America legal training in the colleges was proposed initially to provide liberally educated men with a necessary knowledge of the law for their roles as citizens, not as a means of professional preparation.

This conception of law as a proper part of liberal education persisted well into the nineteenth century and, indeed, it provided a powerful rhetorical justification for forming college-sponsored law schools. In practice, however, the college law schools that achieved success—measured simply by the fact that they kept their doors open—did so by lowering their aspirations and adjusting their curriculum to the pattern set by the economically self-sufficient private law schools, like that established by Tapping Reeve in Litchfield, Connecticut, in 1784. Even those college law schools with the highest aspirations, like Harvard or Virginia, had accommodated their goals to the private school model by the 1830s; it was that fact which made it so difficult by the 1850s to perceive a close connection between the liberal and technical in legal training.

The first attempts to provide for legal study in American institutions of higher learning were the chairs of law and law professorships proposed in the colonial and early national colleges. All of these proposals had as their main intent to give liberally educated men knowledge of the law. With the exception of the professorship proposed by Thomas Jefferson at William and Mary in 1779, these chairs of law at Yale (1777), Philadelphia (1790), Columbia (1794), Transylvania (1799), Harvard (1815) and Maryland (1816) were modeled to a large extent on an English innovation: the series of lectures on the English common law begun by Sir William Blackstone at Oxford in 1753. Blackstone's lectures were the first delivered on the English common law in any university. Prior to that time the English universities of Oxford and Cambridge, themselves modeled after the medieval universities of continental Europe, had cultivated only the Roman and canon law. The English common law, "unsystematized and couched in a barbarian tongue, was outside the range of subjects comprised in the medieval conception of learning." Consequently, the preparation of the "common law" lawyer developed outside the English universities in the famous Inns of Court and, to a lesser extent, in the Inns of Chancery. The Inns of Court served to formalize apprenticeship training in England but, of greater importance for the course of American legal history, the Inns also institutionalized the separation of technical legal instruction from the university community.[4]

It is clear that Blackstone's lectures were not an attempt to alter the pattern of English legal education but instead an effort to broaden the English university curriculum. Blackstone justified this novel expansion of the curriculum in two ways. First, he argued, the study of law was a desirable part of a liberal education. "I think it an undeniable position," Blackstone wrote, "that a competent knowledge of the laws of that society in which we live is the proper accomplishment of every gentleman and scholar; a highly useful, I had almost said essential, part of liberal and polite education." Second, Blackstone argued that the cultivation of the common law in the English universities would improve the content and the administration of English law. Professors of law in the universities would assist practitioners by suggesting improvements to be made in the law and they would also, through their lectures to students, "lay the previous foundations" for the more thorough study of law in the Inns of Court. Since, at the time Blackstone wrote in the middle of the eighteenth century, the Inns had become notably moribund, the university law professorship, far from offering competition to the Inns, would help revitalize those institutions.[5]

Blackstone's justification for university-sponsored legal study on both cultural and professional grounds was adopted in various proportions by those who put forth proposals for American law professorships, though most of the Americans followed the example of Yale President Ezra Stiles who placed major stress on the cultural value of legal study. In a plan for a professorship of law at Yale drafted in 1777 Stiles wrote:

> The Professorship of Law is equally important with that of medicine; not indeed towards educating Lawyers or Barristers, but for forming Civilians. Fewer than a quarter perhaps of the young gentlemen educated at College, enter into either of the learned professions of Divinity, Law or Physic. The greater part of them after finishing the academic course return home, mix in with the body of the public, and enter upon *Commerce* or the *Cultivation of their Estates* . . . . Most certainly it is worthy of great attention the Discipline and Education of these in that knowledge which qualify them to become useful members of Society, as Selectmen, Justices of Peace, Members of the Legislature, Judges of Courts, & Delegates in Congress.[6]

Although Stiles' plan was not implemented, it was followed by the establishment of chairs of law at the College of Philadelphia in 1790 and at Columbia University in 1794. At the College of Philadelphia, James Wilson proposed to "furnish a rational and useful entertainment to gentlemen of all professions, and in particular to assist in forming the legislator, the magistrate, and the 'lawyer.' " Similarly, James Kent's lectures at Columbia were "not designed primarily for professional students."[7] Kent, in the Preface to his *Commentaries on American Law* (an outgrowth of his original Columbia lectures), stated that "the knowledge that is intended to be communicated in these volumes is believed to be, in most cases of general application, and is of that elementary kind, which is not only essential to every person who pursues the science of law as a practical profession, but is deemed useful and ornamental to gentlemen in every pursuit, and especially to those who are to assume places of public trust, and to take a share in the business and councils of our country." [8]

Thomas Jefferson, who was instrumental in the reorganization of William and Mary College in 1779, looked more to the example of the European universities than to Oxford and Blackstone's lectures when he established a Professorship of Law and Police. In Europe, unlike England, there had long existed a close association between legal education and the universities. The rise of the medieval universities had coincided with the introduction of a settled system of law on the European continent. The universities thus became the "medium through which the Civil Law and the Canon Law were diffused throughout the medieval world; and the Civilians and Canonists, who had graduated at the universities of medieval Europe, became the practitioners before its courts both civil and ecclesiastical." [9] Jefferson did alter the European model of higher education in some important respects. He proposed to drop entirely the theological faculty, keep the faculties of law and medicine, and spread the philosophical faculty over four disciplines, thereby creating a university composed of six units. Unlike the college men in the northern states, who gathered loosely attached professional chairs around a central liberal arts college, Jefferson argued that the various faculties should be coordinate and equal. Had Jefferson's plan been followed by American colleges in the nineteenth century, the study of law would have been brought more firmly into the undergraduate curriculum. [10] In fact, his plan did not have great influence, except for a brief period at William and Mary and later at the University of Virginia. And despite the fact that Jefferson looked to Europe rather than to England for his Professorship of Law and Police, that professorship, like the northern chairs of law, was not intended to serve a narrow professional purpose; and, indeed, the course of study owed more to the Blackstone model than Jefferson had intended. Jefferson's own antipathy to Blackstone [11] was not held by the first occupant of the professorship, Chancellor George Wythe, who lectured from 1779 to 1791 at William and Mary, apparently using Blackstone's lectures as the basis for his course. Wythe's lectures were supplemented by moot courts and moot legislatures and, as both the title of the professorship and the presence of moot legislatures suggest, the purpose of the course was to train public leaders, legislators, and magistrates as much as it was to train professional advocates. [12]

Other chairs of law were established in the waning years of the eighteenth century and in the first decades of the nineteenth. In 1799

Transylvania University appointed George Nicholas, a graduate of William and Mary, as Professor of Law and Politics. Isaac Parker was appointed to the Royall Chair of Law at Harvard in 1815 and in his initial lecture promised to deliver a series of lectures that would "best lead the minds of the students to such inquiries and researches as will qualify them to become useful and distinguished supporters of our free systems of government, as well as able and honorable advocates of the rights of citizens." [13] Finally, David Hoffman was appointed professor of law at the University of Maryland in 1812, although he did not deliver his first lecture until 1823. [14] Though differing in the details of the courses proposed and in the specific historical traditions drawn upon, all of these early law professorships were designed primarily to contribute to the education of public leaders. They were viewed as a way to broaden a liberal education, not as restrictive courses of study for future lawyers.

The timing of the proposals for chairs of law also indicates that liberal training constituted their essential purpose. That these professorships were proposed when they were, between 1777 and 1815, reflected a post-Revolutionary consciousness among America's leaders that the United States was engaged in a great, though risky, experiment in government, an experiment that demanded new educational forms through which to educate a rising generation of talent, public spirit and, of course, correct views. The law professorships were only one of many institutional arrangements proposed to assure a future generation of public leaders. During this same period Noah Webster attempted to create a national uniformity through the codification of the English language; Webster and Benjamin Rush were among those who proposed state-supported systems of education in order to, in Rush's words, "convert men into republican machines"; and George Washington, among others, argued for the establishment of a national university in order to make citizens "more homogeneous" and to educate youth "in the science of government." [15] All of these ambitious proposals failed, much like the law professorships themselves (at least in their original form) would fail. The most lasting effect that this concern with training public leaders had in higher education was the expansion of the college curriculum to include offerings in political science, political economy, international law and constitutional law, subjects that most of the law professorships had also included in their purview. [16]

Although the stability and improvement of the American polity was the primary concern of men who took the lead in establishing the early professorships of law, those who served in those posts saw two additional purposes to their labors. They, echoing Blackstone's argument, hoped to improve the content and the administration of law and to lay a better foundation for technical instruction in law. They succeeded in both respects, though not always in the manner originally intended. The textbooks and treatises that flowed from the pens of law professors did a good deal to put the study and administration of law on a scientific basis. That is, these treatises (sometimes in more than adequate detail) classified and arranged legal doctrines in a coherent order. St. George Tucker, successor to Wythe at William and Mary, edited Blackstone's *Commentaries* with notes adapting it to American usage. Tucker's edition of Blackstone, published in 1803, was used extensively by both the office apprentice and the self-trained lawyer. James Wilson's lectures, though not as useful to the beginning law student, were first published in 1804. In Maryland, David Hoffman published his lectures under the title, "Course of Legal Study," in 1817. And the first edition of James Kent's *Commentaries,* a project begun in his years at Columbia, appeared in four successive volumes between 1826 and 1830.[17] Ironically, these textbooks and treatises, especially the American editions of Blackstone, strengthened the apprenticeship system of legal training by setting out in convenient and reliable form a systematic course of legal study. According to Brainerd Currie, "the impression was widespread that the law was contained not only in books but in one book in particular [that is, Blackstone], and that self-education for the bar on the basis of that book was perfectly feasible." [18]

The efforts of the early law professors probably did improve the study of law in the early nineteenth century, but that study was not often carried out within the American college or, when it was, not in the form expected. Almost all the attempts to establish chairs of law floundered, and most eventually failed entirely. The Yale chair of law was never filled. James Wilson, who began his lectures in Philadelphia in 1790, abandoned his efforts before the end of 1792 because of low attendance. James Kent lectured to more than forty students in 1794 but in his second year reported that he "read thirty-one lectures in my office and had only two students besides my clerk." Kent resigned his post in 1798.[19] David Hoffman at Maryland lectured only intermittently and resigned in 1832. At Harvard Isaac Parker was forced to resign in 1828, and was replaced by Joseph Story who turned the law school in a more career-oriented direction. Only the William and Mary professorship, under Wythe and then St. George Tucker, experienced steady success, but that appears to have been because it quickly came to serve a more narrow professional purpose than Jefferson had envisioned. Other law schools later in the century would follow a similar course in order to secure students.

These early proposals for professorships of law failed because they did not meet the career demands of law students for technical instruction in the law. Neither the argument for legal study as a proper part of a liberal education nor as a means to improve the administration of justice seized the imaginations of students. Students simply did not find attractive an abstract appeal to political virtue as a reason to attend a series of lectures on the law. Similarly, the idea that law in the university would be treated as a science proved unattractive to students because the very extent of treatise output in the first half of the nineteenth century appeared to make the "scientific" study of law the task of a lifetime.

Science in the eighteenth and early nineteenth centuries meant basically the orderly arrangement and the logical classification of a body of knowledge. Law professors fully shared that assumption as evidenced by their attempt to inventory legal principles exhaustively. But the attempt to be exhaustive often turned out to be merely exhausting. After David Hoffman, for example, had been appointed professor of law at the University of Maryland he promptly began to organize a curriculum. He did so with such enthusiasm that, when in 1817 he published his "Course of Legal Study," Justice Joseph Story estimated that the full course would take seven years to complete.[20] Story himself did much to impress upon the students and the general public that the study of law was "a laborious undertaking." In his address upon his inauguration as Dane Professor of Law in the Harvard Law School in 1829 Story dwelled at length on the difficulties of treating law as a science. "I know not," he remarked, "if among human sciences there is any one which requires such various qualifications and extensive attainments, as the law." After listing in considerable detail the extent of knowledge required of the lawyer, Story concluded:

> In truth, the Common Law, as a science, must be for ever in progress; and no limits can be assigned to its principles or improvements. In this respect it resembles the natural sciences, where new discoveries continually lead the way to new, and sometimes astonishing results. To say, therefore, that the Common Law is never learned, is almost to utter a truism. It is not more than a declaration, that the human mind cannot compass all human transactions.[21]

While Story's statement certainly provided an abstract justification for the inclusion of legal study in the academic community, as a practical approach his reasoning proved unsatisfactory in two major ways. First, the depth in which law must be studied to satisfy the "scientific" requirements set down by Story and others appeared to preclude the study of law as a part of a liberal education. To essay the study of law in at most a year of lectures was to court superficiality. Thus, Story's rea-

soning served to undercut the primary motive of those who first proposed professorships of law in American colleges. At the same time,
Story did not substitute a practical rationale for more explicit professional training in the college because, by conceiving of legal study in
such broad terms, the scientific study of law became unrealistic for even
those students wholly committed to a career in the law. The prolific
Story perhaps came closest to satisfying his own demands for a broad
and extensive treatment of the law in the treatises he published while at
Harvard Law School, but it is clear that students themselves did not
approach that ideal. To encompass "all human transactions" was hardly
the aspiration of the nineteenth-century student as he began the study
of law. The Harvard Law School flourished during the Story years only
because, after a disastrous decade in the 1820s, the school was reorganized along more practical lines. The prestige and influence of the
Harvard Law School during the 1830s and 1840s derived from the activities of its faculty, particularly Story, and from the social and political
connections of its graduates. However, in other ways the school was
virtually indistinguishable from the many private law schools in the
country, institutions that thereafter would set the pattern for
nineteenth-century law schools.

The most famous of those private schools was that organized by Tapping Reeve in Litchfield, Connecticut, in 1784. Reeve, like many other
lawyers, originally gave instruction in his law office to a small number
of students, then moved his place of instruction to a larger building as
the number of students increased. He retained many of the characteristic features of office instruction "with the students copying precedents
of pleading and conveyance, and reading such books as were at
hand." [22] Although his school was in many respects only an expanded
law office, Reeve proved to be a conscientious teacher and the distinguishing characteristic of his school came to be "its systematic courses
of lectures, delivered daily." [23] Unlike the professors of law in the colleges, Reeve made no pretense of lecturing for the benefit of those who
merely wanted an acquaintance with general legal principles. His
school was devoted exclusively to the preparation of practicing attorneys and the regular lectures and quizzes created a singleness of purpose among students that made the Litchfield School, until it closed in
1833, the leading private law school in the country.[24]

The Litchfield Law School was only the most famous and the most
successful of many private law schools that flourished in roughly the
same period. Contemporary with the Litchfield School were three other
schools in Connecticut, at least three in Massachusetts, three in Virginia, and one each in New York, Pennsylvania, Maryland and North

Carolina. In the third decade of the nineteenth century, private law schools were established in some of the western states. Both Iowa and Ohio, for example, had at least one private law school in operation after 1833, and there is evidence that organization of a private law school was contemplated in Wisconsin in the late 1850s.[25]

These private law schools, which awarded no degrees and existed entirely on the income from student fees, provided the basic model which the successful college-sponsored law schools would follow. Originally conceived as a means to broaden liberal education and to set the study and administration of law on a more scientific basis, the college-sponsored law schools were compelled by pressures from students to offer an intensely practical course of study. The University of Virginia Law School, for example, was organized in 1826 with the intention of treating law as part of the study of government. Yet those expectations were quickly dashed. By 1830 John Tayloe Lomax complained that

The day has gone by when any person was ashamed to appear at the bar under a period of less than three years study. The necessities of some, and the impatience of others, urge most students into their profession after a year's study, or at most two years. They are eager that the period shall be devoted to such instruction as shall practically fit them for their profession. Their demand for the law is as for a trade—the means, the most expeditious and convenient, for their future livelihood. I found myself irresistibly compelled to labor for the satisfaction of this demand, or that the University would have no students of law.[26]

While the University of Virginia followed in the pattern of Harvard by gradually becoming, under the pressures of the demands of law students, a narrow practical school, other colleges simply appropriated existing private law schools. The foundations of the Yale Law School were established in 1824 when David Daggett, a lecturer in a private law school, itself an offshoot of the New Haven law firm of Staples and Hitchcock, was appointed to a chair of law at Yale. Daggett lectured to the seniors at Yale, treating law as part of a liberal education. But he also continued to teach in his private law school to those who wished a more vocational course of instruction. Then in 1826 the Yale catalog formally announced the organization of the Yale Law School by listing the students in Daggett's private school in the College catalog.[27] In effect, Daggett's private school was simply taken under the wing of Yale College, a procedure that many other colleges would follow.

By 1848, then, when the University of Wisconsin was established, a college-sponsored law school was no longer an uncommon phenomenon. In that year fifteen such institutions already existed, including the Harvard, Yale, University of Virginia and Indiana law schools. Thus, it is not surprising that the Wisconsin Charter of 1848 stipulated that the University should consist of four departments: the department of science, literature and the arts, the department of the theory and science of elementary instruction, the department of medicine and the department of law. The direct precedent that was followed to establish the Wisconsin Law Department was probably the proposal for a law school contained in the 1847 Charter of the University of Michigan. Textual similarities suggest that men in Wisconsin simply copied portions of the Michigan Charter when they drafted the University of Wisconsin Charter.[28] But while there were ample precedents for a law school attached to a university, it remained unclear that there was anything that distinguished such a school from the numerous private schools scattered around the country. Although the question of the distinctiveness of the University law school would concern the school's first chancellor, John Lathrop, as it would concern later University presidents, that did not appear to be a problem for the legislators who drafted the University Charter nor for the Regents of the University who approved a plan in 1857 to open a University Law Department. Both groups expected that the Wisconsin Law Department would resemble what the private law schools always had been and what the university-sponsored law schools rapidly became.

The plans for the 1857 Wisconsin Law Department,[29] for example, established no entrance requirements for the school beyond those implicit in the graduation requirements: Candidates for the degree had to be twenty-one years of age and of good moral character. The absence of entrance requirements, however, was not unusual. Harvard, which was typical, required no entrance examination in 1848 and, indeed, stated in its announcement that students could enter in the middle or any other part of the term.[30] Once enrolled, the Wisconsin Regents assumed, the student would present himself for the degree examination after three semesters of study or, if he could present evidence of two years of "private pupilage" (an ambiguous term that may have included solitary reading in its meaning), the examination could be taken after two semesters of attendance. This, too, was typical of schools like Harvard and Yale, and it diverged from the private school model only in the respect that private schools awarded no degrees. Of course, the LL.B. would be awarded only after the candidate had passed a "diligent" examination before four prominent members of the bar appointed by the Regents. That examination, if the experience of other law schools was followed, would be on a course of study that was "almost unrelievedly technical or professional." According to A. Z. Reed, the curriculum in all law schools by the mid-nineteenth century professed to do "little more than cover, more effectively, part or all of the ground traversed by office students in preparation for practice." [31] The uncertain position of legal studies in the university also was reflected in the degree of financial support that most law schools received from their parent school. At Wisconsin in 1857 the Regents appropriated only a token five hundred dollars to the school while also promising to provide "suitable rooms" and the "means for the gradual accumulation of a law library." They clearly stipulated, however, that the professors' salaries were to come from tuition fees "without recourse to the Treasury of the University." This kind of relationship, common to most law schools, had been adumbrated in the University Charter of 1848. That document permitted the University to charge tuition fees of twenty dollars to students in the department of science, literature and the arts and in the department of elementary instruction, but "as soon as the income of the university fund shall permit, tuition in those departments shall be without charge to all students . . . who are residents of the state." [32] No such explicit limits were set on tuition charges in either the law or medical departments because the legislators assumed that the two professional schools would charge tuition rates sufficient to remain self-supporting. The Legislature in 1848, then, like the University Board of Regents in 1857, clearly viewed professional schools as hovering on the periphery of the university.

Collegiate "Friends" and the Defense of the Liberal Arts

Given the uncertain position of legal study in the academic community in mid-nineteenth-century America, it is understandable that when Chancellor John Lathrop suggested in 1857 a strategic alliance between the professions and the University, he did so cautiously and tentatively. Lathrop, together with his closest colleague on the University faculty, Daniel Read (who would first support and then later carry on Lathrop's fight to establish a University Department of Law), knew full well the course along which American university law schools had developed in the preceding three decades. In spite of that, they suggested an alliance with the professions, perhaps out of hope but more likely out of desperation. Their hope stemmed from their own background which made them familiar with legal study in both its liberal and technical dimensions; their desperation stemmed from their efforts to find a way to protect the university from attacks by critics who charged that its course of study was impractical and aristocratic.

Both John Lathrop and Daniel Read had considered law as a career before winding up in the ranks of college teachers and administrators. Lathrop, born in Sherburne, New York, in 1799, attended grammar school and then Hamilton College for two years before entering Yale College as a junior. After graduation from Yale in 1819, Lathrop taught in a grammar school and an academy, then returned to Yale in 1822 where for the next five years he was a tutor. In 1823, while continuing his duties as a tutor, Lathrop entered a private law school in New Haven run by Seth P. Staples. This private school, soon to be taken over by David Daggett, was gradually absorbed over the course of the next four years by Yale College. Lathrop was admitted to the Connecticut bar (the year is uncertain) and, after leaving Yale in 1827, one year before publication of the *Yale Report*, that classic defense of the classical course of study, he opened a law office in Middletown, Connecticut. Within the year, however, he accepted a position as principal at the Gardiner Lyceum in Gardiner, Maine. At this time Lathrop may still have intended to pursue law as his primary profession. It was not uncommon for young men, after their initial preparation for the bar, to take a teaching position for a few years while they attempted to build a professional reputation. If this was Lathrop's intention, his career did not take the expected course because by 1829 he seemed firmly committed to a life as a college teacher. In that year he returned to Hamilton College, where he had spent his first two undergraduate years, as professor of mathematics and natural philosophy. In 1835 he was promoted to the Maynard Professorship of Law, Civil Polity, and Political Economy; in 1845 he was awarded an honorary Doctorate of Law by Hamilton College. Lathrop's appointment to the presidency of the University of Missouri in 1840 signalled the beginning of still another career, this time as a kind of professional college builder. After supervising the development of the University of Missouri during its first eight years of existence, Lathrop was appointed chancellor at the newly established University of Wisconsin in 1848. He left Wisconsin in 1859 to take a position as president of the University of Indiana. After only one year at Indiana he returned to Columbia, Missouri where he became professor of English literature and then in 1865 assumed the presidency of the University of Missouri for the second time. Lathrop died in 1866.[33]

Daniel Read, who was Lathrop's closest (and sometimes only) ally on the Wisconsin faculty in the 1850s and who engineered attempts in the early 1860s to open the Wisconsin Law Department, had a similar background. Born in 1805 on a farm in Ohio, Read entered Ohio University at the age of fifteen and graduated in four years with First Honors. After graduation Read began the study of law, not at a law school as

Lathrop had done, but in the office of an attorney. After only a few months of legal study he became preceptor of the preparatory school of Ohio University. But he continued to read law even while teaching, not an uncommon practice, and eventually was admitted to the Ohio bar. Read, again like Lathrop, never practiced law extensively. His career as a teacher apparently went well, and he quickly gravitated into a college career, serving first as a professor at Ohio University, then successively at the Universities of Indiana, Wisconsin and Missouri. At the latter institution he was appointed president, and in the estimation of one historian, Read's tenure at Missouri "marked a new era in the development of the institution; the old-fashioned liberal arts college with a preparatory department gave way to a real university with professional divisions." Among those professional divisions was the University of Missouri Law School, the kind of institution that Read, like Lathrop before him, would fail to establish at the University of Wisconsin.[34]

John Lathrop's efforts to form a law department at Wisconsin in 1857 and two similar proposals by Daniel Read in 1863 and 1866 were clearly attempts to protect the University, and especially the school of liberal arts, from its critics who claimed the institution was impractical, aristocratic, and godless. The men who guided the University of Wisconsin during its first decade were not necessarily opposed to supporting scientific or practical studies. Indeed, the Board of Regents often appeared more open to such new areas of the curriculum than did Chancellor Lathrop and members of the faculty. Yet even the Regents agreed that the development of the liberal arts college should be given priority over more technical schools. The first Board of Regents argued that the classical course may be expected "to prepare liberally educated young men to become good and useful citizens of the republic," an entirely traditional view. The Board recognized that the classical course traditionally had been taken by sons of the upper class, but they hoped that at Wisconsin the sons of farmers, shopkeepers and tradesmen would also attend the school of liberal arts. The sons of the middle class would be drawn to the University by its low tuition and by its practical offerings in civil engineering, practical surveying "and other field operations."[35] Once at the University, however, these young men would be irresistibly drawn by the lures of the liberal arts and they, too, would become good citizens of the republic. Using practical pursuits as a lure, then, the Regents hoped that the University would recognize and reward talent from all levels of society and also create ties of social and intellectual affection that would bind that society together. Moreover, the beneficial social effects of this policy would be carried to all parts of the state by means of the normal department. Through its teacher training activities the University would become "the nursery of the educators of the popular mind . . . . It is by making our University the *school of the school-master* that a corps of competent instructors is to be best provided, and that all the educational agencies of the State, from the highest to the lowest, may be made tributary to the great end of training up the mind of Wisconsin to intelligence and virtue." [36]

Although few men would have quarreled with these sentiments, the chief barrier to their implementation was money. The founders of the University of Wisconsin had assumed that direct state aid to the school would be unnecessary, believing that sufficient money to meet operating expenses and to provide for expansion of the educational program would be generated by the sale of the land granted to the state by the federal government for the support of higher education. But, except for a brief period during the middle 1850s, the proceeds from the land fund proved disappointing.[37] Lathrop and the Regents therefore concentrated on the development of what they believed to be the central mission of the University: the college of liberal arts. Thus when critics of the University claimed that the school was not providing a practical, vocation-oriented education for the sons of Wisconsin citizens, a criticism that became vociferous by the mid-1850s, they could make a good case. The school did not provide courses in agriculture, geology and the like so that the sons of tradesmen, businessmen and farmers would find the school of immediate practical use.

In addition to those who criticized the University for its impractical course of study, some critics condemned the school for its secular nature. The 1848 Wisconsin Constitution had provided, and the University Charter had affirmed, that the State University was to be free of any sectarian bias. Yet the close link between religion and morality that existed at the time led many to insist that a nonsectarian school whose purpose was to build character and instill principles of morality was a contradiction in terms. While they accepted the Regents' basic premise that the function of the University was to build character, they charged that the University was a godless institution and therefore could serve no useful moral or social function. This line of attack was especially threatening since supporters of the various denominational colleges in the state brought these charges into the state legislature in the middle of the 1850s. In 1855 petitions were circulated among state legislators asking that the University Charter be repealed and that the money from the University fund be distributed among the private colleges. In the following year a bill to that effect was introduced in the state legislature.[38]

Although the bill for the repeal of the University Charter was soundly defeated, the Regents were obviously responding to that threat when they created a number of new University departments in the years 1855 to 1857. A law department, a medical department, a department of civil and military engineering, and a department of physics and astronomy were established on paper, while proposals for an agriculture department and a commercial department were put forth but not enacted. The arguments in behalf of the medical department were the most explicit in indicating the political motivations of the Board of Regents. The Regent Select Committee on the Organization of the Medical Department urged its speedy opening not only on the grounds that young men in the state would be provided with a sound medical education but also because a medical department sponsored by the University would

> Do more to satisfy those complaints of the public which acting through our legislature are crippling our efforts, and rendering uncertain our progress, than any other investment of the same amount. Throw open your medical department to students free of cost, and it will fill not only your rooms but your city to such an extent that your legislature will have constantly before its face a full and satisfactory answer to the Stereotyped but troublesome question, "What is the University doing with the large means in its hands." [39]

The Regents were not so frank in discussing their motives in proposing the establishment of the University Law Department in 1857, but there can be little doubt that they acted for essentially the same reasons: to give clear evidence of the University's interest in practical, vocation-oriented training and, in the words of John Lathrop, to secure to the parent school "a more potent influence and a better assurance of success." [40] And that the Regents were seeking to cultivate the interest of the legal profession rather than responding to any demand from lawyers for the establishment of a law school is made clear by the legal profession's lack of interest in earlier overtures to open such a department. As early as 1850 Lathrop and the Board of Regents had taken the initiative in suggesting that a law and medical school be created in the University. "Under the advice of members of the Board," the Regents announced in their annual report for that year, "the Chancellor has addressed communications severally to the Medical Society of the State, and to the Court and Bar, inviting suggestions from them relative to the most suitable plan of organization of each of the faculties of Law and Medicine." [41] The chancellor's inquiry elicited no response from any member of the Wisconsin legal profession. [42] In 1851 the Regents simply recorded that "the attention of the Court and Bar has been called to the subject" of a law department; [43] subsequent reports reiterated that notice. In 1855 Chancellor Lathrop could only suggest that "preliminary action" with regard to the organization of a law department would not be "premature," a proposal that was greeted by the Regents and the state legal profession with silence.[44]

When the Board of Regents passed a resolution on January 29, 1857 that provided for the organization of a law department, perhaps the most surprising aspect was that they had found two lawyers in the state who agreed to give instruction in the department. Yet even the men selected revealed the essentially political motivation behind the establishment of a law school. Timothy O. Howe was a prominent Green Bay attorney and a former justice of the Wisconsin Supreme Court while Edward G. Ryan was a young lawyer from Milwaukee, a former newspaper editor and publisher and a rising politician. Howe, a Republican and Ryan, a Democrat, were obviously chosen with an eye to sectional and political appeal. Yet the appointments also must be viewed against the background of a dispute over the governorship of Wisconsin that flared up in 1855. In that year the Republican candidate for governor, Coles Bashford, lost to the Democratic candidate, William A. Barstow, in an election marred by charges of voting fraud. Bashford filed suit against Barstow and, after a long court fight, the Republican Bashford was declared the winner of the election. Timothy Howe was one of Bashford's attorneys, and he was joined by the Democrat Edward Ryan in presenting the case before the Wisconsin Supreme Court. The case of fraud proved so egregious that Ryan afterward maintained his appeal among most Democrats, but he was also immensely popular among Republicans for breaking party ranks to defend Bashford. The Regents could hardly have picked two men with broader political appeal.[45]

The strategy devised by people in Wisconsin to align the interests of the professions on the side of the University was not unique. The same tactic was tried more successfully a decade later in Iowa. John P. Irish, who styled himself a "friend" of the University of Iowa, recalled his role in the establishment of the Iowa College of Law in 1868. Irish, then editor of the Iowa City *Press*, was elected to the lower house of the Iowa legislature in 1867 and quickly discovered that the condition of the University, founded in 1847, had sunk to an all-time low: "Its income was depleted, it had long been without a President, and it was in a helpless condition." When he attempted to raise money for the University of Iowa in the Legislature, Irish was accused of "intending to establish 'an aristocracy of learning' that would serve the rich while supported by the poor." Throughout the legislative term he "was stirred by the apathy on all sides toward the University." This situation led Irish to "plan for the wider influence of the University, to the end that it might have powerful friends, and I conceived the idea of allying it with the two most influential professions by attaching to it the schools of law and medicine." Irish accomplished part of his plan by simply transferring a private law school in Des Moines, Iowa, founded by William G. Hammond, to the University of Iowa. And "so it came to pass that when the University opened its fall term in 1868 it had a law school with more than a score of students." [46]

Irish was successful where those in Wisconsin were not. The organization of the Wisconsin Law Department in 1857 proved premature. At a meeting of the Board of Regents on March 24, 1857, the appropriation of five hundred dollars to the law department was rescinded because of the anticipated cost of building Main (now Bascom) Hall which, interestingly, was to provide better housing for the liberal arts college. A week later, on April 1, the resolution that had organized the law department was itself revoked. [47] For a time, the subject of legal education in the University was ignored. Then, in 1863 and again in 1866, Daniel Read, professor of mental and moral philosophy in the University and Lathrop's closest colleague during the 1850s, attempted to spark interest in the establishment of a University department of law. Read's efforts on behalf of a law department were almost a replica of the 1857 arguments, though his orchestration of events in 1866 was nicely conceived, even if ultimately unsuccessful. In 1863 Read submitted a brief report to the Board of Regents in which he reminded them that a law school even "if at first continued but three or four months, and conducted at first by a single professor with such aid as might be rendered gratuitously by members of the Bench and Bar, would add much to the respectability and usefulness of the University." Read observed that "each year a portion of our students, not merely graduates [of the University] but others who have completed the course which they have prescribed to themselves, enter upon the study of law. Other young men even now to some extent resort to the City of Madison to pursue legal studies." [48] Despite Read's hint that there was a large group of students waiting to be enrolled by the University, the Regents ignored his proposal. Undeterred, Read convinced Professor John W. Sterling, acting president of the University, to broach the subject to the Regents once again in 1866. Sterling rehearsed the familiar arguments. The law school itself would be inexpensive because it would be composed of a single professor, supported entirely by tuition fees, whose efforts would be supplemented by "volunteer lectures on select titles" by local lawyers. Sterling also reminded the Regents, in language more blunt than Lathrop had ever used, that "the advantage of such a Department in our University would be not only its usefulness as a means of professional culture, but it would also tend to conciliate the support of a profession always powerful in every free state." [49] Finally, Sterling played his trump card. He informed the Regents that Madison was already a center for legal education. A number of young men, "mostly . . . former students of the University" who were reading law in the offices of city attorneys, had formed a "voluntary" club "for mutual improvement in legal knowledge." These students, whose activities probably involved informal discussions and quite possibly more formal moot court arguments, from time to time invited speakers to lecture on various legal topics. Conveniently (and one must assume by design), Daniel Read was the invited speaker on January 17, 1866. Sterling therefore invited the Regents to gather with members of the law club in the Wisconsin Supreme Court chambers to hear Read's address on "The Dignity of Law as a Profession." [50] Unfortunately, there is no record that any member of the Board attended the meeting. Shortly thereafter Read left the University of Wisconsin to join the faculty at the University of Missouri where, eventually, he became its president.

The Nineteenth Century Law School in Legal Historiography

Historians have not recognized that college men expected that law schools would shelter the central college by providing a veneer of practical training and that they would also broaden the base of collegiate support by erecting a bridge to a powerful professional group. Instead, legal historians have begun with the assumption that a university (and in the case of state universities, the state itself) has a responsibility to provide higher education in the professions. Their studies have concentrated on the early recognition of that principle and they have understandably focused on the emergence of an intellectual tradition which justifies in the twentieth century the existence of university-sponsored legal education. [51] In brief, such histories argue that tradition represented the coalescence of three major elements. First, some men like Blackstone and Jefferson believed that legal training should be part of a liberal education. But since that argument only justified law on the undergraduate level, not as a professional course of study, it quickly recedes in importance in most writing on legal education. [52] More important were the dual motives of the lawyers and judges who lectured in the early law schools. These men wanted both to improve legal education and to advance the science of the law. That some men acted from all three motives is undeniable but to focus almost exclusively on such statements is to oversimplify the process through which law schools gradually became attached to the American college. Willy-nilly, one ignores other motives that did not contribute directly to the elaboration of the central twentieth-century rationale for the university law school. One value of the early Wisconsin experience, then, is the virtual absence of arguments for the establishment of a law school on professional grounds, an absence that forces one to search for an explanation in other areas. And at Wisconsin in the 1850s and early 1860s, less obvious, though no less important, motives stand nakedly revealed: A law school (along with other professional and practical schools) would offer testimony to the University's interest in practical pursuits and it would, in the words of John Sterling, act as a means to "conciliate the support of a profession always powerful in a free state."

Because the history of legal education has been written from a professional's perspective, it is difficult to tell whether the Wisconsin experience was common in other states. Although direct evidence remains buried in institutional archives, it is plausible that men in other states acted from a similar sense of institutional self-interest when they moved to attach law schools to the college of liberal arts. Certainly the phenomenon was familiar to observers in the nineteenth century. George W. Swasey of the Boston University Law School remarked in 1889 that "most of the law schools in America have not originated so much from a real public demand for them as from a desire upon the part of college authorities and their friends to add new departments to those already attached to their respective institutions." [53] And certainly John Irish's account of the establishment of the Iowa College of Law, even if it inflates his own role, indicates that the Wisconsin experience was not unique. At both schools friends of the state university explicity suggested a strategic alliance with the professions in order to advance the fortunes of the institution as a whole.

Nor was it unusual for colleges to forge simply and quickly a connection with the legal profession by adopting, as Iowa did, an already existing private law school. As mentioned above, John Lathrop's alma mater, Yale, gradually annexed a private law school between 1824 and 1826. In a similar fashion, the Cincinnati Law School, a private school founded in 1833, was taken over by Cincinnati College in 1835; the Lumpkin Law School was founded and then almost immediately incorporated into the University of Georgia in 1843; the University of North Carolina adopted in 1845 a private school organized two years earlier by Judge William H. Battle. [54] Although the majority of colleges (by 1860 thirty colleges had sponsored a law school of which twenty-one still existed) [55] did not act in such a direct fashion, those schools which did organize their own law departments usually left them to operate on the fringes of the institution. The effect was not so different from annexing a private school and allowing it to continue to operate on the income from student fees. (The only colleges that provided salaries to the law faculty prior to 1860 were Harvard, Virginia and Michigan.) Moreover, students in the various college-sponsored law schools were rarely subjected to the same rules and regulations that governed the traditional academic departments. They, along with the faculty, were isolated (often physically) from the intellectual life of the institution. In matters both of finance and governance, then, the antebellum college law school had only a nominal connection to the parent school, a pattern that is certainly consistent with and possibly reflects a cautious stance similar to that taken by Wisconsin's John Lathrop when he promoted professional education.

College men saw sponsorship of a law school as only one—and clearly not the most important—means to defend the liberal arts. But it was an intriguing tactic since it could be used in two ways. Because law was obviously a vocation-oriented subject, a law school could testify to the college's interest in practical pursuits. Sponsorship of such a school might fend off those who wanted the college to devote a major portion of its resources to other kinds of practical pursuits, especially in science, the mechanic arts, commerce and agriculture. Such demands, of course, were ultimately impossible to resist, and colleges moved, reluctantly in many cases, to set up practical courses in those areas. As in the case of law schools, however, college authorities often isolated those courses on the fringes of the academic community and, indeed, in some cases organized entirely separate schools (as did Yale with the Sheffield Scientific School and Harvard with the Lawrence Scientific School). Those schools began their existence on the fringes of the college because of fears that their curriculum, with its practical emphasis, and their clientele, who were of a lower social class than the usual university student, would contaminate the liberal arts and the culture that supported such study. In contrast, the early law schools had a nominal connection to the colleges, not because law itself necessarily represented a threat to the liberal arts (although the actual narrow course of study that emerged in the university-sponsored law schools may have given some supporters of the liberal arts pause) but because college authorities believed it hazardous to argue for the allocation of scarce resources to support training in what many people, especially legislators, perceived as an aristocratic profession. To sponsor a law school might be an intriguing means by which to defend the liberal arts from more extensive attack but the sponsorship had to be kept financially nominal. If it were not, the alliance between the university and the professions might itself become the subject of attacks by a state legislature already attuned to charges that the university served the interests of the upper classes.

It was not enough, however, simply to defend the college from attack. Throughout the nineteenth century, colleges were concerned with broadening the base of support from a local to a state or even national level. David Potts has demonstrated that many colleges sought to achieve this goal by strengthening and then formalizing their ties to religious denominations.[56] It is not difficult to see how the sponsorship of a professional school could serve a similar purpose and that it might have been especially useful in the cases of the new and usually underfinanced state universities. Prohibited by their charters from any denominational ties, the colleges found that a sensible alternative was to seek closer connections with powerful secular groups like lawyers and doctors.

While this was a logical strategy, it was probably nowhere immediately effective, and certainly not at Wisconsin where a law school was not opened until 1868 and where medical education did not begin until the 1890s. Other tactics proved much more successful. In 1866 the Wisconsin legislature reorganized the University, making its charter more flexible so that the school would be eligible for funds made available through the Morrill Act. Equally significant, the legislature changed the method of selecting the Board of Regents. Prior to 1866 the Board, then elected by the legislature, was composed largely of men from the southwestern part of the state and particularly from the Madison area. Although this was a natural consequence of the population pattern in the state, the situation reinforced the image of the University as a local school serving primarily a Madison constituency. Under the terms of the 1866 reorganization act the power of selection passed to the Governor who was required to choose two Regents from each congressional district and three from the state at large. The success of these moves can perhaps be indicated by the fact that the state gave direct aid to the University for the first time in 1867.[57]

The major difficulty with the strategic alliance with the professions proposed by Lathrop and Read was the reactions of professionals themselves. The legal profession was largely indifferent to the formation of a law school, whether sponsored by a university or not; the medical profession, though intensely interested in the formation of a medical school, especially one attached to the university, was so splintered intellectually that it could not agree on the content of the course of study. The circumstances of professional life which determined those significantly different attitudes are examined in the next chapter.

CHAPTER TWO

Education and Professional Life Styles: Law and Medicine in the Nineteenth Century

The majority of American lawyers during most of the nineteenth century were indifferent to the fortunes of the few law schools in existence because such institutions served no important professional purpose. Law schools were viewed by those students who did attend as a useful supplement to the apprenticeship experience. But the law schools had little or nothing to do with certifying professional competence nor did they have much to do with regulating entry into the legal profession. Instead, the process of certification and regulation depended upon the circumstances of legal practice which, organized around life on the judicial circuit, brought together judges, lawyers and even those preparing for the bar into an intimate professional relationship.

The outstanding feature of the professional life style that emerged was its conviviality, a characteristic which provides the key to understanding the highly personalistic way in which the nineteenth century legal profession was organized and controlled. Admission to the bar did not depend upon meeting formal educational requirements but instead was controlled by lawyers who selected and sponsored young men on the basis of a personal assessment of their character and talent. Similarly, professional discipline was invoked not through selective admission requirements or through formalized bar associations or disciplinary hearings but instead within that convivial social and intellectual matrix created by the judicial circuit.

The decisive impact that professionals' life styles had upon the development of institutions for professional training can be shown by comparing the development of the legal profession to that of the medical profession. An analysis of those two professions, centering in particular upon Wisconsin lawyers and doctors in the middle third of the nineteenth century, indicates that doctors, unlike lawyers, were confronted with enormous problems of professional discipline. Those problems not only involved the regulation of economic competition but also the very definition of "professional" medical practice itself. For doctors, then, professional schools did serve an important professional purpose: They were "schools" in a quite literal ideological sense and they were created as part of an effort to exclude alternate theories of medical practice from the marketplace.

For that reason, the expansion of American medical schools began in the 1820s, while American law schools greatly increased in number only after 1870. The energy that American physicians expended can be grasped from the fact that in the years 1800 to 1910 over 450 medical schools were established in this country. During that same period only a hundred and seventy-one law schools were founded and the vast majority (one hundred and forty) opened after 1870.[1] This astonishing proliferation of medical schools reflected an almost equally astonishing proliferation of medical sects in the nineteenth century. That indicated a growing instability within the medical profession and that, in turn, stemmed from the fact that for doctors there existed no institution comparable to the judicial circuit which had the potential to unify the medical profession either socially or intellectually.

Sociality and Conviviality

A study of the Wisconsin legal profession, particularly during the years between 1830 and 1860, indicates that professional life was regulated and controlled outside the sphere of formal admission requirements and without recourse to formal disciplinary proceedings. Instead, discipline was maintained through the social life of the judicial circuit, and professional ability was certified in the oratorical contests of the courtroom. It was within that context that the image of the lawyer as advocate emerged to dominate professional consciousness.

To argue that the effective and important regulation of the bar took place after each member had been admitted to practice challenges one of the central themes of legal historiography. The standard interpretation of professional development in antebellum America pictures a bar in disarray. In all states the regulation of admission to the bar, at least as measured by statutory barriers, declined in effectiveness. This general dilution of professional regulation and certification procedures has been attributed to many factors: the removal of Loyalist lawyers to England during the American Revolution, which seriously depleted the leadership of the bar; the general unpopularity of English-based institutions, including the common law; and the animosities generated among debtors as lawyers acted to recover property in the depressed years after Independence. Most important of all, "the imperious demands of the democratic opinion which gathered force in the Jeffersonian years and came to full expression in the Jacksonian 1830's, brought extreme relaxation of professional standards." [2] A combination of anti-intellectualism and suspicion of privilege in general worked to lower bar standards and these forces, it is generally argued, were at their most virulent in the intensely democratic frontier areas.

There is no doubt that formal admission standards to the legal profession were diluted in the half century after 1800. A survey of the laws governing admission to the Wisconsin bar fully supports this interpretation. [3] Moreover, the few surviving records that give a glimpse into the examination process stress the informality of such examinations. In 1906, for instance, James G. Jenkins recalled how bar examinations were undertaken in the middle of the nineteenth century.

> When one desired to be admitted to the bar in those days he got a lawyer to move the court to appoint a committee, and of course the court appointed the mover of the proposition and whoever the mover and the judge might select, and then the duty of the applicant according to this tradition of the bar, was to invite this committee to a wine supper. . . . The examination took place after supper. [4]

That the examination process was not always taken seriously also is indicated by the experience of Mr. Lucius M. Miller of the Winnebago County Bar. Miller, according to Moses M. Hooper, "was admitted to the bar . . . simply as a matter of courtesy to him and in order to relieve him from duty as a juryman." [5] Anecdotal evidence, then, corroborates satutory evidence to confirm that admission to the Wisconsin bar in the territorial and early statehood periods was not difficult to achieve.

However, to assume that formal admission standards are a valid indication of the strength of professional organization is to impose twentieth-century views back upon the nineteenth century. Historians have ignored other evidence, also anecdotal in nature, which suggests that on the Wisconsin frontier professional discipline was imposed after a lawyer was admitted to practice. The evidence is found in the various reminiscences written by Wisconsin lawyers in the last three decades of the nineteenth century.[6] These accounts were recorded mainly by that generation of lawyers who had begun legal practice before 1860 and who had thus participated directly in the life of the frontier bar. A younger generation of lawyers, relying more on anecdote and research, also contributed substantially to the historical record. The purpose of both groups, however, was essentially the same: to record for posterity a style of professional life that was rapidly receding into the past.

Conviviality was one of the central characteristics of that older style of professional life. Moses M. Strong, in an address to the Wisconsin State Bar Association in 1881, noted that

A generation has passed since the days of the first supreme court of the state, and it is impossible for the present generation fully to realize all the surrounding circumstances which affected the character and conduct of the bench and bar of that day. Perhaps the most influential and in some instances the most baleful of those surroundings was the large degree of sociality and conviviality which marked the intercourse of the members of the profession with each other and with the rest of mankind.[7]

Thirty years earlier Moses B. Butterfield, a lawyer from Racine, Wisconsin, had recorded his impression of the Wisconsin bench and bar in terms remarkably similar to those used by Strong. In 1852 Butterfield attended a session of the State Supreme Court at Madison and in a letter to his wife wrote that "The bar of Wisconsin are fine looking men, as fine as I ever saw anywhere—but one or two ordinary looking men. But as a general thing, I should say they are not too much given to hard study. Some appear to have spent much time in study but most appear to enjoy sport and pleasure and are apt to try to live by their wits." [8]

The devotion of frontier lawyers to "sport and pleasure" is confirmed by other sources. One of the most popular accounts of early Wisconsin legal history (it was repeated by several writers) concerned Judge David Irvin, Associate Justice of the Wisconsin Territorial Supreme Court. Judge Irvin "was not considered a profound lawyer," though he did have "a strong vein of practical common sense and a natural love of justice." But the characteristic that most captured the imagination of his chroniclers was Irvin's "keen relish for field sports," and his "particular interest in his horse, his dog and gun." [9]

Irvin's interests were somewhat unusual, perhaps even a little exotic, for a Wisconsin lawyer. But that was due to the Virginia-born Judge's cultivation of the image of the Southern gentleman. More common, particularly as towns and cities witnessed a growing concentration of lawyers, was a fondness for whiskey and cards. Roujet D. Marshall remembered the bar of Chippewa County as composed during the 1870s of "a lot of good fellows who readily turned aside from the business of their profession at most any time during business hours to enjoy a social game of cards with more or less drinks by the side." Most members of the local bar considered young Marshall a "drudge." He was "at the office from seven o'clock in the forenoon until ten o'clock in the evening, . . . and [he] was always at . . . work while in the office." Marshall spent no time "visiting or loafing, as was customarily the case at most other offices in the city, nor was any time spent at saloons." Such industrious habits, he later recalled, were "very unusual." As a consequence, Marshall was not regarded by members of the Chippewa County Bar as "in any sense a mixer or desirable companion for recreational enjoyments." [10]

The conviviality that so fascinated Wisconsin lawyers later in the century provides a key for understanding the structure of legal practice before 1870. For conviviality invariably occurred within the institutional webbing created by the court system, and on the frontier the influence of the court was structured and extended into the community by the journey of judge and lawyers from county to county over the judicial circuit. "Court days," according to one recollection, "were the event of the season at the county seat, and with the arrival of the presiding judge came a string of lawyers trooping in on horseback, in stage, on prairie schooner or sleigh, and sometimes on foot; to remain until the term was closed and then on to the next assize." [11] The judge and his retinue of lawyers resembled a troupe of actors, traveling from town to town and presenting at each stop a spectacle that differed from others along the route mainly in the circumstances arising from new litigations.

For the people of the surrounding area, court days were times of entertainment and sociability. Judge Romanzo Bunn recalled that "the court houses were filled with people. . . . They came in from all over the country. They filled corridors, stairways, window cases and every place full." [12] And the court day itself was long, with trials frequently being held from 8 A.M. to 10 or 11 P.M. [13] According to Burr Jones the trials of the frontier days served a purpose similar to the football games of a later generation. [14] And Nels Wheeler wrote that "A Justice Court supplied a great variety of wants of a large body of people: for an exciting trial presented under one tent the ravishing beauty of a circus, the majestic grandeur of a caravan, the spiritual fascination of a camp meeting and the bewitching horror of a well conducted dog fight." [15]

Court days also provided the occasion for lawyers to prove that they were the most able and effective members of the bar. On the frontier men did not choose a lawyer because he called himself a lawyer, or because he had passed a bar examination or exhibited a diploma from a law school. Instead, lawyers were selected on the basis of their court-room ability. A lawyer achieved eminence at the bar because of his effectiveness as a courtroom advocate. This informal, immediate and personal selection procedure that existed on the circuit meant that lawyers found oratorical ability more important than legal learning in establishing a reputation among clients and potential clients. This kind of lawyer "despised exceptions and motions and all the technicalities of pleadings and evidence" and depended instead on his "power to cross examine witnesses and to win the jury by . . . oratory." [16] If in the course of a trial, the lawyer was able to heap ridicule on his opponent, so much the better for his reputation.

There were, of course, many types of lawyers on the frontier. The "natural enemies" of the orator "revelled in Tidd and Chitty and gloated over their success in upsetting the verdicts won by their eloquent rivals." [17]

There were [also] the devotees of Blackstone whose shining faces and mottled noses showed that they were also the devotees of Bacchus.

There were those whose courtly manners and careful dress gave evidence that they were not strangers to the conventionalities of the old families of the East or South.

There were others whose fine disdain of dress won a certain notoriety. But even they were apt to have some peculiarity of dress which would distinguish them from the common herd.[18]

Though many kinds of lawyers existed on the frontier, the lawyer as an effective courtroom advocate emerged as the dominant image of the successful practitioner. This image gained strength, not because all lawyers were advocates, but because the major form of certification of professional ability, the courtroom battle, affected, at least initially, the career of almost every lawyer. Even those lawyers who later gained renown as learned legal counselors, and who capped their careers as judges, often established their initial reputation in the lower trial courts. E. G. Ryan, for example, was later known among Wisconsin lawyers as a man of superior force in expounding the law but in his early days of practice two of his contemporaries, Thomas Arnold and Matthew Carpenter, "could much surpass Mr. Ryan in ability to obtain a verdict" because of their ability as courtroom advocates.[19] Yet even Ryan, who was uncomfortable in the role of courtroom advocate, achieved his initial reputation in a trial case concerning rape in which he defended the outraged woman with a sustained burst of oratorical fervor.[20]

Liberal admission requirements to the bar on the frontier were therefore countered by the existence of post-admission certification procedures. Men did not yet rely upon the anonymity of professional certification methods like law school diplomas or bar examinations, but instead depended upon first-hand knowledge of the legal skills of the various attorneys, knowledge based upon years of watching courtroom contests. These courtroom spectators, potential clients for the lawyers, judged a lawyer competent or incompetent, good or bad, mainly by his manner in the courtroom: did the lawyer win his cases? was he entertaining? and could he be counted on through effective use of wit and sarcasm to give a measure of revenge beyond what the purely legal forms would render?

While the actual court contest introduced the young lawyer to the public and to the profession, he was even more fully integrated into professional comradeship by the social life of the circuit itself. The circumstances of circuit life—judges and lawyers often traveled together and usually ate and slept at the same hotels—encouraged the development of a "professional fellowship" among members of the bar.[21] Some sense of that fellowship is suggested in the following account of Judge Charles Dunn's role in the structure of Wisconsin's fifth judicial circuit.

Charles Dunn was appointed Chief Justice of the Wisconsin Territorial Supreme Court in 1836 and served in that post until the State Judiciary was organized in 1848. After his retirement from the bench in 1848 Dunn returned to active practice and hence to the circuit. There he quickly became the informal leader of the bar.

> Judge Dunn's room was always the best room in the best hotel of the town where court was in session, and was universal headquarters for members of the bar, no matter how distinguished or humble. Frequently every facility for seating his guests, even to his bed, would be taxed to the utmost capacity, and there long evenings were spent in social communion, eminently satisfying to all, in which the judge was principal actor.[22]

There is an indication, too, that such social gatherings would on occasion be turned to the enforcement of professional standards. Although every "worthy member" of the bar received Judge Dunn's friendship, "he had no use for the unworthy members of the profession and they instinctively knew it." [23] Men like Judge Dunn served as professional and moral examples to both the new and experienced lawyer on the circuit. A word, a gesture, a favor from a lawyer of Judge Dunn's eminence could be an effective check on unwarranted conduct.

The arrangements of circuit life tended in other ways to enforce group standards. The pressure to conform "made itself felt in the long discussions and exchanges of professional talk as horses stumbled or wagons bumped their way over the indifferent roads between courthouses." Similar pressures "were expressed through the mock courts that were held of an evening at the tavern, to call one of the brethren to account for conduct that day in courts." [24] Burr Jones reported that "More than once I have heard the older lawyers tell of mock trials in which judges of the Circuit Court and even Supreme Court in early days were arraigned and tried before a midnight court at chambers in the hotel, for some alleged judicial misdemeanor." [25]

Social and professional intimacy was thus one of the outstanding characteristics of circuit life. Group standards were defined and enforced in an immediate and personal manner. However, a clear threat to the stability of the circuit was the danger that pressure to conform might easily degenerate into personal hostility and recrimination. The effectiveness of the circuit as a means of imposing professional discipline therefore depended upon the ability of the member lawyers to mute personal hostility. The sociability of the frontier bar, which so impressed lawyers later in the nineteenth century, was almost certainly useful in achieving that end. An atmosphere of conviviality took the sting from a basically serious disciplinary proceeding. Professional regulation on the frontier was well served by good fellowship.

The Danger and Dreariness of Professional Isolation

The image of conviviality seized upon by lawyers to describe changes in the practice of law provides a perspective from which to analyze the nineteenth-century medical profession. Although Wisconsin doctors did not produce anything like the large body of reminiscence written by lawyers, scattered memoirs do indicate that doctors experienced little of the sociability and conviviality that characterized relations among the bar. Doctors did not find medical practice convivial primarily because they lacked professional institutions that played a function comparable to the judicial circuit. These same memoirs suggest that even in more settled areas of the state doctors were continually confronted with problems of professional regulation. Indeed, for doctors the growth of cities only seemed to exacerbate the basic problem of defining "professional" practice because urban areas brought together a number of doctors who were still without benefit of social or professional arrangements that might have provided an integrating professional force.

Dr. John Reeve, who began medical practice in Wisconsin in the 1860s, had few fond memories of that past age as he set down his recollections. "With pen and ink," Reeve wrote, "it is impossible to convey an idea of the dreariness, the isolation, and the dullness of life in my chosen village. Absolutely deprived of professional companionship, and with little of any other kind, traveling over wretched roads through the intense cold of winter and storms of summer, bearing as best might be the innumerable privations of domestic life, the dreary time dragged slowly away, week by week, month by month, varying only with the changing seasons." [26]

To some extent, Reeve's memoir only reflects the hardships imposed by the harsh frontier environment, hardships shared equally by Wisconsin lawyers. Alexander Meggett, for example, recalled the life of the frontier in similar terms: "The drudgery of the [legal] profession in those early days," Meggett wrote, "would now be intolerable. It then imposed upon the lawyer himself, all the mechanical and scribe work of the office, demanded often, short and long tedious journeys by slow and uncomfortable conveyance in the parching heat of summer, the intense cold of winter; exposure to rain, snow and chilling winds, over rough roads and through wilderness—the sleeping upon floors and uncomfortable beds, often infested with vermin, the eating of ill-cooked and unpalatable food." [27] Yet there is an important difference. What distinguishes Reeve's recollections from those of lawyers is his insistence on the "dreariness, the isolation and the dullness" of professional life.

This sense of isolation from fellow professionals, absent in accounts of frontier law practice, was deeply imbedded in the external patterns of medical practice. The nineteenth-century physician almost always treated patients in the confines of their own homes or in the privacy of his office. Unlike the lawyer who rode the circuit and who performed in the courtroom, the doctor practiced his profession isolated from the view and to a large extent therefore from the influence of fellow practitioners. More important, there was no easy and familiar way to break through the screen of isolation. Arrangements that encouraged familiarity and intercourse among doctors barely existed in the nineteenth century. Consultation was sporadic and irregular; office clinics were unknown; partnerships, though not uncommon, did not provide for a broad professional companionship; and the hospital, the one institution that might have served an integrative function, was an unimportant facility. Except in some large cities, the nineteenth-century hospital did not give an institutional focus to medical practice. The hospital was a custodial institution for the incurable, the insane, the infectious, and the poor. Admittance to a hospital did not signify the point at which a wide range of medical talent and knowledge could be brought to bear upon illness; rather, such admittance normally meant that the doctor had relinquished further responsibility for treatment.[28]

The absence of an institutional focal point for the practice of medicine also posed difficulties for the young doctor who wanted an introduction to the community and to the profession. Thus, according to Daniel Calhoun, "the practitioner who most impressed an ordinary community was apt to be the man who came in, administered overdoses of dangerous chemicals, then was lucky enough to have his patients pull narrowly and therefore dramatically through to recovery." [29] These "heroic" therapies, as they were then known, are reminiscent of the florid oratory of the young lawyer. In both cases, the aim was to exhibit one's professional talents in as spectacular a manner as possible. Both heroic therapy and courtroom advocacy were designed to push one forward in a society in which regular channels for advancement, such as a hierarchical school system, were either absent, incomplete or obscure. But legal oratory became a recognized procedure for certification because it could be sustained and its potential excesses regulated by the court and the convivial life of the judicial circuit. Heroic therapy, in contrast, was not so reliable because it had no institutional control, except that of the community at large. Its usefulness therefore depended upon luck, personality, and individual initiative rather than any regular professional practice; and because heroic therapy thrived outside regular professional channels, its excesses could neither be curbed nor controlled.

Given the lack of informal arrangements in the medical profession that would aid professional discipline, it is not suprising that doctors were early concerned with organizing professional associations, with lobbying for statutes restricting entry into the profession, and with the establishment of medical schools. However, there is an additional factor that affected the practice of medicine in the nineteenth century which not only further explains the medical profession's preoccupation with formal institutions of schooling, certification, and regulation, but also explains why, ultimately, those persistent efforts to enforce professional discipline bore so few permanent results until the first decades of the twentieth century. That factor, establishing yet another point of contrast with the legal profession, was the absence of any agreed-upon definition of sound medical treatment.

When an American medical profession began to coalesce in the late eighteenth and early nineteenth centuries, there already existed a wide variety of medical practitioners. Although sharp distinctions among these practitioners cannot always be maintained, generally doctors can be placed into two groups: regular and irregular physicians. The regular doctors, or allopaths, were convinced that the treatment of disease should proceed through the use of remedies that produced effects different from or opposite to those produced by the disease. Thus, they relied heavily upon such remedies as bleeding, purging, sweating and massive doses of drugs, often heroin- or mercury-based compounds. The irregular doctors were a more motley group consisting, at least in the view of the regulars, of all doctors who did not subscribe to the doctrines of allopathy. The irregulars went under a variety of names— herb, botanic, hydrotherapist, empiric, among others—but they generally based their treatment on experience and folk wisdom rather than the latest scientific theories. Though some were intrigued with the possibility of electric or magnetic cures, most used in their practice substances like roots or herbs.[30]

In the early nineteenth century the distinctions between doctors were reinforced by social class differences. Regular doctors were well educated, usually with a medical degree and often with a college diploma. The irregulars, in contrast, had little formal education. The regular doctors were from the middle, sometimes upper, strata of society; the irregulars were ordinarily of the lower classes. The regulars spun vast theories by which they could explain the course of a disease and prescribe for treatment; the irregulars had few scientific pretensions but instead explained and prescribed on the basis of tradition and their own experience.

In one important respect, however, the distinction between regular and irregular physicians was never very clear: Both groups were about equally ineffective in curing illness. In fact, the mild practices of the irregular were probably safer than the harsh doses of a regular doctor. The irregular, usually relying on mildly beneficial folk practices and on drugs derived in most cases from harmless substances, did not at least impede the recuperative powers of nature. That was more than could be said of the methods of the regular doctors. Their reliance upon bleeding, purging, and heroic doses of mercury was, at best, unpleasant and, at worst, deadly.[31]

The professional reputation of the regular physician was therefore based to a large degree on general education and social rank rather than on any obvious therapeutic advantage to the patient. But after about 1825, when the first homeopathic practitioners appeared in America, the distinction between regular and irregular physicians began to blur. The emergence of homeopathic and, later, eclectic practitioners undermined the class division of medical practice.[32] Homeopaths and eclectics rejected the massive dosing and painful bleeding procedures of the regular doctors and hence were able to attract patients by their painless and pleasant remedies (the eclectics made it a practice to sugar-coat their nostrums). Moreover, the homeopaths, unlike other irregulars, were usually well educated, possessed social standing in the community and could present "scientific" theories of medical treatment. They therefore appealed to the middle and upper classes of patients, a fact recognized by regulars when they derided homeopathy as "the quackery of the drawing-room." [33]

The challenge posed by these new medical sects, particularly homeopathy, helps explain why regular doctors became so concerned by the 1850s with professional regulation. The basic problem was not simply the proliferation of medical sects or the breakdown of regulatory machinery. These were only symptoms of a more fundamental intellectual readjustment in medical practice. The very meaning of orthodoxy was being redefined in this period.[34] Not until well after the Civil War, following a series of advances in medical science, were most doctors even modestly successful in treating illness, and probably not until after 1900 did most patients have a better than even chance of benefiting from medical treatment.

With notions of professional competence in doubt, doctors—allopaths, homeopaths and eclectics alike—responded by heightened attention to the task of defining and enforcing competing conceptions of orthodoxy. To achieve that goal, physicians of all sects turned to the formation of medical societies, the passage of legislation and the establishment of medical schools. Although none of these strategies really achieved their primary purpose—the enforcement of a particular view of professional medical practice—they did eventually provide a regulatory framework for the medical profession in the twentieth century.

Wisconsin doctors formed numerous local societies in the 1840s and 1850s. The Dane County Medical Society, for example, organized doctors in the area as early as 1850. In Milwaukee at least six short-lived medical societies were formed prior to 1855. More ambitious efforts preceded even these early local attempts. Only five years after the Wisconsin territory was organized in 1836, doctors established the Wisconsin Territorial Medical Society. The State Medical Society was organized in 1848 when Wisconsin was admitted to the Union.[35]

The meetings of these societies served as a forum for the exchange of new medical knowledge and their members acted as interest groups to petition the state legislature for the legalization of dissection and the tightening of admission standards to the profession. The societies' efforts at regulating the profession, however, were not very successful and at times bordered on the comic. In 1850, for instance, the State Medical Society attempted a census of all state doctors as a first step in arriving at a plan for regulation requirements. The Society quickly abandoned the idea when it was found that reliable information could not be obtained, since "in many cases irregulars were appointed [as census takers] and as a consequence irregulars would be reported as graduates, quacks as doctors, and so on." [36] The Society's aims were hindered also by the tendency of regular doctors to convert at an alarming rate to the principles of homeopathy.[37]

The Territorial Medical Society and its successor, the State Medical Society, persisted in trying to gain legislation that would provide standards for admission to medical practice. In 1849 the Wisconsin legislature did write into law rigid standards for membership in medical societies, requiring, among other things, three years of medical study. One clause, however, greatly weakened the power of the medical societies: "This chapter shall not be so construed, as to prevent any person from practising physic and surgery within this state, who is not a member of any of said societies." [38] A revised version of this law adopted in 1878 provided that no doctor should have the right to collect fees through court action nor to testify in court as an expert unless he was a member of a county or the State Medical Society.[39] By that time, however, the major irregular groups had incorporated medical societies of their own (the Wisconsin homeopaths in 1864, and the eclectics in 1877), and so the statute affected only scattered village herbalists.

Eventually, political reality dictated cooperation between the regulars and the homeopaths and eclectics. As early as 1880 these three groups jointly drafted a bill "to prevent unqualified persons from practicing medicine in the state of Wisconsin." [40] Although that bill was postponed indefinitely in the legislature, the cooperating societies finally engineered passage of a similar bill in 1897. The 1897 statute set up a Board of Medical Examiners to pass upon the qualifications of any person wishing to practice medicine in Wisconsin. The law provided that homeopaths and eclectics, as well as regular doctors, be given representation on the board, and that "the Examination in materia medica, therapeutics and practice of medicine shall be conducted by members of the said board representing the school of medicine which the applicant claims to follow." [41] By 1897, then, the legal definition of "regular" practice included two schools of medicine formerly classified as irregular.

Medical societies, as it turned out, proved largely ineffective as regulatory agencies, and legislation simply served to place homeopaths and eclectics on a par with regular practitioners. Wisconsin doctors accordingly began to follow the example of their colleagues in other states by establishing medical schools that would train young men in "sound" medical principles. By 1900 Wisconsin doctors had attempted on at least nine separate occasions to establish a medical school. For all the energy expended, their efforts could point to only two operating medical schools (both private and both located in Milwaukee) and a premedical course at the University of Wisconsin in Madison.[42]

That doctors were concerned with medical schools primarily as regulatory devices is clear from the unsuccessful efforts dating from the early 1850s to establish a Medical Department in connection with the University of Wisconsin. Dr. Alfred Castleman, the most active promoter of a University Medical Department, obviously viewed the proposed school as a means to rid the profession of irregulars and quacks. Castleman told the State Medical Society in 1855 that "Schools must be established and their chairs filled with professors of high moral, as well as professional worth." The primary duty of these professors would be to "impress upon the student the important fact that quackery as often exists under cover of a diploma as under the dogmas of Thompsonism [a variety of botanical practice] or the feeble vagaries of Hahnemann [the founder of the homeopathic school of medicine]."[43] In a letter to the University Regents, apparently written after the Board had informed the Medical Society that insufficient funds were available to support a medical school, Castleman reiterated his views:

> We deem it a great misfortune that the finances of the University are not in a condition to warrant the immediate organization of that department with an appropriation sufficient to bring it full grown & at once into existence—A feeble and sickly start of such a school is for many and obvious reasons to be deprecated, and yet the immediate organization of such a department seems the only way to arrest the growth of the many fungous schools, which all around us, are springing into existence from bad legislation.[44]

In addition to lack of money, the University Regents also may have been reluctant to open a medical department when it became clear that Castleman and the State Medical Society wanted only regular medical doctrines taught in the school. Castleman finally withdrew his support from the project when the Regents refused to grant the medical society control over the school.[45]

In 1868 University authorities approached the Medical Society with a proposal for a university medical school to be located in Milwaukee. University President Paul A. Chadbourne appeared before the Society at its annual meeting in 1868 to ask that the Society act upon such a proposal. No reaction to the president's offer was recorded by the Society's secretary and no official action was taken by the members present.[46] In 1875 still another initiative by the University was dismissed by the Medical Society. This time, however, it is clear that the Society refused to act because of their fundamental disagreement with the University's position that, in the words of President John Bascom, "the establishment of a medical department at the University [must be] on a basis of equal privileges to all systems of medicine." [47] The Society first passed a resolution deeming the establishment of a medical school in Madison "inexpedient," and then, perhaps thinking their position unclear, the members adopted a second resolution expressing their "disapprobation of any movement looking towards the future establishment of mixed schools of medicine in connection with the state university." [48] Regular physicians thus faced a dilemma. They could either choose to support a mixed medical school which would further legitimize the doctrines of homeopathy and eclecticism or they would have no state-supported medical school at all. That dilemma could not have arisen in the legal profession because lawyers, unlike doctors, did not splinter into warring sects in the nineteenth century.

The Persistence of Personalism

Throughout the nineteenth century Wisconsin lawyers would continue to view legal training as essentially a process whereby practicing attorneys sponsored worthy young men in their efforts to enter the legal profession. They also continued to believe that the discipline of the profession's members was best done through the informal invocation of group standards. This highly personalistic approach to preparation and regulation, however, became harder to maintain after the decline of the convivial life of the judicial circuit. Some lawyers therefore began to argue for more stringent standards of admission to the profession and for the establishment of more formal bar associations to maintain the opportunity for convivial association and professional regulation. Yet the transition to a more formally regulated bar was so gradual as to be almost imperceptible to the profession. One important reason for the persistence of the old attitudes even after the influence of the judicial circuit had almost disappeared was the widespread agreement upon the sources and the nature of the law. Unlike the splintered medical profession, the legal profession was not ripped apart by scientific sectarianism.

The effectiveness of the circuit as a means of professional discipline depended upon the extent to which it included most lawyers in its web. Its effectiveness gradually was diminished, however, for as villages and cities grew, and the volume of legal business also expanded, the more successful lawyers began to leave the peripatetic life of the circuit to pursue their calling in a single location. Also, as the most prominent members of the bar found their practice centered around a few courts of the city rather than around the series of courts on the circuit, they found their professional influence considerably lessened.[49] To meet these problems, new means of professional regulation began to be devised.

The bar association was the most obvious of these new modes of professional regulation. Indeed the establishment of local bar associations may give a rough measure of the transition from an itinerant to a stable bar. In Wisconsin the first local bar associations of any permanence were formed in the late 1850s. The Brown County Bar Association was organized on April 4, 1857, and on June 11, 1858, the Milwaukee Bar Association was formed. The Dane County Bar Association, which included lawyers from the Madison area, was organized in July, 1858.[50] It was reorganized under the name of the Dane County Legal Association in 1869. In 1878 the State Bar Association was finally organized. The immediate and primary professional concern of the early bar associations was the regulation of economic competition among member lawyers. To that end all appear to have adopted a fee bill detailing the minimum charge for various types of action.[51] The Milwaukee Bar Association also formed a law library for the use of its members, and all the local bar associations served to bring together at least some members of the bar for occasional social meetings. It is probable, too, that these local associations were effective in securing passage of those laws in Wisconsin that after 1860 provided for slightly more stringent entrance requirements to the legal profession. In 1861 the legislature approved a statute which required that the applicant, in addition to being a resident and of good moral character, submit to an examination in open court to determine whether he possessed "sufficient legal knowledge." [52]

Neither the local nor state bar associations were noted for disciplining their members after admission to the bar, apparently because they remained uncomfortable with a rebuke that would be both formal and enduring. In 1898 John R. Berryman complained that "there seems to be a profound reluctance on the part of members of the bar to take action looking towards disbarment of unworthy members, even though it reaches a point at which further tolerance would seem almost paramount to complicity." The State Bar Association, he found, "has never yet acted upon a single case, and but very few have ever been reported to the association for action." [53] The bar associations in the nineteenth century, then, existed more as potential regulatory agencies than actual forces for professional control. Indeed, the State Bar Association did not even meet regularly prior to 1900; and as late as 1911 only twenty-nine of seventy-one Wisconsin counties had local bar associations.[54]

Lawyers did not flock to join bar associations or to press for more stringent and formal standards of admission to the bar because their professional lives were not characterized by serious and sustained professional disputes. The success of such an informal means of regulation as the judicial circuit had always depended upon the fact that definition of the intellectual foundations of legal practice was never seriously in question in the nineteenth century. Of course, lawyers did disagree, often vehemently, over important questions like the applicability of the English common law to American situations, the merits of codification of the law, or on the interpretation of legislative intent. Such disagreements, however, did not cause permanent breaks in professional solidarity, partly because some of those issues could be handled in the political arena (and therefore were not narrowly professional questions at all) but even more because settlement of disputes was the essence of legal practice. The professional impact of disputes was softened and usually dissipated by the judge acting as the arbitrator of disagreement. Through a succession of court cases judges "defined" (however temporary that definition might be) the point of law in question. A figure comparable to the judge did not exist in the medical profession.

Moreover, the validity or "truth" of the law did not depend, as it did in medical practice, upon a complex relationship between scientific coherence and practical effectiveness. Since each court case was, for that moment, "The Law," there existed a close connection between the latest developments in law and the practice of the ordinary lawyer. In medicine, scientific investigation could and did proceed independently of ordinary medical practice. In addition, medical practitioners were constantly confronted in the nineteenth century with the discord between scientific principles and practical effectiveness. The truth, the "scientific" way to treat patients, could not be shown to be better than other truths, or systems of medical treatment. In contrast, law was, almost by definition, and certainly in practice, an ongoing process of verification (or exposure) of legal principles.

Though nineteenth-century lawyers were continually concerned with defining and refining conceptions of law, that professional preoccupation was inherent in the nature of legal practice and it did not therefore lead to widescale professional disruption. Among medical practitioners, however, neither regulars nor irregulars could prove to the public that they possessed an exclusive right to medical wisdom. Pressed on all sides by competing theories of medical practice, all of which seemed to work equally well (or equally ineffectively), doctors turned to the creation of institutions, like medical societies and medical schools, that would impose some semblance of rationality and order on their professional lives. Nineteenth-century doctors, unlike lawyers, were forced to concern themselves with more than the regulation of their profession.

They had also to define professional conduct itself. Lawyers had no compelling professional stake in the development of law schools, in the organization of bar associations or in the support of stringent standards for admission. Therefore, law schools grew mainly in response to student demands; bar associations met irregularly, when at all; and the formal admission standards gradually reintroduced into the statutes posed no real barrier to entry into the profession in the nineteenth century.

CHAPTER THREE

Apprenticeship and the Law School: A Harmonious Arrangement

Because the function of the law school in the nineteenth century has not been made sufficiently clear, the nineteenth-century law school has appeared to observers in the twentieth century as an institution with abysmally low, even irresponsible standards. The admission requirements were minimal or nonexistent; the faculty consisted of one or two practicing lawyers supplemented by a number of occasional lecturers; the brief two- or three-term course of study did not pretend to be exhaustive; and the LL.B. was granted after attendance for a year. Even that requirement, however, was further diluted by the practice of extending credit for study in another law school, reading under the direction of an attorney or even for unsupervised reading of legal treatises.

Such standards become much less shocking—and should even be seen as sensible—when it is understood that the nineteenth-century law school did not serve any of the functions that we have come to associate with the twentieth-century law school. It was not intended to serve as the sole or even primary mode of legal training; it was not intended to regulate entry into the legal profession; and it was not intended to certify the professional competence of lawyers. Instead, the nineteenth-century law school was designed to blend in harmoniously with other arrangements for legal training and to operate in the context of other methods of professional regulation and certification.

William F. Vilas. (*University of Wisconsin Archives*)

The Nineteenth-century Law School

The University of Wisconsin Department of Law, opened in the fall of 1868, was typical of the law schools in the nineteenth century both in the circumstances of its establishment and in the conditions of its organization. The initiative to open the school was taken by University authorities, not by the legal profession. The lawyers who did participate in its establishment appear not to have been moved by any crisis within the legal profession but simply by the fact that they had attended a law school and thus perceived the advantages that such a school could offer to other young men. Finally, the organization of the school—its nominal relation to the University, its reliance upon part-time faculty and its academic standards—departed in no significant way from other schools in the United States at the time.

The initiative to organize the Wisconsin Department of Law was taken by Paul Chadbourne, shortly after his appointment as president of the University of Wisconsin. On the last day of October, 1867, Chadbourne wrote to William F. Vilas, a twenty-eight-year-old Madison attorney, asking for assistance in forming the University Law Department.

> This is a matter which I desire to lean very much under the direction of the Alumni, who are members of the bar. It seems to me that some of them can aid much by giving courses of lectures on specific subjects without interfering with their business. But in reference to all this, I wish to consult with you [and] shall feel obligated to you if you will give it some thought and aid me what you can in organizing and carrying on such a school.[1]

William F. Vilas would prove to be a key figure in the organization of the University of Wisconsin Law Department in the fall of 1868. He also would play a major role in the development of the school over the next two decades as a teacher and as a member of the University Board of Regents and its Committee on the Law Department. Later Vilas would achieve some measure of national prominence, serving as Postmaster General (1885–1888), Secretary of the Interior (1888–1890), and United States Senator (1891–1897). When Chadbourne contacted him in 1867, however, he was still a young lawyer of only local eminence.[2]

A number of factors obviously recommended Vilas to Chadbourne. The Vilas family long had maintained an active interest in the fortunes of the State University. Levi Vilas, William's father, had served on the University's Board of Regents during the 1850s and had sent two of his sons, including William, to be educated there. William F. Vilas had graduated at the top of his class in 1858, received a master's degree from the University in 1861 and, in that same year, helped organize (and served as the first secretary of) the University Alumni Association.[3] In addition, Vilas was also popular in the Madison area because of his distinguished service record during the Civil War (he was mustered out in 1863 at the rank of Lieutenant-Colonel and would thereafter be known as Colonel Vilas). He also had gained the reputation as a young man who was always ready to defend the interests of the common man against the power of the large corporations. Later in his career Vilas would be closely associated with the growth of the corporate economy—his professional energies shifted to corporation law when he became attorney for the Chicago and Northwestern Railroad in 1874— but during the 1860s Vilas was known as "the people's lawyer." [4] If Chadbourne was concerned that the University might be criticized for educating an aristocratic elite if it opened a law department, then Vilas was the perfect person to counter such attacks. Finally, Vilas was one of the few attorneys in the state (and perhaps the only one in the city of Madison) who had been trained in a law school. In the fall of 1858, immediately after graduation from the University of Wisconsin, Vilas had entered the Albany Law School in Albany, New York, where he studied law for two years and received the LL.B. in 1860.[5] By virtue of that background Vilas was viewed as an authority on law school organization and practice.

The deliberations which led to the organization of the Wisconsin Law Department are not recorded. President Chadbourne certainly talked with Vilas and perhaps with other members of the bar during the winter of 1867. Those discussions led the University Regents on February 14, 1868, to appoint a committee to consult with Chadbourne on the organization of the law department and to authorize them "to take the proper steps to procure a Professor thereof and to establish that department." The three Regents appointed to the committee were Angus Cameron, Henry Barron and Frederick O. Thorpe.[6] Both Barron and Thorpe had been on the Board since its reorganization in 1866, and Thorpe had served on a committee appointed in June 1866 to study the possibility of opening a law department. At that time, however, the Board was preoccupied with finding a new University president and so the committee never submitted a report. Angus Cameron, a newcomer to the Board in 1868, and Henry Barron were both lawyers and both graduates of the State and National Law School in Ballston Spa, New York. Founded in 1849 by John W. Fowler in a resort village, this obscure school's "brief but brilliant" career lasted no more than five years.[7] (Ironically, its life was cut short by competition from the Albany Law School established in 1851, the school from which William Vilas would graduate in 1860.) The law school background of Cameron and Barron meant that they, like Vilas, were judged expert in the proper organization of the proposed law department. For the details of operation, however, Chadbourne apparently relied most heavily on the judgment of Vilas. That the Vilas influence was dominant was later made clear when the Regents noted that "our present regulations as to scholarship for entry and graduation are copied from the regulations governing the justly celebrated Law School at Albany, New York." [8]

By late June 1868 arrangements for a law department were substantially complete. On June 23 President Chadbourne expressed to the Board of Regents his hope that "the proposed organization will prove acceptable . . . and that the school will essentially strengthen the University." [9] The following day the Regent Law Committee recommended that a law department be established immediately "at an expense to the University fund not exceeding two thousand dollars." [10] While that may seem a large sum, especially when the 1848 University charter and the proponents of the law school in 1857 had assumed that such a department should be self-supporting, it did not represent any basic change of view. Even though the University would gradually raise its contribution to the law school every few years, the assumption that the school should be self-supporting was not challenged directly at Wisconsin until the twentieth century. Indeed, in 1880 two members of the Regent Committee on the Law Department (both lawyers and one a graduate of the Harvard Law School) recommended that the annual appropriation, which had grown by that time to three thousand dollars, should be gradually reduced so that the "original intention" of the Board—that the school "should eventually be a self-sustaining department, as is usual in similar institutions of learning"—would be carried out.[11] The two thousand dollars appropriated in 1868 simply reflected the determination of the Board to subsidize a law department until a clientele sufficient to support it could be developed. To that end, the most important requirement was to ensure regular lectures; therefore the Board devoted the entire two thousand dollars to pay the salaries of the two faculty appointed to the school.

Jairus H. Carpenter, a forty-six-year-old Madison lawyer of "the true judicial temperament," was designated dean of the Law Department and its only full-time lecturer.[12] William F. Vilas was appointed as lecturer to be supported by the income from student fees. The Regents reported that if "the fees paid by the students in this department will not pay Col. Vilas a salary of $500 per annum," then "Mr. Carpenter and Col. Vilas have agreed to divide the sum of $2000 between them," an arrangement that was to continue until the student fees were sufficient to pay Vilas the full sum of five hundred dollars. In addition to Carpenter and Vilas, the three justices of the Wisconsin Supreme Court agreed to lecture without payment "when their other duties will permit." [13] The listing of Chief Justice Luther S. Dixon and Associate Justices Orsamus Cole and Byron Paine was clearly intended to provide the school with instant prestige. They apparently gave no lectures and as Burr Jones, later a professor in the school, remarked, "the influence of their names was all that was ever expected."[14]

Carpenter was the mainstay of the staff. He was assigned courses in contracts, criminal law, personal property, real property, wills, and equity jurisprudence. Vilas, in contrast, was expected to lecture only on evidence and pleadings. This kind of arrangement was typical of many nineteenth-century law schools, especially in the first decades of their existence. At Harvard in 1829, for example, Joseph Story was appointed a professor while he continued to serve on the United States Supreme Court, but to ensure a regularity in the lectures John Hooker Ashmun was brought in from a private law school to oversee the day-to-day operations of the institution.[15] At Wisconsin, Vilas, along with the state supreme court justices, probably was expected to become one of the major attractions on the early law faculty. Already he fitted the mold of the nineteenth-century legal advocate and the courses assigned to him—evidence and pleading—reflected that reputation. However, the person to whom the Regents turned for regular instructional duties was Jairus Carpenter, that man of the "true judicial temperament." That phrase is significant because in the nineteenth century it contained the implication that Carpenter was unable to hold his own in the rough and tumble of the courtroom. Given the importance in this period of courtroom advocacy as a means of professional advancement, Carpenter's position within his profession must have been an uneasy one, as it would have been for any lawyer with his particular talents. (G. G. Wright, writing in the *Western Jurist* in 1867, advised students that they could become good lawyers without being great advocates but he warned them not to get the reputation of being only a legal counselor.[16]) Men like Carpenter who did not fit the mold of the courtroom advocate could aspire to a position on the bench but the "judicial temperament" would also be a positive advantage in a law school. And, in fact, most of the men appointed to full-time positions in the Wisconsin Law School during the nineteenth century would show a similar aversion to the hectic life of the trial court and an attraction to the intellectual side of the law.[17]

The University of Wisconsin Law Department opened on August 26, 1868. The Regents agreed to provide a room in Main Hall for its use but instead classes were held in the State Capitol Building located about a mile from the University campus. Though the law school would relocate often in the next two decades, it remained physically isolated from the University community until 1893 when a separate building on campus was completed for its use. This arrangement persisted because the faculty and the students, "who, at the time, were all in law offices in the city," [18] found a downtown location more convenient. It also meant that law students would have access to the state law library, a privilege that sharply reduced the University's expenditures for law books.

Because time was so short for notice of the school's opening to be circulated, President Chadbourne had warned the Regents that they should expect "no great number of students" the first term. Still, the new department attracted fifteen students that first year; twelve of them completed the course and graduated the following June. [19]

The purposes of the Wisconsin Law Department were set forth in the 1868–69 University catalog in a statement that would remain virtually unchanged for the next two decades. The beginner in legal study, the catalog stated, "wants . . . to obtain a comprehensive general view and analysis of the whole system" of the law. He also needs "to learn, without the careful reading which would occupy a lifetime, what the books contain, and where to search for more particular and detailed information." Finally, the beginning student "must acquire the habits and methods of legal study and thought." [20] The catalog listed courses in contracts, criminal law, personal and real property, wills, equity jurisprudence, evidence, pleadings, domestic relations and practice. It is clear that the school aimed at breadth rather than depth. Indeed, in one year it would have been impossible for a student to study anything in detail. Readings and lectures, supplemented by occasional moot court work, formed the basis of instruction. The emphasis throughout the course was on the general principles of the law rather than on practical work like the drafting of legal documents. Exposition of legal doctrine, both in the assigned textbooks and in the lectures, was abstract and theoretical. Thus, for students in the University Law Department prior to the 1890s the course provided an introduction to legal study, a broad overview of what the student eventually would have to learn in greater detail.

But the catalog announcement was misleading in one respect. It stated that the course was organized around what the beginning law student needed. In a broad sense, that was true, if one saw the study of law as the work of a lifetime; but in reality many of the students were not beginners in legal study. Many had already had some acquaintance with the work of the lawyer, either through independent reading or a term in a lawyer's office. Others would use the law school to supplement concurrent study in a law office. The law school curriculum, therefore, was designed deliberately to complement other arrangements for legal instruction. For that reason lawyers in the nineteenth century were little concerned about admission and graduation requirements in the law school. It was not yet an important institution for the certification of professional competence.

Patterns of Nineteenth-century Legal Preparation

The limited and supplementary role that law schools played in legal training can be grasped better through a detailed examination of the educational preparation of a Wisconsin lawyer, Roujet D. Marshall, who never attended a law school. Marshall's educational career indicates that apprenticeship, usually assumed to be the dominant mode of legal training in that period, comprised only the most formalized part of a long introduction into the rules, techniques, and values of the legal profession. Thus Marshall's experience, while not typical, begins to suggest the range of educational possibilities open to the beginning law student, and it creates a context for understanding the sharply proscribed role of the nineteenth century Wisconsin Law Department.

Roujet D. Marshall, who would later become a justice on the Wisconsin Supreme Court, began legal study in Wisconsin during the late 1860s at about the time the University Law Department was established. Marshall's early interest in law derived from reading accounts of famous trials and biographies of renowned lawyers. That interest was probably heightened by watching lawyers argue their cases when the circuit-riding judge came to town. As he reached his late teens Marshall determined to become a lawyer himself, and he asked a lawyer who lived nearby for advice. This attorney told Marshall to pursue a college education and then "in the course of a year or two, to commence and pursue, as diligently as practicable, a course of reading law at home." Marshall accepted the advice and the offer of a loan of some law books and returned home. During the next three years Marshall worked on the family farm, attended Baraboo College and read law in his spare time. By the spring of 1868, when he was twenty-one years old, Marshall had "finished reading and reviewing Blackstone's Commentaries and was quite confident of having become well versed in all the principles dealt with." He "next took up the reading of Kent's Commentaries which [he] purposed mastering before entering a law office." Marshall wanted to become familiar with the principles of law before entering a law office, not only because that familiarity would make his formal apprenticeship of greater use to himself, but also because his learning would "be of some value to the person who might see fit to take me in as a law clerk and student." [21] The poverty-stricken Marshall probably also hoped to be able to avoid any fee for his instruction by increasing the value of his services.

Also in the spring of 1868 Marshall ran for the office of justice of the peace. His election to that office proved to be an important step in his legal education because it gave him "possession of a copy of the Statutes of the State and some other law books, and a court docket, running back several years, including the period when men of considerable ability held the office." He held the post of justice of the peace for two years and though he "was seldom applied to for the exercise of official duties, anticipating that I might be, I endeavored to fit myself therefor." Marshall later recalled that "by familiarizing myself with the books and records mentioned, I derived much benefit." [22]

In 1870, at the age of twenty-three, Marshall finally decided to enter a law office. He was certain that he should choose an office near the county seat "where courts were frequently held," but he was less certain about whose office to enter. The choice was between the offices of Cyrus Remington and N. W. Wheeler. Remington was "regarded as the head of his profession in the county" and was much nearer than Wheeler to Marshall's ideal of what a lawyer should be. Remington was "more profound in the law than Mr. Wheeler and more successful as a practitioner, especially where an appeal to a jury was less important than logical presentation to the court of cold questions of law." Wheeler, in contrast, was "well-read but rather indolent." He "relied more on his oratorical ability and logically and convincingly presenting questions to the court and jury than on his knowledge of law. As what was commonly called a jury lawyer, he had no superior in the country around, if in the state." [23] The choice, then, was between a lawyer of superior legal knowledge and a lawyer with superb oratorical ability, between a counselor and an advocate.

Although Marshall's own sympathies were with Remington, the counselor, he chose not to enter his office. Perhaps Marshall realized that as a young lawyer, he would build his own reputation, at least initially, on the trial circuit and hence would make better use of the legal skills to be learned from Wheeler, the advocate. (As a matter of fact Marshall did build his early, though local, reputation on the strength of a successful defense of a murder suspect. Marshall's impassioned plea on the accused's behalf, he later recalled, caused some jurors "to brush away a tear." [24]) Marshall, however, thought the personalities of the two men more important. Remington was "dignified and difficult of approach." He was also "very self-confident, so much so that he was quite disinclined to entrust anything but matters of a merely clerical nature to a law student." In contrast, Wheeler had a "natural disinclination" for hard work and thus "was ever willing to permit any young man with him who had obtained a fair knowledge of legal principles and was ambitious to learn by doing things, to have ample opportunity to do so. There was hardly anything that Mr. Wheeler was not willing to farm out to the boy, as he was wont to call his office assistant, only taking time to go over the young man's work for approval or disapproval before using it." [25] The opportunity for learning law was greater in Wheeler's office and Marshall would therefore put himself under Wheeler's tutelage.

The decision was not an easy one, and Marshall apparently put it off for about a year. In the interim he worked as deputy clerk of the circuit court, again using a judicial office to further his acquaintance with legal doctrine and court procedure. Marshall finally entered Wheeler's office in the fall of 1870, where he began to pursue his legal reading with greater concentration and intensity. He began to read Greenleaf on *Evidence*, Roscoe's *Criminal Evidence*, Russell on *Crimes* and "standard works on contracts and commercial law." [26]

Marshall worked in the law office only during the winter. Each spring he returned to work the family farm, reading law after the day's work was done. This combination of supervised and unsupervised reading continued for three years, until 1873, and by the end of his term in Wheeler's office Marshall was doing a considerable amount and variety of legal work. "I did more practice work, drew papers, to a considerable extent, and tried cases in justice court, besides reviewing in a general way, all I had gone over before, particularly all relating to criminal law, contracts, commercial law, and real estate." [27] In the spring of 1873 Marshall applied for admittance to the bar, underwent a "rigorous" examination in open court, and was admitted to the legal profession.[28] His education, of course, would continue as he entered the convivial life of the circuit.

Evidence gathered from a study of the biographies of Wisconsin lawyers suggests that Marshall's training was not exceptional. By the time Marshall was admitted to the bar at the age of twenty-six, he had undergone a number of distinct educational experiences: solitary study, service as justice of the peace and clerk of the circuit court, practice in the arena of justice court (where no license to practice was then required), and reading and office work under the supervision of a practicing attorney. That variety was perhaps unusual to find in a single career but the length of time—nine years—devoted to part- and full-time preparation was not at all unusual.

The careers of 464 eminent Wisconsin lawyers are detailed in two massive volumes published in 1898. The age at which admission to the bar occurred can be determined for 385 (83 percent) of those lawyers. The average age at bar admission is twenty-five years, or one year less than Marshall's age when he was admitted to the bar. This was the case whether the lawyer attended a law school or not. For the 216 lawyers who used apprenticeship as the main path to the bar, the mean age at the time of admission to practice is 25.4 years (the median is 24); for the 116 who combined apprenticeship with law school training, the mean age is 25.2 (the median is 25). Finally, there are fifty-three lawyers whose mode of preparation is uncertain but whose age at the time of admission still can be established. The mean age for that group is 26.6 years (median = 25).[29]

Those figures support the argument that preparation for the bar in the nineteenth century was a slow and gradual process of training and initiation. That pattern of extended legal training was enforced by the practitioners themselves who selected, advised and sponsored those young men who desired to become lawyers. Apprenticeship, then, was a formal mode of legal training in the nineteenth century, but it was commonly combined with solitary study, observation of court proceedings, service as a court clerk or justice of the peace, practice in justice court and, with increasing frequency, a brief period in a law school. That latter experience gave order and coherence to the other modes of preparation.

To argue that office apprenticeship was a formal mode of preparation, however, does not necessarily imply that the experience itself was logically organized. One of the more persistent complaints of students in law offices was the absence of any overall design to what they studied. To some extent that problem could be alleviated by the explanations of the supervising attorney but the reminiscences of law students suggest that far too often the lawyer was too busy or too indifferent to provide the explanations needed. Moreover, the problem of unsystematic study was inherent in the nature of apprenticeship itself. The flow of office work tended to determine the order in which the beginning law student first approached many legal concepts. There was, of course, no assurance that clients would bring their legal problems to the attorney in any kind of logical order. Clerical and research duties of widely varying kinds might be required of a law student in the course of a single day. In addition, the trend toward legal specialization in the nineteenth century began to detract from the value of apprenticeship. That is, as lawyers concentrated their efforts in certain fields of law, like tax law, railroad law or patent law, the value of study in their offices declined precipitously. The beginning student needed a broad variety of legal problems, problems that ideally would be approached in order of increasing complexity and difficulty.

The vast outpouring of legal treatises in the nineteenth century probably mitigated the worst effects of office reading and unsupervised study. Those treatises did impose a logical order on many fields of law and they possibly also slowed the expansion of law schools by enabling students to pursue with greater profit a course of reading. But even here students faced problems. The treatises stated the law abstractly, logically and definitionally. "Few textbooks," the Wisconsin law catalog advised in 1871, "are written for students. The most elementary works are designed as exhaustive treatises for the use of lawyers and embrace not only the history of the growth of the doctrine, but also a discussion of the subject in far more detail than the student can advisably pursue so early." [30] And as single treatises went through many editions, changes and refinements in the law naturally appeared. Did the student have the latest edition of the work? Did other legal scholars agree with the edition in hand? Did the law as defined in the treatise apply to local conditions? These and other questions demanded the attention of an experienced lawyer; if one was not available in a law office, then lectures by a practitioner in a law school were a sensible substitute. The abstract nature of the law school curriculum thus became the major attraction of the school. Law students received, in the time spent in the law school, a systematic exposition of knowledge they were confronting in less organized fashion elsewhere. The three aims of the Wisconsin Law School announced in the 1868 catalog—to give the student a "comprehensive view" of the legal system, to introduce him to the literature of the law, and to train him in the "habits and methods" of legal study—nicely complemented office reading or other methods of legal preparation.

Most students who attended the Wisconsin Law Department during the years between 1868 and 1888 shared the assumption that the mission of the school was to supplement other forms of preparation. All the evidence available indicates that many students, in most years a majority, worked in a law office at the same time that they were enrolled in the Wisconsin Law Department. And of those students who did not study in the office and school concurrently, many used the law school either before or, more commonly, after a period of office reading. Levi Bancroft, who entered the Wisconsin Law Department in the fall of 1882, and shortly thereafter accepted a position in the law office of P. L. Spooner, remarked that "it is customary for the students *when they can* to enter the law office of some practitioner in the city who directs their reading, [and] gives them the use of his library." [31] Burr W. Jones made an arrangement with Madison lawyer John D. Gurnee to work in his office while Jones attended the Law Department in 1870. For doing "such work as might be necessary" Jones was paid thirty dollars a month, though he noted that it was highly unusual for a student to be paid for office work.[32] Other students who attended the Wisconsin Law

Department also spent time in a law office. John M. Olin studied law for a summer before entering the Wisconsin Law School; [33] Robert M. LaFollette was admitted to the bar after five months' study, "part of the time in the office of R. M. Bashford and part of the time in the university law school"; [34] and John B. Winslow studied in a law office for two years before entering the Law Department. [35]

An analysis of attendance patterns at the University of Wisconsin Law Department between the years 1878 and 1895 corroborates the testimony of the individual lawyers cited above. After 1878 two years of legal study were required for the LL.B. at Wisconsin. Time spent in a law office or another law school, however, could still be used to fulfill one year of that requirement. In each year after 1878, then, the number of students new to the senior class had at least one year of prior training in a law office or a law school. Given the fact that few students entered any law school at that time, and assuming that the number who transferred from another law school was small,[36] the students new to the senior class provide a rough estimate of the number of students combining office work with law school lectures. As Figure 1 indicates, the number of seniors who were new to the school exceeded the number returning from the previous junior class in seven out of ten years between 1878 and 1888. The figures drop below fifty percent only in 1881 and 1882 (the first two years of a formal two-year program) [37] and in 1886, near the end of the period when the pattern begins to change. During the 1890s (with the exception of 1894, the last year before a three-year program was instituted), this trend was reversed. Now the number of seniors who were continuing students outnumbered new seniors. Although some students did continue to work in law offices,[38] the change in the trend, as the next chapter will argue, was largely the result of the inability of students to find openings in Madison law offices during the 1880s.

The central point to grasp is that the nineteenth-century law school was orginally perceived as simply one additional pathway through which a student might receive a part of his legal preparation. While men at Wisconsin who established the Law Department and who guided its development during the decades of the 1870s and 1880s obviously thought it was an important institution, they did not view it as the central institution for legal preparation nor did they expect it to become such an institution. The curriculum in the school was intentionally broad and it was deliberately designed to complement, rather than compete with, office apprenticeship. Moreover, these men did not believe that the law school had a central responsibility for certifying to the public or to the profession the competence of its graduates. Lawyers, they expected, would continue to establish their professional

Figure 1

Year	1877–78	1878–79	1879–80	1880–81	1881–82	1882–83
Total Attendance	31	48	52	64	49	48
Junior Class	31	17	18	24	21	20
Senior Class		31	34	40	28	28
Junior Class Returning		7	15	12	19	15
New Seniors		24	19	28	9	13
% New Seniors		79%	56%	70%	32%	46%

Year	1883–84	1884–85	1885–86	1886–87	1887–88	1888–89
Total Attendance	36	38	60	70	113	119 [1]
Junior Class	13	20	27	35	54	44
Senior Class	23	18	33	35	59	43
Junior Class Returning	9	7	12	19	23	41
New Seniors	14	11	21	16	36	2 (32) [1]
% New Seniors	61%	61%	64%	46%	61%	5% (79%) [1]

Year	1889–90	1890–91	1891–92	1892–93	1893–94	1894–95
Total Attendance	112	118	126	166	169	266 [2]
Junior Class	51	51	73	86	87	157
Senior Class	61	67	53	80	82	93
Junior Class Returning	40	48	36	60	65	69
New Seniors	21	19	17	20	17	88
% New Seniors	34%	28%	32%	25%	21%	95%

[1] A one-year course, apparently designed specifically for students who were combining law office study with the law school, attracted 32 students this year.

[2] This total includes 16 students who entered on the first year of the newly established three-year program. The huge influx of students into the junior class this year represented the effort of many to evade the three-year program by enrolling in the last two-year sequence to be offered at Wisconsin.

credentials after admission to practice as evidenced by their ability in the courts and through their growing acquaintance with their professional brethren.

Professional Standards and the Diploma Privilege

In 1870 the Wisconsin legislature passed a "diploma privilege" law. This statute granted all graduates of the University Law Department automatic admission to practice in any court in the state upon presentation of a Wisconsin LL.B. and the payment of a nominal fee.[37] Precedents for the Wisconsin diploma privilege existed in other states. Virginia had been the first state to adopt such a law, in 1842, although the statute was repealed in 1849. In the 1850s the New York legislature favored the Albany Law School with the diploma privilege and in the early 1860s extended it to the Columbia Law School and the New York University Law School. The New York statute was probably the general model for the Wisconsin diploma privilege, for many former New Yorkers lived in Wisconsin, and the number of lawyers in the state who had attended the Albany Law School was quite large.[40] William F. Vilas, of course, was quite familiar with the New York law. In the west, the Michigan Law School, Wisconsin's nearest competitor, gained the diploma privilege in 1863 (and would maintain it until 1881 and again in the years between 1895 and 1913). By 1870, then, when the Wisconsin diploma privilege law was passed, nine schools in seven states (including Wisconsin) had secured a similar right.[41]

The Wisconsin diploma privilege was passed because the Regents were disappointed in the attendance at the school, and its passage almost certainly was the major factor in the growth of the student body in the Wisconsin Law Department during the 1870s and 1880s. The enrollment jumped from thirteen in 1869 to an average enrollment of twenty-eight in the years between 1870 and 1875. The increase in the number of graduates almost kept pace, from nine in 1870 to an average of twenty-six over the next five years. Thereafter, the attendance continued to rise, reaching fifty-two in 1879 and seventy in 1886; but the number of graduates leveled off after 1875, ranging between ten and thirty-eight in the following decade.[42] Despite the increased attendance, the diploma privilege did not attract enough students to place the school on a self-sufficient basis.

The act of granting the Wisconsin Department of Law the diploma privilege simply indicated that the legal profession remained indifferent toward formal admission requirements of any kind during this period. After 1861, formal entrance to the Wisconsin legal profession was governed by a statute which required that the applicant be a resident of the state, of good moral character, and able to pass an examination in open court "to ascertain whether [the] applicant possesses sufficient legal knowledge."[43] Not only were these examinations apparently quite easy but it was also a common practice for young men who found an examining judge in one judicial district too strict to journey from court to court until they found a judge lenient enough to admit them to the bar. The practice was finally barred in 1881 when a revised law required an applicant to be a resident of the judicial district where he applied for admission.[44] Not until 1885, however, when a statewide Board of Bar examiners was established, did the state formally require at least two years of legal study prior to bar admission.[45]

In 1870 the rules which governed admission to and graduation from the Wisconsin Law Department did not differ in any degree from the statutory regulations for admission to the bar. Applicants to the school were required only to be of good moral character, to which was added in 1872 an examination in "the ordinary English branches." [46] It is doubtful that that exam was any more rigorous than the judgment made by an attorney before he took a student into his office. These admission rules remained in effect until the late 1880s. Graduation from the Wisconsin Law Department was also fairly easy. Students needed to attend the school for one year (three terms), though students who attended only for the final term "may be graduated if they have pursued a course of study elsewhere equivalent to that required here." [47] Again, the apparent looseness of this requirement simply reflected the common assumption that the LL.B. was largely honorary and that even automatic admission to the bar following a minimal period of preparation did not threaten professional standards when controls were maintained after admission to the bar.

Nevertheless, the diploma privilege did represent a potential threat to professional standards. As long as the traditional means of policing the legal profession—notably the "convivial life" of the bar—were effective, and as long as students shared the assumption that law school lectures were meant to complement the office experience, then the scholastic standards of the Wisconsin Law Department had quite a marginal effect on the legal profession. But the founders of the Wisconsin Law Department could not foresee that the 1870s and 1880s would be a period when regulation of lawyers after they were admitted would begin to dissolve and when the harmonious relationship between law school and law office would be severely challenged. Under the pressure of such changes the Wisconsin law faculty, along with the state bar itself, would be forced to reexamine their assumption about the role that the law school played in professional life.

CHAPTER FOUR

The Drift Toward Formalism

Lawyers did not show any concern about the academic standards of the nineteenth-century law school until the harmonious relationship between the law school and the apprenticeship system began to break down. Three developments undermined the fragile connection between school and office. First, the growth of the legal profession in some areas of the country, particularly in the smaller towns, did not keep pace with the number of students who were beginning to attend a law school. The overcrowding in local law offices that resulted made it much more difficult, as a practical matter, to combine law school training with apprenticeship. Second, the regulatory functions of the judicial circuit diminished in strength as prominent lawyers established a practice in one locale. The disengagement of the more prestigious lawyers from the convivial life of the circuit made it increasingly difficult to enforce standards of professional conduct in an immediate and personal way. Third, these same prominent lawyers began to shift the focus of their professional practice to serve corporate and business interests, a shift that demanded different professional skills. Now it became more important to be able to arrange a client's affairs so as to prevent subsequent court challenge than to be at the ready to defend the client's interests in the courtroom itself. Not only did this fundamental shift from advocacy to counseling further undermine the professional life of the circuit, based as the latter was upon the courtroom battle, but eventually it also would make the abstract and theoretical training provided by the law school a more important and practical kind of professional knowledge.

Facing, though never fully understanding, these profound shifts in professional life, members of the bar began to search for ways to restore the familiar patterns of professional training and organization. All their experiments—the establishment of bar associations, the passage of laws setting more stringent standards for admission to the bar and the movement toward higher admission and degree requirements in the law schools—represented a drift toward a greater formalism in professional life. Though the pace of change varied from region to region, the trend was visible everywhere after 1870. In Wisconsin, more formal modes of training and regulation appear first in the late 1870s. In 1878 a small group of lawyers formed the Wisconsin State Bar Association. By 1885 these men had succeeded in establishing a State Board of Bar Examiners and in revising the statute governing admission to the bar to require two years of formal legal study. The faculty in the University Law Department, themselves among the leaders in the Bar Association, lengthened the course of study from one year to two, began to standardize the admission and degree requirements in the school and even experimented with ranking students according to academic achievement. By the late 1880s, then, the informal standards of behavior previously enforced through the convivial life of the circuit had begun to be engraved in more formal and explicit codes of professional training and conduct.

A Plethora of Law Students

The possibility that opportunities for young men to enter Madison law offices diminished during the 1870s and 1880s was suggested in a letter that Levi Bancroft, who had just enrolled in the University of Wisconsin Law Department, wrote to his family in 1882. Bancroft said that it was "customary for the students *when they can* to enter the law office of some practitioner in the city who directs their reading, [and] gives them the use of his library." [1] Bancroft supplied the emphasis to underscore his own good fortune in securing such a position. But an analysis of the growth of the legal profession in the Madison area indicates that other young men were not so fortunate.

The number of lawyers and the number of law offices in Madison began to decline sometime in the late 1860s and continued to drop until the late 1870s. The disruption caused by the Civil War was perhaps a factor, but the pace of economic development combined with natural settlement patterns were probably more important. In Dane County, where Madison and the University of Wisconsin were located, the total number of lawyers dropped between 1860 and 1870 from fifty-nine to fifty-four; but the total number of lawyers in cities and villages other than Madison increased by four while Madison experienced a drop of nine lawyers.[2] The reason for this is that as the state population grew, settlement patterns tended initially to fill out the area around Madison rather than in the central city itself. These same years, moreover, were characterized by an economic recession in the area, a period of stagnation reflected in the slow population growth during the years between 1865 and 1880. In 1865 the Madison population was 9,191; fifteen years later the population was only 10,341.[3]

The effect of this on the Madison legal profession was striking. In 1858 there had been forty-two lawyers in the city and they were organized into twenty-seven law offices. In 1871 (the next year for which comparable figures are available) Madison had only thirty-five lawyers dispersed among twenty-four offices. This decline reached bottom in 1876 when the University Regents first considered, only to reject, a proposal to extend the law school course to two years. In that year there were only twenty-nine lawyers in Madison organized into twenty-one law offices. Thereafter the number of lawyers began to increase, and by 1880 there were forty-four lawyers organized into twenty-eight law offices.[4] Still, this was an increase of only two more lawyers and one additional law firm than Madison had boasted in 1858.

While the number of lawyers remained stable or declined during the 1860s and most of the 1870s, the number of law students in the new University Law Department increased significantly, and there can be little doubt that the demand for apprenticeship positions created by sheer numbers of law students was increasing. The appearance in the middle of the nineteenth century of a new occupational category—the permanent office clerk—only made matters worse. The state census of 1870 for Madison listed for the first time four law clerks. These four men ranged in age from thirty to forty-eight and, according to the census, possessed real property ranging in value from one thousand dollars to thirty-five hundred dollars.[5] These were not the characteristics of law students, who also often were called "clerks," but of stable, middle-class citizens. And with the appearance of full-time law clerks, the lawyer's traditional need for law students to copy documents and run errands correspondingly declined.

The general dimensions of the problem of overcrowded law offices is suggested by information contained in the 1880 City of Madison Directory. The Directory for that year (and only for that year during the nineteenth century) included "law student" as a category. These men were listed not because they were attending the Wisconsin Law Department (though many were) but because they were students in the office of a local attorney. Thus, a sample listing would run: "Henry Kessenish, Student, Sloan, Stevens & Morris, Res. Francis [Street]."

Seventeen such students were listed in the 1880 *Directory:*[6] five were in their second year of law school; seven were in their first year of law school; two would later enter the Wisconsin Law Department; and three were never listed in the law school catalog.[7] Only twelve of the seventeen students can be assigned to specific law offices and these twelve were scattered among nine of the twenty-eight law offices in Madison at that time. If the twelve law school students who can be assigned to a specific office are deducted from the total attendance of sixty-eight in the Wisconsin Law Department in 1880-81, then fifty-six law school students remain to fill spaces in nineteen offices. Even if it is assumed that each of those offices could handle two students (probably not a reasonable assumption), then it is still the case that eighteen law school students would have had difficulty securing an apprenticeship position. And—to posit a totally unreasonable assumption—even if most of these students in 1880 did in fact find places in a law office, it must be remembered that each year the attendance at the Wisconsin Law Department rose and each new influx of students (the majority in any one year were usually from outside the Madison area) created a backlog of students waiting for office space. All this suggests that when in 1888 *The Aegis*, a student newspaper, noted that less than a third of the law school students were in offices in the city, that estimate was probably close to the mark.[8]

The timing of this overcrowding was significant. The low point of available office openings in Madison occurred during the middle 1870s at exactly the time that the University Regents ruled that two years of legal study, one under the direction of the law faculty and one under the supervision of a practitioner, were necessary to obtain the LL.B. Although the Regents were attempting to reaffirm the traditional role of the law school as a supplement to office reading, the new regulation came at precisely the moment that the institution of apprenticeship in Madison was least able to handle more law students. The fact that office openings were more difficult to secure after 1875, when combined with a rule that the LL.B. required two years of legal study if only in part in law school, created a situation where the law faculty and the Regents were forced to find a way that would make it feasible for at least some young men to complete all the work for the degree in the Law Department itself. In 1881, therefore, the University law course was lengthened to two years.

Local peculiarities—for example, the long period of economic stagnation and slow population growth in the Madison area—certainly accentuated the seriousness of the problem of overcrowding. But the establishment of a law school in any community during the nineteenth century brought with it an increase in the concentration of law students, and most of those communities and their law schools experienced similar pressures upon the harmonious arrangement between school and office. The only exceptions appear to have been in large cities; and, indeed, it is in the large cities, like New York, Chicago, and, in Wisconsin, Milwaukee, that the practice of combining law school attendance with study in a law office persisted, in some cases well into the twentieth century. The problems created by a shortage of law office openings, however, became most severe in the two decades after the Civil War because by that time there were signs, indistinct and not always recognized, that there were now other pressures on apprenticeship, pressures that derived from broad shifts in the nature of legal practice.

From Advocacy to Counseling

After about 1870 the image of the successful lawyer began to change from courtroom advocate to office counselor. According to Willard Hurst, this "shift in emphasis from advocacy to counselling was the most basic change in the nature of lawyers' professional work" in the nineteenth century.[9] The shift was given major impetus by the growth of corporations in the years after the Civil War. Corporations, in an effort to monopolize the finest legal talent available, retained lawyers on a long-term basis. In turn, lawyers were expected to represent the corporation in the courtroom when the occasion arose. This arrangement had a number of advantages, not the least of which was the assurance given the corporation that a good lawyer would not appear in court as an opponent. Even more important, lawyers now began to be expected to devise ways to keep their clients out of court. The contentious life of the frontier, from which the convivial life of the judicial circuit drew its sustenance, had developed in large part because of the fact that only small sums of money were usually at stake. According to one nineteenth-century observer, "in the early days when many clients were execution proof, and had everything to gain and nothing to lose by litigation, when a judgment for costs had no terrors, it was natural that law suits should be a popular remedy." But as the consequences of defeat grew more serious lawyers were increasingly asked for legal advice, especially in contractual arrangements, that would preclude later court challenge.[10]

This shift in the image of the lawyer from trial advocate to office counselor had profound effects on both the role of the law office in legal preparation and on the development of the American law school. One consequence for the system of apprenticeship has already been mentioned. As lawyers retreated from the courtroom to the office, they often began to develop special areas in which to concentrate their legal practice. This was a natural movement because effective legal counseling depended not upon the oratorical skills necessary to sway a jury but upon a profound grasp of complex issues of law. As it became more and more necessary to cultivate thoroughness and depth of knowledge, it also made sense to narrow the scope of one's area of expertise. The beginning law student, however, did not find in a specialized law office that broad range of issues and problems which would make his office reading most useful. Specialization of function in legal practice thus tended to undercut the law office as a center of legal preparation.

But the shift from advocacy to counseling affected office apprenticeship in a more subtle, and perhaps much more important way. Recall the discussion by Roujet D. Marshall as he explained why he chose Wheeler, the advocate, instead of Remington, the counselor, when Marshall finally decided to enter a law office. Even though Marshall was much more in sympathy with the ideal of the lawyer represented by the counselor, Remington, he picked the "indolent" Wheeler because he would give Marshall much greater responsibility. Marshall explained the differences between the two men largely in terms of their personalities: Remington was "dignified and difficult of approach" and was "very self-confident" so that he entrusted only matters of a "merely clerical nature to a law student." Wheeler, in contrast, had a "natural disinclination" for hard work and therefore was willing to farm out to his apprentice almost anything, "only taking time to go over the young man's work for approval or disapproval before using it." While the personalities of the two men were probably important, it is also essential to note that their attitudes toward their law students corresponded nicely with the image of the lawyer that each man had adopted. The counselor, concerned with technical legal doctrines, with "cold questions of law," in Marshall's phrase, would be understandably reluctant to turn over to an inexperienced law student matters that might cost a client thousands of dollars if a mistake were made. The advocate who "relied more on his oratorical ability and logically and convincingly presenting questions to the court and jury than on his knowledge of law," [11] did not expect profound analyses of the law from his apprentice. Moreover, the advocate, who plied his skills more often on the local level, usually had clients with much less at stake financially and in that situation it was natural and feasible to give the law clerk greater responsibility. The shift from advocacy to counseling, then, had a further effect on the nature of the law office as a center of legal preparation: It tended to isolate the apprentice from the main business of the lawyer and threatened to turn the clerk into at best a researcher of cases.

It is important to understand that this significant change in the nature of the lawyer's duties occurred over decades and that during these years the image of the advocate and the counselor jostled each other for dominance. On the national level Willard Hurst dates the shift in favor of the counselor from roughly after 1870. [12] In Wisconsin, a benchmark of sorts was established in 1878 in the case of Brown vs. Swineford. The Wisconsin Supreme Court decided in that case that circuit court judges had a duty to intervene when lawyers, in the full flush of oratory, based their arguments on facts not appearing on the record or "appealing to prejudices irrelevant to the case and outside of proof." [13] This decision represented an effort to curtail the excesses of the courtroom advocate, excesses that were in reality an important part of his legal talents; and it therefore rendered recognizable a movement away from the image of the lawyer as a powerful advocate.

The shift in the image of lawyers from trial advocates to office counselors was obviously paralleled by a new emphasis on legal knowledge rather than oratorical skills as the key to professional reputation. And here the law school, where the abstract and theoretical curriculum had always nicely, if briefly, complemented the practical skills learned in the office and courtroom, had the decided advantage. It would eventually become the dominant mode of training because its very bookishness made it well suited to teaching detailed and technical knowledge of legal principles. Eventually, too, the manner in which professional competence was established also changed, from public advocacy in the courtroom to evidence of mastery of legal knowledge through the bar examination and the law school diploma. Law schools would not only train this new lawyer but they would also assume a major responsibility for certifying to the public and to the profession his competence.

But these changes, it cannot be stressed enough, occurred gradually. The image of the lawyer as advocate did not suddenly disappear overnight, and for many law students it still represented an attractive and perhaps even a dominant ideal during the last three decades of the nineteenth century. This should not be surprising because the expanding corporate economy, upon which the emergence of the counselor so much depended, did not secure its legal talent from among the very young lawyers but from older, established attorneys. In the 1880s and even later young lawyers still established their initial reputation as often in the local trial courts as they did in the corporate office. Recognizing this, they maintained an interest in honing the skills of the advocate.

The slow pace at which this shift in the nature of the lawyer's duties affected the law school and the law student is nicely indicated in the history of the student law clubs at the University of Wisconsin. These clubs, which began to appear in the 1880s, reflected what law students perceived as the skills important to the successful lawyer. The first of these clubs, the E. G. Ryan Society, was organized in 1883. This society was modeled upon the undergraduate literary and debating societies that were so important a part of college life in the nineteenth century.[14] The law students who organized the E. G. Ryan Society declared in the preamble to the club constitution their belief in "the advantages to be derived from exercise in debate and parliamentary practice." [15] And the topics assigned for discussion in the Ryan Society were essentially the same as those debated in the undergraduate clubs. Typically, the topics dealt with broad questions of social, economic or political policy. In March, 1884, for instance, the following questions were debated by Ryan Society members: "Resolved, that gold should be the only standard of value"; "Resolved, that the electoral franchise should be based upon educational qualifications"; "Resolved, that Nihilism in Russia is justifiable"; and "Resolved, that the U.S. Banks, as the Banks of Issue, should be abolished." Only one question in that month dealt directly with a narrow legal topic: "Should insane persons be held liable for their Torts?"; and that discussion was recorded in the minutes as an "impromptu debate." [16]

The obvious similarity between undergraduate debating societies and the E. G. Ryan Society is hardly surprising. Apart from the fact that the college literary societies were the most readily available models for law students,[17] college students generally in the nineteenth century assumed that in adult life they would have the primary responsibility for political and social leadership. The extent of their influence, they further assumed, would be broadened immensely by training in oratory and debate. Law was simply a more specialized area for participation in local, state or national affairs and, indeed, the close connection between law and politics hardly even implied specialization. The art of advocacy, whether in the courtroom or in the legislative chamber, formed the technical basis of lawyers' and politicians' influence.

Almost from its inception, however, the E. G. Ryan Society experienced difficulty in drawing law students to its meetings, a fact which might suggest that law students even then may have been questioning the image of the lawyer as advocate. At the April 19, 1884, meeting of the society the members decided (by a vote of four to two) to "discuss the condition of the society." After a "lively discussion" the members decided to "rise and report, that the Ryan Society is still booming." [18] With only six members present and voting the boast had a hollow ring. The following year, when the condition of the society was again discussed, "no definite conclusion was arrived at." [19] *The Aegis* remarked in the fall of 1886 that "it is strange that with a membership of nearly 50 the E. G. Ryan should be so poorly attended." The puzzlement over the decline was obvious.

Perhaps it is due to the fact that the new students have not yet settled down and cannot spare the time; still another fact is apparent, namely, that the old students do not manifest that lively interest in society matters which was evinced last year. Let all members turn out and have a regular old-time meeting, such as we enjoyed so heartily heretofore.[20]

Members of the society were in fact secretive about the reasons for the decline in attendance: "At times, on account of the increase in class work together with other causes unnecessary to enumerate, the usual high standing of the society was not maintained." [21]

It is certain that one cause of this decline was the emergence of other college activities, like football and social fraternities, which not only filled leisure time but also provided an alternate form of "entertainment," a favorite word used to characterize the literary society meetings.[22] But it also seems clear that fewer students, both in the College of Letters and Science and in the Law Department, were finding debating skills an important part of their preparation for the future. As far as law students were concerned, the image of the legal advocate, so central to the formation of the E. G. Ryan Society, did not vanish suddenly. With the establishment of a new student law club, The Forum, however, there is a hint that that image was being challenged by the idea that the lawyer should be first and foremost a careful legal technician.

The Forum was organized on April 18, 1889 when seven law students met in the office of a Madison attorney named Richmond to "consider the advisability of organizing a new society connected with the law college at the University of Wisconsin." These students took this action because the E. G. Ryan Society "seemed to be forsaken by its members." [23] As the name of the society indicated, the students agreed with the members of the Ryan Society that the art of oratory and debate should be cultivated by law students. The Forum, they believed, was "an appropriate name" for a society "whose members are destined to rank foremost in the *fora judicilia* of our Republic." But The Forum founders also hinted that there would be a distinct difference between the activities of the new society and those of the E. G. Ryan group. "The debates are characterized by common sense and careful preparation, and the discussions show exhaustive research." Members of The Forum "seem to feel that the work of the lawyer consists in a systematic search for truth rather than in attempts at old-style oratory." [24] The question debated at the first meeting of The Forum indicated in concrete terms what the differences between the two clubs would be: "Resolved, that common carriers should not be allowed to limit their common liability by special contract or notice." At a later meeting they discussed whether the "Petit Jury system should be abolished." [25] Such questions were more oriented to a discussion of legal principles than the broad social policy issues debated in the E. G. Ryan Society.

The organization of The Forum in 1889 marked only the beginnings of this important shift in the attitudes of law students away from oral advocacy. In the years between 1897 and 1902 five new law clubs would be formed by students in the Wisconsin Law School. The Luther S. Dixon Law Club was established in 1897, the Andrew A. Bruce Law Club in 1900, the John Marshall Law Club in 1901, and the Edwin Bryant and the Chancellor Kent Law Clubs in 1902. [26] These five clubs (modeled upon similar organizations at Harvard) [27] were not primarily debating or discussion societies. These clubs instead were each organized as a hierarchical series of courts. The Luther S. Dixon Club, a model for the other four, was "divided into three courts: Appellate, Supreme, and Superior, the first being composed of Seniors, the second of Middles [second-year law students], and the third of Juniors." The object of the Dixon Club was "to determine the method of working cases, to get acquainted with the process of pleading under Wisconsin rules, to give training in parliamentary practice, and in oral argument." [28] The purpose of the John Marshall Club was similar: "The society will try cases according to the supreme, circuit, and justice court procedure and all the formalities of practice and pleading will be followed as nearly as possible." [29]

Although some of these law clubs survived into the first decade of the twentieth century, they do not appear to have flourished for long. The Law School *Bulletin* of 1906 noted that "The practice court is supplemented by a number of club courts, voluntary student organizations, where legal questions are argued and debated." [30] The following year the reference to the club courts was dropped. By 1911 the catalog contained only the terse notice that "A number of law clubs are maintained by the students, in which questions of law are argued and determined." [31] By 1918 all references to law clubs, student courts and debating societies were dropped from the law catalog. To some extent, the student law clubs withered away because the activities they sponsored entered the formal curriculum of the law school but an even more important cause of their decline was that a debating club, even if its members attempted to confine their discussions to formal legal questions, simply was not the appropriate agency through which to develop the skills of the office counselor. The counselor was noted for thorough research and closely reasoned opinions more appropriately rendered in the form of a written legal brief than in oral debate. In the twentieth century (though at the University of Wisconsin not until 1920) the ideal environment for the cultivation of such skills would be the law review.

New "Machinery" for Regulation and Training

The shift after 1870 from advocacy to counseling as the major task of
the lawyer also further undermined the informal arrangements for regulation of the legal profession that had characterized the frontier bar.
Eminent lawyers retreated to their offices and in the process relinquished the opportunity to act as models for or to influence the actions
of younger lawyers. Less and less did the judicial circuit provide an
institutional nexus for professional conviviality. In truth, the influence
of the circuit as a means of professional discipline had been declining
for decades. As pointed out earlier, the inclusive membership which
was a feature of the circuit at the peak of its influence tended to be
rapidly diluted by the growth of small towns and cities. A denser population provided a concentration of legal business in one area which
made it possible for lawyers—especially eminent ones—to leave the
circuit permanently. By the decade of the 1870s, then, professional regulation based upon conviviality and organized around the judicial circuit
was clearly on the wane. As yet, however, alternate ways to control the
legal profession were weak and ineffective. In most areas of the state
local bar associations were just beginning to appear, and even where
they did exist these local associations did not attract a broad membership nor were they able to establish a pattern of regular meetings. Thus
the decades of the 1870s and 1880s were years of transition for the Wisconsin bar, years in which the leaders of the legal profession began to
be concerned about professional standards in a way that would have
been inconceivable a generation earlier.

The remarks of E. G. Ryan concerning bar admission standards in
1846 and again in 1878 provide an impressive measure of how much
attitudes changed. In 1846 during the debates over the proposed Wisconsin State Constitution, the question arose as to what standards
should be required for admission to the bar. The debate centered
around a proposal to restrict the practice of law to those who possessed
"the requisite qualifications of learning and ability." Lawyers lined up
on both sides of the debate, but one, Ryan, expressed the hope "that
whichever the convention should decide to do, they would do one thing
or the other—either shut the door [to the legal profession] close or open
it wide. For his own part he didn't care much which." [32] Ryan, who
would later be listed as a member of the Law School faculty and who
would become perhaps the most learned justice on the Wisconsin Supreme Court in the nineteenth century, probably expressed the feelings
of most men at the time. The upshot of the debate was that the issue of
admission to the bar was largely avoided: The convention passed only a
provision allowing "any suitor in any court of this state . . . the right

to prosecute or defend his suit either in his own proper person or by an attorney of his choice." [33] Because the 1846 Constitution was never ratified and because the 1848 Constitution failed to deal with the question of admission to the bar, one has to wait until 1849 to find an expression in law of the general attitudes toward admission standards. The 1849 legislature required only that the applicant be a resident of the state and of good moral character. No examination of legal knowledge was mandated.[34] From 1850, when that law took effect, until 1861, the standards for admission to the Wisconsin bar remained at this low point. Then in 1861 there began a gradual movement to strengthen the formal admission standards. An act passed in that year retained the requirements of residency and character testimonials but added a minimum age requirement of twenty-one years and an examination in open court "to ascertain whether the applicant possesses sufficient legal knowledge." Fines ranging from fifty dollars to one hundred dollars and ten to sixty days in jail were provided for those who disobeyed the law.[35] This is where matters stood in 1878 when E. G. Ryan, now chief justice of the Wisconsin Supreme Court, warned those lawyers who had gathered in Madison to organize a state bar association that "the rule of admission is unfortunately lax. The doors are not ajar, but wide open." [36] But, except for a brief period during territorial days, the formal rules governing admission to the bar in Wisconsin had always been lax. What had changed Ryan's attitude were shifts in the conditions of legal practice itself. As the older, more personal methods of regulating the legal profession became more and more ineffective, leaders of the bar looked to more formal ways to maintain professional standards.

The organization of the Wisconsin State Bar Association in 1878 provided the principal forum from which lawyers expressed their concern with the quality of the bar. Those lawyers responsible for the organization and operation of the University Law Department took the lead in Association affairs. Supreme Court Justice Edward G. Ryan, listed as a lecturer in the University Law Department catalog from 1874 to 1876 (though he may not have actually delivered any lectures), was elected chairman of the 1877 committee that had been established to advise on the organization of a State Bar Association. William F. Vilas, professor in the Law Department since its opening, was elected secretary of that same organization committee. When the Association finally was formed in January, 1878 members of the law school faculty and their close allies continued to play central roles. Edwin E. Bryant, Vilas' law partner from 1872 to 1883 and later, from 1889 to 1903, dean of the Wisconsin Law School, was elected the first secretary of the State Bar Association; Law School Dean Jairus Carpenter was elected the first treasurer; and William Vilas was elected to the executive committee. John B. Cassoday, also a professor in the Law Department, became a member of the four-man Committee on Legal Education.[37] Cassoday, who had attended the Albany Law School, was also beginning in 1878 a two-year term on the University Regent Committee on the Law Department (and in 1881, when a two-year law course was given formal approval, William F. Vilas would begin a four-year term on that Regent committee).

The focus of discussion at the initial meeting of the State Bar Association was not so much on changes in existing rules governing admission to the bar but upon complaints that such rules as did exist (character references and examination in open court) were not being enforced. One of the first orders of business was a resolution which proposed that "the several circuit Judges of this state be respectfully requested to strictly observe the laws of this state with reference to the admission of members of the bar." Significantly, this resolution was rejected by the membership (with no vote recorded) because the complaint was too specific. The Association felt that the judges it was designed to rebuke would take exception to being singled out in such a manner; at the conclusion of the meeting the members could only agree to resolve blandly that "the Association is in favor of the strict enforcement of the laws of this state regulating the admission of attorneys." [38] In earlier days that admonition to the circuit judges would likely have been administered at a mock trial where feelings could be soothed by whiskey and conviviality. But when the rebuke was administered impersonally and engraved in the permanance of print, there was no way to remove the sting except by directing the complaint at no one in particular. This reluctance to direct complaints at specific lawyers would in the future continue to characterize the State Bar Association, so much so that in 1898 John R. Berryman observed: "There seems to be a profound reluctance on the part of members of the bar to take action looking towards disbarment of unworthy members, even though it reaches a point at which further tolerance would seem almost paramount to complicity." [39]

But if the new methods of regulating the profession made it more difficult to discipline members of the profession, it was not so difficult to lay down and enforce rules for those who were not yet members of the profession. The decline of the convivial life of the circuit, then, had an additional effect on the legal profession. The bar changed its policy of trying to regulate lawyers after they had been admitted, by means of mock trials and the like, to a policy of selecting only worthy candidates for membership in the profession. Accordingly, the Wisconsin State Bar Association during the nineteenth century was concerned mainly with the passage of stricter laws governing admission to the bar; in the twentieth century, when the law school had become the dominant form of legal training, lawyers would begin to concentrate on standards of admission, not only to the profession, but to the law school itself.

The concern with admission standards received full expression in 1881 in a report submitted to the Wisconsin State Bar Association by its Committee on Legal Education. This committee relied heavily on an article in the *American Law Review* by Francis L. Wellman titled "Admission to the Bar." [40] Wellman, drawing on a study of bar admission rules in all the states, on his research into the legal education required in England, France and Germany, and on his own experience as a professor in the Boston Law School and private tutor to Harvard Law School students cramming for the bar examination, proposed a series of reforms in the rules governing admission to the bar in the various states. He concluded that to be eligible for admission to the legal profession a young person should be of good moral character, twenty-one years of age and a citizen of the United States. These three regulations, Wellman noted, were the only ones common to every state in 1881. Wellman also argued that three years be designated as the minimun time of legal study and, reviving a distinction between college and noncollege applicants that had been common in some localities in the late eighteenth and early nineteenth centuries, he recommended that noncollege graduates be required to study law for five years and to take strict preliminary examinations in history and general literature before beginning legal studies. Finally, Wellman recommended that admission to the bar be administered by a central board of law examiners in each state. [41]

The recommendation that central examining boards be established was central to one of Wellman's primary concerns: the strengthening of American law schools. Wellman thought that "it would hardly be practicable to require a law school diploma of every applicant for the public examination for the bar" but "given a good board of examiners, a proper selection of subjects for examinations, and a high standard of knowledge, . . . it will certainly follow that the students will seek suitable instruction; in other words, that they will be driven into the law schools." [42] Wellman neither wanted nor expected that law schools would replace office apprenticeship. He did, however, recommend that one year in a law office should follow, not precede, as was more commonly the practice, two years in a law school. [43]

The Wisconsin Bar Association Committee on Legal Education agreed, in the main, with Wellman's recommendations, and they advised all members of the Association to secure a copy of the *American Law Review* and read the article in its entirety. [44] The Committee did insert a summary of the Wellman regulations in the annual report of the Association, but, in doing so, they tended to mute Wellman's strong stand on the importance of broadening the role of American law schools in legal training. Because Wellman did not recommend that law school attendance be made mandatory for admission to the bar, the summary of the rules he had prepared mentioned law schools only once: "But time spent in a law school in any State, as proved by passing its examinations, shall count toward admission to the bar like time spent in an office." [45] Unless members of the Wisconsin Bar Association made the effort to search out and read the entire article, the report of the Committee on Legal Education probably left them with the impression that law schools were only to be considered equal, not superior, to office apprenticeship. In fact, that was probably a fair reflection of the prevailing opinion among members of the legal profession in Wisconsin although for some, most assuredly, even that statement was too radical. Indeed, not until the 1890s would members even of the Wisconsin law faculty venture to maintain that a law school education was decidedly superior to reading law under an attorney.

Judging from subsequent events, the endorsement given the Wellman article by the Wisconsin State Bar Association had an important effect. The resolution which recognized the essential equality of training in either a law school or a law office probably strengthened the case of Jairus Carpenter, dean of the Wisconsin Law Department, when he appeared a week later before the University Board of Regents to argue for formal extension of the law school course to two years. Moreover, the other recommendations in the Wellman article were adopted in Wisconsin to a remarkable extent during the course of the following fifteen years. One of the more important steps was taken in 1885 when the Wisconsin legislature, with the active support of the Bar Association, established a central Board of Bar Examiners and set a two-year minimum period of study before entrance to the bar could be gained.[46] The creation of a central examining board, together with the requirement for a written examination preceded by a two-year period of legal study, had the effect in Wisconsin that Wellman had predicted: It drove students into the law school. It is not clear whether students responded primarily to the threat of a written examination supervised by the Board of Examiners or that they simply recognized that two years in the law school with its diploma privilege was now no more a hardship than two years in a law office. It is clear that law school attendance increased immediately after passage of the 1885 legislation. Between 1885 and 1888 attendance at the University Law School almost doubled, from sixty students in 1885 to one hundred and thirteen students in 1887.[47]

Not all lawyers approved the movement toward more formal rules and regulations governing the profession; nor did the increased reliance upon the law school as a training ground for new members of the profession gain unanimous support. It cannot be stressed enough that the State Bar Association itself contained only a small minority of Wisconsin lawyers, ranging in the most optimistic estimate between twenty and thirty percent in the nineteenth century.[48] Moreover, only a minority of that minority attended the meetings of the Association. And of those who did appear with regularity at the meetings (the meetings themselves were not held annually until 1900), there was disagreement over what policies to pursue. Many of the reminiscences published in the *WSBA Reports* reveal a desire to somehow return to the older, personal methods of regulating the bar rather than to devote time to developing new, more methodical procedures for professional control. Even as late as 1899 Elisha W. Keyes, a member of the University Board of Regents during the 1880s and 1890s, complained that "The Easy going methods of entering the profession at the present time are in strong contrast with the early system." Keyes went on:

> Now, office study and hard work is not in vogue. It is out of the common school, the High school or the University, into the College of Law, and soon with a jump, it is out of the latter place into the profession, no contact with the business world, and generally very poorly equipped to make a success of their chosen profession. It is not strange that so many of them fail—that so few of them succeed in achieving eminence as lawyers. I contend that the hand-made article, the old-fashioned formulation, was more likely to win the battle of life, than those who were turned out during the later years by the manipulation of machinery, so to speak.[49]

Keyes, and others like him, might look back yearningly to "the hand-made article," but that did not actually bring back that older style of professional life. The major thrust of all legislation affecting admission to the bar and the central theme of all the State Bar Association meetings during the 1880s was the need to replace the variety of admission procedures, based on a system of personal sponsorship by experienced attorneys, with regular and standarized means of regulating entrance to the profession.

Formalism in the Law School

Leaders of the Wisconsin legal profession first faced the problems stemming from the breakdown of traditional modes of regulation and training when they strengthened the requirements for the law school diploma and when they standardized and extended to two years the law school curriculum. The halting and uncertain manner in which they implemented these changes, however, indicates that they had no long-range vision of an increased role for the law school in professional preparation. Certainly they did not expect that the institution one day would dominate legal training. Such an expanded role for the university-sponsored law school was already being articulated at Harvard under the leadership of Charles W. Eliot and Christopher Columbus Langdell; significantly, men at Wisconsin clung to the model of the Albany Law School in New York State. Curricular and organizational changes at Wisconsin in the 1870s and 1880s, then, did not represent the rejection of traditional arrangements and values. Instead, those changes that were made were designed to preserve as much of the past as possible.

That professional considerations, not a search for academic respectability, led to the reorganization of the Law Department in the 1870s and 1880s is indicated by University of Wisconsin President John Twombly's failure to argue successfully for higher admission standards in the law school. Twombly, a Methodist minister, did not understand the limited role that the law school played in preparing candidates for the bar, nor did he clearly perceive its marginal function in weeding out undesirable members of the profession. His support for more stringent admission requirements and a longer course of study derived from a traditional academic outlook that valued a well-articulated course of study and clearly defined standards of achievement.

In 1872, after the spurt in attendance which followed passage of the diploma privilege law of 1870, Twombly first recommended to the University Regents that "the course of study in the Law Department be extended to two years, or that students be admitted to it only on condition of having a good academical education." [50] The Regents ignored Twombly's suggestion that a two-year course be established although they had previously modified the original admission requirements, which had consisted only of credentials of good moral character, to include an examination in the "ordinary English Branches." [51] Twombly was not satisfied. He told the Regents in 1873 that the examination "has had an excellent effect" but the "standard fixed upon at that time I consider quite too low, for now, as formerly, students who fail in their examinations for admission to the Preparatory Department go into the Law School without condition." Such low admission standards, Twombly warned, represented "an injury to the reputation of the university as a whole and, as I think, to the Law Department itself." Twombly even hinted that the quality of the state legal profession would eventually suffer "especially as all graduates have a right by virtue of having the diploma of the University to demand admittance to all the courts of the state." [52]

The Regents and the law faculty ignored this argument for even more stringent admission standards. Credentials of good moral character and evidence of a fair English education would remain the only barriers to entrance into the Law Department until the late 1880s. As for Twombly, his imperious manner quickly earned him the enmity of many of the Regents and he was fired from his post in early 1874. Thus he did not have the time nor, after about 1873, the influence to press for higher admission standards in the Law Department.

Twombly's support for a two-year course of study proved more prophetic but only because the law faculty and the Regent Committee on the Law Department were concerned with ensuring that the original conception of the law school as a complement to apprenticeship would endure. In the years between 1875 and 1881 they gradually implemented a longer course of study. The groping and uncertain manner in which they moved toward a two-year course of study, however, is remarkable when one considers that they had readily at hand clear organizational models for a two-year course. By 1870 thirty-one law schools existed in America and already seventeen had expanded their course to two years; and by 1880, one year before the Wisconsin Law Department would officially establish a two-year course, twenty-nine of the fifty-two law schools then in existence offered two years of instruction and four had extended their course to three years. [53] That men at Wisconsin moved so uncertainly to implement the two-year course suggests that the example of other institutions was of much less importance than the attempt to adjust the organization of the law school to meet problems posed by changing local conditions.

Clearly, one impediment to the establishment of the two-year course was financial. In 1875 the Board of Regents briefly considered the adoption of a two-year course but, upon the recommendation of the law faculty and the Regent Committee on the Law Department, abandoned the idea. [54] Such a course, the Regents explained, "would require the carrying along of two classes at the same time and thus double the labor of the professors, or it would make it impossible for students to start the course, except once in two years." Those problems could only be overcome by additions to the faculty, a move which the Board was not prepared to finance. "The Department is new and lengthening the course will deter many students from attending, and we should greatly fear that the revenues would be greatly diminished, and this we cannot permit until we are able to increase our standing appropriation." In the meantime, the Regents took comfort from the fact "that our present regulations as to scholarship for entry and graduation are copied from the regulations governing the justly celebrated Law School at Albany, New York." [55]

The following year the Regents again took up the subject of degree requirements. In June of 1876 they determined that "no student shall hereafter be graduated from the Law Department who has not devoted two years to the study of Law; one year of which shall be under the direction and supervision of the Faculty of said department." [56] This regulation simply confirmed and institutionalized the relationship between school and office that had characterized the operation of the Wisconsin Law Department since 1868. Students, however, were not happy with the new requirement, and at this point evidence begins to appear which suggests that some law students no longer assumed that the law school should be used only to systematize other avenues of legal preparation, like the law office experience. In 1877 a group of students petitioned the Regents asking that the two-year rule be suspended and that students be allowed to graduate in one year after taking appropriate examinations. The Regents refused the request.[57] Even so, some students tried another way to circumvent the two-year regulation by claiming private, unsupervised reading of law as the fulfillment of the second year of legal study. In 1878 the Regents explicitly outlawed that practice, ruling that "anytime devoted to the study of law shall not be deemed a compliance herewith unless the same is under the direction of the faculty, or of a reputable practicing attorney." [58]

Apparently these efforts to formalize the school and office pattern of legal education were unsuccessful because in the fall of 1878 there is the first indication that the Wisconsin Law Department might adopt a two-year course of study. Although there is nothing in the Regents' records to indicate that such a move was even under consideration, the University catalog for 1878–79 listed two classes of law students: first year and second year.[59] It is not certain that these classes took different courses. The catalog continued to list a curriculum lasting for one year that was substantially the same as previous years and the records of the Regents are mute concerning any planned reorganization of the courses offered. It is possible that the Wisconsin law faculty had adopted the system, once in vogue at the Michigan Law School, which crowded all the work into a single year but asked students to spend a preliminary year watching seniors recite.[60] What is clear is that the experiment tried was deemed unsuccessful. In the spring of 1879 the law faculty again recommended that "the class should be divided into two distinct classes, the one to be termed the Junior and the other the Senior Class." [61] But what emerged from this recommendation was yet another variation on a two-year course. According to the catalog, the plan was not for a course in which two classes would be taught simultaneously but instead a two-year course with the junior year offered one year and the senior year offered the following year.[62] This was essentially the alternative that the Board of Regents had rejected in 1875.

There is one revealing peculiarity about the two-year course instituted in 1879. First- and second-year students were so designated according to the year in which they had entered entered the law school, not by the courses taken. A different portion of the curriculum was offered each year, and students who entered as new students simply picked up the course at whatever stage had been reached. There was, in other words, no clear sense of hierarchy among the subjects under this organization (a scheme that obviously was a solution to the objection in 1875 that students would be able to enter a two-year course so organized only once every two years). But this notion, which was already beginning to change, was simply an extension of the earlier assumption that law students could enter the course at any time during the school year; it reflected the conception of the law school as a service for students, a collection of lectures from which students picked and chose as they themselves determined. This is not to argue that the Wisconsin law faculty had no sense of a hierarchy among legal studies but it is certain that in the 1870s attempts to enforce hierarchies went no further than informal advice. Prerequisites for entering certain law school courses were not formally institutionalized until the 1880s, and, indeed, the Wisconsin law school catalog did not even "urge" students to enter at the beginning of the collegiate year until 1885.[63]

If the law faculty and University Regents appear to have been confused about the direction the school should take during the late 1870s, it also should be noted that the experiments described above may not have been implemented. Though the evidence in the catalogs is unmistakable that trials with the form and organization of a lengthier course were at least under consideration, there is nothing official in the records to verify that any changes actually were effected. Not until June 1881 did the Regents clearly mandate a change in the organization of the Law Department. The dean of the school, Jairus H. Carpenter, initiated the action by asking the Regents to consider "the necessity of making two classes in the Law Department"[64] (and the language of his request suggests that two classes did not then exist). Carpenter and the law faculty were supported in their recommendation by the Law Alumni Association, a group of former University law students. The Association was represented at the June meeting of the Regents by Burr W. Jones, a young practitioner who would later have a long and distinguished career as a professor in the Wisconsin Law School. Carpenter's recommendations were referred to the Regent Committee on the Law Department and on the following day, June 22, 1881, the committee recommended the adoption of the following resolution:

> Resolved, That the Faculty of the Law Department are hereby directed and required to arrange the course of study in that department so as to extend over two years, that they divide students attending that department into two classes, one to pursue the course for the first year, the other for the second year, and that a separate course of lectures and instruction be hereafter given to both such classes during each term throughout the year . . . . That no student shall hereafter be received into the class for the second year of the course until he shall have pursued the entire course of the first year in the Law Department and have passed a satisfactory examination, or unless he shall have pursued in other schools, or for two years in a respectable lawyer's office the studies prescribed for the first year, and have passed a satisfactory examination; and that two full years of study in this department, or the full second year's study therein after admission thereto as aforesaid, with satisfactory examination in either case at the close, shall hereafter be required to graduation in the course to the Degree of Bachelor of Laws.[65]

The Committee also recommended that the tuition fees in the Law Department be raised to eighty dollars for two years and fifty dollars for one year; and that the University enlarge its appropriation to the Department to forty-five hundred dollars in addition to all fees. The report was adopted by the full Board without recorded debate or vote.[66]

In retrospect, the expansion of the law program to two years seems such a simple and logical move that it is difficult to understand the groping manner in which the law faculty and the Regents acted. It would be easy to explain this apparent floundering as a reluctance to commit any substantial funds for the expansion of the school's operation, an explanation that gains force when it is recalled that two members of the Regent Committee on the Law Department recommended in the year before the two-year program was implemented that the annual appropriation to the school be reduced. But financial considerations, while they played a part, probably were not a dominant factor. In the last half of the 1870s the University was in reasonably healthy financial shape. In 1876 the state legislature had passed a bill which granted annually to the University the proceeds from one-tenth of a mill tax per dollar on the assessed value of all taxable property in the state, an action that gave the University much greater security and which permitted

University of Wisconsin Law School graduating class of 1885. The woman is Mrs. Robert M. (Belle Case) LaFollette, the first woman graduate of the Law School. (*University of Wisconsin Archives*)

more long-range planning.[67] The 1880 proposal to reduce the annual appropriation to the Law Department thus did not reflect a weakening financial position but rather the reassertion of the traditional assumption that a law school should be self-supporting. That the course was lengthened to two years in 1881 (with the increased financial commitment that that involved) in the face of that assumption suggests that the law faculty and the Regents were acting out of desperation. The more fundamental explanation for the confusion and hesitation which marked the implementation of a two-year course is that lengthening the course of study was a tentative solution to a problem that itself was ill-defined. When students in the late 1870s and early 1880s began to use the law school to evade a longer period of legal study and when leaders of the bar began to complain that professional standards were slipping, then something was out of phase.

Whether more mechanical modes of regulation and training could restore the informal arrangements that had existed in the past, however, remained unclear. The law faculty, for its part, continued to experiment throughout the 1880s with more formalized means of organizing the law course. The University catalog in 1885, for example, announced that students would continue to be admitted to the law school at any time during the school year but, for the first time, all students were "urged to enter at the beginning of the college year." [68] That phrase at least suggested that the faculty was reexamining its view of the curriculum as a collage of courses that students might choose among according to their own personal needs. The 1885–86 catalog also noted, again for the first time, that the two-year course could be taken in one year by "passing an examination on the subjects pursued in the junior year." [69] Previously students apparently had been allowed to enter the second year immediately if they could present proof that they had spent one year in the office of an attorney, and they were expected to pick up any information covered in the first year of the course as best they could. That change in policy also reflected the sequential view of the courses that was beginning to emerge. These minor catalog changes, then, suggest that the law faculty was beginning to view the law school course as possessing an integrity even apart from its obvious usefulness in supplementing office work. The course was now increasingly viewed as a sustained, methodical way to prepare for the work of the lawyer.

The clash between an objective, test-oriented and impersonal method of certification and that older means of establishing professional credentials, immediate and personal, where a young man "proved" himself in the arena of the courtroom after admission to legal practice, was nicely illustrated in an 1885 proposal to publish the class standing of students in the Wisconsin Law Department. Since 1870 when the Law Department secured the diploma privilege the school had been engaged in the business of certifying students' legal competence. In the absence of ranking procedures, however, such certification could not indicate whether students were good, bad or indifferent. Whatever sorting of students according to ability the law school faculty did was akin to the personal sponsorship available to apprenticed law students.

Then in 1885, Professor Ithamar Sloan, dean of the school, announced in one of his classes that "the faculty had under advisement the adoption of a rule to direct the publication of class standings of the students, the standing to be determined by means of examinations at the end of the term." [70] Once before the law school faculty had assigned rankings to the law school graduates [71] but that 1879 experiment had been quietly dropped. In 1885 student opposition to the ranking proposal was immediate. In the *Press and Badger,* a student newspaper, one law student argued against the proposal in this way:

The only reasons urged in favor of the adoption of this rule, are, that thereby the students might be influenced to do better work, and that the students who have done excellent work should receive proper recognition. The weakness of these reasons is manifest, and needs no further explanation. Suppose that by means of this rule all students would be influenced to do better work, would this appear in their favor if the relative standings were published? The fact is that, no matter how good the work done by the class, there would only be a few who would succeed in carrying off the honors. While the distinction gained by the few might be of advantage to them, it would be an advantage gained by great injustice done all the remaining members. A young lawyer starting out for himself does not, as a rule, jump into a large practice; indeed, in the majority of cases, it is only after long and patient waiting and working for a practice, that his efforts meet with reasonable success. To publish to the world the names of three-fourths of the members of the class as poor students, would be a unjustifiable proceeding on the part of the faculty, for it would add another obstacle to the many difficulties the young practitioner will naturally have to encounter. Besides, the honor system or any competitive system with a view to securing marks running up in the nineties, is at best a "survival," and while such a system may be well enough for a high school, it is certainly out of place in a college having for its object the training of professional men. [72]

The proposal for ranking students according to academic ability was not adopted in 1885 and, in fact, it was never formally proposed to the University Board of Regents. But like the rule requiring students to pass examinations in the junior year studies before entering the senior class of the law school, and like the suggestion that students enter the law school at the beginning of the year, the ranking proposal reflected the belief of some lawyers that bar admission procedures had to be administered more formally. These innovations in the organization of the law school course therefore were of a piece with the establishment of a Board of Law Examiners in 1885 and the passage of a statute, also in 1885, that mandated two years of formal legal study for applicants to the bar.

These experiments with more formal modes of regulation and training did not represent a different sense of professionalism. Instead, they reflected an effort to preserve, in a different institutional framework, traditional values. The legal profession, lawyers hoped, would remain a guild bound together by mutual respect and good fellowship. Bar associations, both on the local and state level, would provide a context for regulation that was at once effective and personal. Older and more experienced practitioners would continue to select and sponsor worthy young men who desired to become lawyers. They would do so not only through the traditional apprenticeship arrangement but also through the law school. In fact, nowhere would the persistence of traditional values be more evident than in the University Law School during the 1890s. Under the leadership of Dean Edwin E. Bryant the Law Department, even as its organization became more formal, would be conceived as the ideal law office.

CHAPTER FIVE

Practical Training and Legal Scholasticism

The proponents of two models for the organization of a law school competed for supremacy in the years between 1870 and 1900. Although supporters of both models agreed that the law school provided a legal education that was decidedly superior to apprenticeship alone, they disagreed on the reason for that superiority. One view, supported mainly by practitioners and part-time law teachers, argued that if the links between the law school and the law office could not be preserved, then the law school itself should be remodeled upon the apprenticeship experience. The law school would become the ideal law office by combining theoretical instruction with a wide range of practice courses all carried out under the watchful tutelage of eminent practitioners and professors. The competing view, supported by academics and career law professors, argued that the law must be taught and studied as a science and that the methods of legal reasoning rather than a broad knowledge of law and legal practice must be the focal point of the curriculum. Christopher C. Langdell first articulated this view when he began in 1870 to reorganize the Harvard Law School curriculum around the intensive analysis of leading cases. Langdell's case method gained ground slowly, even at Harvard, but by the 1890s many were convinced that case study was the distinguishing characteristic of the better university law school.

The significance of these two models of organization has been overlooked because the reforms promoted by the two groups were often the

same: a longer course of study, more stringent admission and graduation requirements, a closer attention to administrative detail and the
replacement of part-time lecturers with full-time law professors. This
surface agreement on the nature of the reforms necessary to expand the
role of the law school in legal education obscured the underlying issues.
Not only were the goals of the law school debated in this period but, of
even greater importance, the debate over those goals involved a fundamental disagreement over the professional image of the lawyer that the
law school ought to promote.

University Leadership in Law School Reform

The transformation of many American liberal arts colleges into universities in the decades after the Civil War profoundly affected the
development of American law schools. Basically, that transformation
infused those academic communities with a new set of scholarly expectations based upon a spirit of scientific investigation and research. Men
like Charles W. Eliot of Harvard, Andrew Dixon White of Cornell and
Daniel Coit Gilman of Johns Hopkins, trained in the leading European
universities where they committed themselves to the values of scientific
research, began to replace men with ministerial training as the leaders
of major American universities.[1] These new university leaders were not
content with injecting into the traditional classical collegiate curriculum
a greater emphasis on scientific and technical training. They also took
the initiative in reforming the professional schools attached to their
institutions and, in the case of the law schools, that meant that the
influence of the university administration would be thrown on the side
of those who promoted the scientific model for organizing law schools.
The importance of that influence on the development of the American
university law school was clearly shown by events at the University of
Wisconsin in the late 1880s and throughout the 1890s.

For almost four decades after its founding in 1848 the University of
Wisconsin had been almost indistinguishable from other private liberal
arts colleges in the state. It did have one professional school—the Department of Law—loosely attached to it but the major portion of the
University's resources continued to be devoted to the traditional liberal
arts curriculum. The first presidents of the University were completely
in accord with this stress on the liberal arts. These men recognized that
a state-supported university might be expected to do more than a private liberal arts college in the way of supporting professional preparation and scientific investigation but always, they assumed, the focus of
the school's program must remain instruction in the traditional liberal
studies.

When Thomas C. Chamberlin replaced John Bascom in 1887 as president of the University of Wisconsin, however, the emphasis on the classical curriculum and on character training began to be counterbalanced by a major commitment to research and vocational preparation. Chamberlin, one of the leading geologists of the day, stated in the first University catalog prepared under his direction that the aims of the University should be to provide "amply for disciplinary training," to provide "trustworthy technical training in the leading professions," to contribute to the "advancement of knowledge and to train students in investigation," and, finally, to contribute "directly to the higher education of the people." Under Chamberlin's leadership and, after his resignation in 1892, the guidance of Charles Kendall Adams, the University of Wisconsin began the transition from a small liberal arts college to a university of national reputation. The research activities begun in a modest way under Bascom were greatly expanded, and in the 1890s the University became an important center for scientific investigation. Its reputation was secured especially by the discoveries emanating from the Washburn observatory and by the findings of researchers in the field of agriculture. With the hiring of new faculty like Frederick Jackson Turner, Richard Ely and John Commons, the liberal arts also were infused with a new investigative spirit. Vocational and professional studies were expanded: Both the engineering and the agriculture departments drew impressive numbers of students; the teacher training program grew steadily; and a premedical course was established.[2]

For the Law Department, Chamberlin's commitment to "trustworthy technical training in the professions" meant that the school in the future would be drawn much more tightly into the institutional orbit of the University. The need for such a change was first expressed in 1888 in a report by the University Board of Visitors, a group of private citizens appointed each year by the Governor to comment on University programs. The group assigned to the law school noted that "the relation of [the Law Department] to the University at present is not unlike that of a stray child. The committee would recommend that this department be found and taken home." Specifically, the Visitors wanted rooms assigned on campus for the use of the Law Department so that the school would "be more closely identified as a department of the University." The Visitors also recommended that admission requirements to the school be raised and that a full-time dean be appointed to run the school.[3]

The movement to integrate the law school into the university community, which even in its early stages was orchestrated by President Chamberlin, would have a decisive impact on the law school's development. Among other things, it meant a repudiation of past policies and traditions. That was shown in June, 1888, when the committee on the Law Department of the University Board of Regents, in a highly unusual move, rebuked the dean of the Wisconsin Law Department, Ithamar C. Sloan, for what they termed a "looseness" in the financial management of the school. "We find that it has been customary to allow students to enjoy all the benefits of the school for months and in some cases down to the final examination without their having paid the matriculation fee required by the regulations . . . . The methods [the original word, crossed out in the manuscript, was "negligence"] of the Dean in this matter are such that it is practicable for any young man to have all the advantages of the department except that of receiving a diploma and not pay any part of the matriculation fee." The Regents also found a looseness in the academic records of the Law Department. They thought it essential "to preserve for reference the standing of all students on all subjects upon which such students are examined during their course of study," but the Regents could find no such records. All of this, they concluded, "is largely the fault of the Dean of the faculty and . . . should not be allowed to exist in the future." [4]

Although Dean Sloan may have had some intimation that changes in the policies of the law school were under advisement (he had a few years earlier hinted to his law class that ranking procedures might be introduced in the school), he was probably stunned at the severity of this rebuke. He had, after all, merely continued the policies of his predecessors in the deanship. Student records had never been systematically kept, and the policy of allowing poor students to attend classes without paying fees had been in effect since 1871 when Dean Harlow S. Orton told the Regents:

> The Students many of them are poor and have struggled to attain a legal education to enter at once upon the duties and compensations of the profession. To those who for the time are unable to pay for their tuition the full benefits of the course have been liberally extended trusting them to pay when able to do so. None who could pay for their board and support in the City have been turned away on account of their inability to pay for their instruction. [5]

The Regents never officially approved of this practice. The Board rejected a proposal in 1875 that would have authorized the dean to "exempt poor, extra-ordinarily meritorious law students from the payment of the entire matriculation fee, or such part thereof as he may see fit." [6] Even though the Regents refused to sanction formally the actions of the deans, the practice continued into the early 1880s. [7] By 1888, however, the Board was becoming more and more reluctant to allow the dean such a free hand in the administration of the school. Convinced by Chamberlin that the school must "move forward in a well defined line of improvement," the Regent Committee on the Law Department made two recommendations.

First, they proposed to increase the amount of money allocated to the law school. Part of that money would be raised by an increase in tuition fees but, more important, they recommended that eleven thousand dollars be appropriated out of the general fund of the University for the use of the Law Department, a figure that was truly astonishing in view of the prior support given the law school by the University. Second, the Committee proposed to employ "a competent person as Dean of the Law Faculty who shall devote his entire time to the duties of the position and in the instructional work of the department." The experience of other institutions, the Committee argued, "shows that dependence cannot be placed on any person for such a position if he is to be allowed to carry on the active practice of his profession. We ought long ago to have recognized this fact and acted accordingly." [8] Although the Regents recommended no one specifically for the dean's position, the tone of their report suggested that Ithamar Sloan would not be the prime candidate.

The Board of Regents delayed final action on the committee report but they did authorize President Chamberlin to begin the search for a dean of the Law Department. Chamberlin consulted various people in the summer of 1888 and reported in the fall that he had been unable to find an appropriate person to fill the position. He therefore recommended that Sloan be continued in the position for the present and that no further changes be made in the regular faculty. However, Chamberlin also reported that "my study of the problem of the law school has led to the conviction that a somewhat general reorganization is to be desired, involving new requirements for admission; and extension of the course on the part of all who do not come with advanced preparation; the addition of subjects not now taught, and the fuller treatment of some subjects presently touched upon." [9] Chamberlin recommended that an extension of the course be undertaken immediately through the employment of special lecturers "on subjects of which they are masters." Striking a familiar chord to those who remembered when supreme court justices were listed in the early catalogs for reasons of prestige, Chamberlin argued that "very considerable benefits would accrue to the school from the personal influence" of these men as "well as from the reputation of talent so employed." Shortly thereafter the Regents named the following men to give special instruction in the Law Department for the year 1888: Judge James G. Jenkins (negligence, admiralty, and trademarks); Judge John B. Winslow (topic unannounced); Judge George Clementson (estoppel); Judge Samuel D. Hastings, Jr. (taxation and tax titles); Judge George H. Noyes (common carriers); and Hon. William E. Carter (damages).[10]

Chamberlin thus had turned the search for a full-time dean of the Law Department into the occasion for a general study of institutional organization. Although the Regents in 1888 had called for a "well defined line of improvement" in the Law Department, it was Chamberlin who took the initiative in defining the content of the improvements needed and in outlining the specifics of the reorganization. During the school year of 1888 Chamberlin visited the law schools at Michigan, Cornell, Harvard, Yale and Columbia and he also "advised with a large number of legal gentlemen of our own state." As a result of that investigation, Chamberlin prepared a series of recommendations for the reorganization of the Law Department which he submitted to the Board of Regents on June 18, 1889. He proposed, for example, that the admission requirements to the school be raised gradually and that the course of study, "which is now nominally two years, but which a considerable percentage of the students take in one year," be made "in reality a two-year course." He also recommended that the system of special lectures be maintained but that examinations be required in each of those courses. As to the "instructional work in the school," Chamberlin asked "leave to make a verbal statement." Finally, Chamberlin recommended that the Regents name Edwin E. Bryant Dean of the College of Law at a salary of $3500 a year.[11]

That last recommendation, accepted immediately by the Regents, was critically important because it set the stage for a confrontation between two visions of the future university law school. The appointment of Edwin E. Bryant as Dean,[12] in fact, represented a compromise between Chamberlin and the Regents. Chamberlin's vision of what the Wisconsin College of Law should become derived from the examples of the university law schools that he had visited during 1888 and 1889 and, in particular, from the example of Harvard where the ideal of the law school as a center of scientific study was most fully developed. The Regents' vision was more parochial and also more imprecise. Attuned to recent warnings within the legal profession of imminent professional decline, they believed that stricter controls over entry to the profession were needed and that the law school's role in legal education ought to be expanded and formalized. Precisely what they expected the law school to become was less clear. It would remain for Edwin E. Bryant to articulate a theory of law school organization that would meet the problems posed by changing conditions of professional life while still preserving the values of a passing era.

The Law School as an Ideal Law Office

As dean, Edwin E. Bryant attempted to fill the role of an experienced practitioner who supervised a vast law office. That law office was designed not to dispense legal services to clients but to dispense legal knowledge to students. Bryant's conception of the law school as an ideal law office was particularly noticeable in two areas: in the formal curriculum and in his administrative style. Bryant reorganized the curriculum so that in addition to more work in legal theory, which had always been the speciality of the law school, he introduced immensely detailed and thorough work in legal practice, the kind of "practical" knowledge that students previously had picked up outside the law school. Less obvious, but equally important, Bryant successfully maintained a personal administrative style even amidst a rapidly developing formal administrative framework in the school. Admission requirements, for example, were increased and made more objective but Bryant continued to rely upon his own personal and professional judgment in admitting young men to the law school. His actions here, as in other respects, bore an obvious similarity to the immediate and personal process of selection and sponsorship that had marked the admission processes of the judicial circuit.

Bryant's background and professional connections underscored his commitment to the traditional functions of the law school in legal preparation. Moreover, the selection of Bryant as dean reflected the continued influence of that small group of lawyers around Madison who had determined the Law Department's fortunes since 1868. Chamberlin, in fact, could not have recommended any one who did not have the approval of that powerful group. William F. Vilas was, without doubt, the central figure among those lawyers even though he had not taught in the law school since 1885. Indeed, President Chamberlin initially approached Vilas with an offer to assume the dean's position. Vilas, according to his later recollection, "pointed to Bryant as a prize. Senator [John Coit] Spooner, who intimately knew his fitness, cordially joined in effective commendation." [13] It was fitting that Vilas recommend Bryant for the dean's post because Bryant's law partnership with Vilas, formed in 1872, had been Bryant's entree into that small circle of Madison lawyers who controlled the Law Department.

The thirteen men who taught for varying lengths of time in the school prior to 1885 formed the core of this influential group. Two men, William Vilas and John B. Cassoday, served not only on the faculty but also on the University Board of Regents; both men, Cassoday from 1878 to 1880 and Vilas from 1881 to 1884, were members of the Regent Committee on the Law Department. Even more extensive ties were established through personal and professional association between the law faculty and members of the Board of Regents. For example, Jared C. Gregory was a Regent during much of the 1870s and 1880s, and in 1874 and again between 1878 and 1880 was a member of the Regent Committee on the Law Department. Gregory's law partner from 1858 to 1879 was Silas U. Pinney, a member of the law faculty from 1871 to 1881. Gregory's first law partner in Madison had been Levi B. Vilas, father of William F. Vilas. Gregory was also the father of Charles N. Gregory who would join the law faculty as associate dean in 1894.[14]

Jared Gregory and William Vilas were important powers in the Democratic party but the law faculty also had solid connections to the higher councils of the Republican party, at that time the dominant political organization in the state. Philip L. Spooner, who served as dean of the Law School from 1872 to 1876, and who continued to lecture in the school until 1881, was at the hub of these connections. His son, John Coit Spooner (who would later concur with Vilas that Bryant ought to become dean in 1889) was a member of the Regent Committee on the Law Department in 1881. A second son, Philip, was a member of the so-called "Madison Ring" which controlled the congressional district for the Republicans in the Madison area. The "Madison Ring" was run by Elisha "Boss" Keyes who during the 1880s was a member of the powerful Executive Committee of the University Board of Regents.

To be appointed to the law faculty itself during this period it obviously helped to know someone who was a member of the faculty or a member of the Board of Regents. J. C. Hopkins, appointed to the faculty in 1876, was a former law partner of Harlow S. Orton, dean of the school from 1868 to 1872 and a lecturer in the department for a number of years. A. L. Sanborn, appointed to the faculty in 1885, was a law partner of Silas Pinney. Sanborn later formed a partnership with John C. Spooner, a Regent and the son of Law School Dean Philip L. Spooner. Burr M. Jones, also appointed to the law faculty in 1885, had clerked in Vilas' law office for a time and was a political protégé of Regent Jared C. Gregory. John Bashford, who also joined the faculty in 1885, had worked with both Vilas and Pinney in the preparation of the *Revised Statutes of Wisconsin* in 1878. By 1885, too, it was common for appointees to the faculty to have attended the Wisconsin Law Department as students. Bashford and Jones graduated from the school in 1871 and Sanborn had attended the school in 1879–80, though he never received the LL.B.

Edwin E. Bryant had not attended the Wisconsin Law Department (nor any other law school) but throughout the 1870s and 1880s his career had been closely linked with that of the hub of the law school coterie, William F. Vilas. A writer for the *Chicago Times* remarked in 1892 that the period in which Vilas achieved "his greatest success as a lawyer . . . was when he was associated in practice with Gen. E. E. Bryant. . . . These two gentlemen made a complete law firm. One was the complement of the other, and together they established an enormous practice." [15] Vilas' great skill, of course, was as a courtroom advocate while Bryant, as his career outlined below will show, was the careful legal scholar who researched and prepared the briefs.

Bryant, like Vilas, was a Democratic politician. He was elected to serve in the State Assembly in 1878 and, in 1880, possibly through the recommendation of Congressman Burr W. Jones (the former clerk in the Vilas law office) Bryant went to Washington as a clerk to the Committee on Public Lands. He returned to Madison in 1883 (after the defeat of Jones for reelection), purchased an interest in a Madison newspaper, the *Democrat* and for the next two years assumed responsibility for that paper's editorial management. Then in 1885, after Vilas had been appointed Postmaster General in the cabinet of President Cleveland, Bryant returned to Washington as Assistant Attorney General for the Post Office Department. He served in that post for four years, returning to Madison along with Vilas in 1889. It was at this point in his career that he accepted the position of dean of the Wisconsin College of Law. [16]

Although Bryant's appointment could not have been better designed to emphasize continuity with the law school's past, there were other reasons for his selection. He had had no direct experience with law schools, either as a student or as a teacher, but he was certainly familiar with the operations of the Wisconsin Law Department. His association with Vilas and other Madison lawyers, as well as his early involvement in the State Bar Association, made it certain that he had kept abreast of developments in legal education in the state. Moreover, Bryant had gained a reputation as a scholarly man. The outlines of his career confirm that he found the intellectual side of the law, as contrasted to the hectic pace of the trial court, more congenial. In 1869 Bryant had published with John C. Spooner an edition of *Town Laws* with forms and instructions for town officers of Wisconsin. He and Vilas in 1875 revised, edited and supervised the printing of the early volumes of the *Wisconsin Supreme Court Reports*. While in Washington Bryant edited a *Postal Guide* and compiled a volume of *Postal Laws and Regulations*. Later in his life, while dean of the College of Law, he would write a number of textbooks, including one on *Code Practice* and another on the duties of the *Justice of the Peace*. In addition to his instructional writing, Bryant also worked on a newspaper in two separate periods: during the late 1850s on the Monroe, Wisconsin *Sentinel* and in the mid-1880s on the Madison *Democrat*. Thus, in the two major activities of his life—law and

Edwin E. Bryant. (*University of Wisconsin Archives*)

politics—Bryant operated mainly in the realm of ideas. Vilas would later remark that "there was in Bryant a natural aptitude for literature. . . . In my estimation, Bryant's gifts were more addressed by nature to this pursuit even than his profession." [17]

Bryant's vision of the law school as an ideal law office began to emerge in the revisions he introduced into the first law school catalog prepared under his direction. He began by revising the initial sentence of the general statement of aims which, since 1870, had proclaimed the "great advantage of professional schools for the rapid and thorough elementary training of professional men." Bryant's catalog, in contrast, asserted the "superior" advantages which law schools held over all other methods of preparation for the bar. If the law school were to be truly superior to all other forms of training, however, the curriculum had to incorporate all that the law office had claimed to do. The school must engage students in the activities that "they will be required to do as lawyers." To achieve that end, Bryant added to the course description an extremely long and detailed paragraph describing the "unusual pains" that the Wisconsin College of Law would take "to make the students familiar with the preparation of all kinds of legal documents."

In common law pleading they are required to practice in drafting pleadings in the entire series. In equity practice and pleading they are also required to conduct suits from beginning to end, thus becoming familiar with all the steps in a suit. In code practice and pleading a thorough course of instruction is given and practical exercises conducted in the draft of pleadings, the preparation of papers of all kinds, especially affidavits, motion papers, orders, findings, exceptions, judgments, bills of exception. To illustrate the practice and familiarize students with the actual work of the lawyer, cases are submitted, and the student is required to prepare, under supervision and instruction, all the papers in actions on simple contract, actions for divorce, to wind up partnerships, for reformation of deeds, actions with proceedings in attachment and garnishment, actions in which injunctions and writs of *ne exeat* are issued, receiver appointed, etc., actions of ejectment, foreclosure, partition, and for the enforcement of liens on real property; and other actions are conducted from original process to judgment, instructing the student in each step.

In criminal law, the class is exercised in the drafting of complaints, indictments, informations, warrants, pleas, and in all the steps of a criminal prosecution. All papers are examined, errors pointed out, and students required to perfect them. [18]

Bryant eventually came to view the emphasis on practical work as the distinguishing feature of the Wisconsin College of Law. In an address to the Wisconsin State Bar Association in 1895, Bryant told the lawyers present that the "Wisconsin Law School devotes more time to the subject of practice than is usual in law schools, and requires more work akin to that done in a law office to be done by the students." [19] Yet had the number of law offices available to students in the 1880s and 1890s kept pace with the number of students flooding into Madison to study law at that time, Bryant likely would not have made the important changes in the law curriculum that he did. Significantly those law school students who were combining law lectures with work in a local attorney's office were excused from this practice work.[20] Bryant's detailed justification for the "superiority" of law school preparation over other methods of legal study was, in fact, nothing more than the logical extension of the organizational changes of the 1870s and 1880s which had as their aim to support the relationship between school and office. When that proved impossible because of the shortage of office space, the remaining step was to recreate the law school in the image of the ideal law office: The regular, personal attention of the law faculty would provide training both in the theory of the law and in the techniques of practice.

If the law school was the efficient law office, then the dean was simply an eminent practitioner who selected, guided and encouraged those students who showed promise of becoming worthy professionals. The growing formality of the rules and regulations governing the school did not mean, then, that a more impersonal atmosphere should pervade the school. The manner in which Bryant administered the rules governing admission to the institution provides a clear example of how he acted both as preceptor and as judge in his contacts with students.

In 1889 the Regents, following President Chamberlin's recommendation of the previous year, approved stricter admission requirements. In addition to the usual character testimonials, candidates for admission to the school would now "be examined in English literature (leading works and authors), in American and general history, and in the constitution of the United States and of Wisconsin." In addition:

The candidate will also be expected to possess at least a fair knowledge of the other common English branches. Candidates will be admitted without examination upon presenting a certificate of graduation from a reputable college or university, State normal school, or accredited high school or academy; or upon presenting a first or second grade teachers' certificate. Candidates from outside the state may be admitted without examination on presenting certificates of graduation from any high school of good standing.[21]

These entrance requirements were substantially the same as those required by the Yale Law School, although they were less rigorous than the entrance examinations of Columbia, Harvard, Pennsylvania, Hastings and Ohio State. Even so, the new regulations put the Wisconsin College of Law among the most restrictive law schools at the time. In 1890 there were sixty-one American law schools and only eighteen reported any entrance requirements at all.[22]

The requirements for admission approved in 1889 were not basically altered during Bryant's term as dean. Until 1903 evidence of good moral character and a high school diploma or its equivalent admitted students to the law school. The only change, under Bryant's leadership, was a recommendation, printed for the first time in the 1892 Law School catalog, that "candidates ought not to rest satisfied with the minimum requirements imposed but secure the highest practicable general education . . . . A college course is eminently desirable." [23] That, however, was only a recommendation, not a requirement. In 1895 the Board of Visitors recommended that the admission standards be made equivalent to those required of students entering the undergraduate College of Letters and Science but if that were "deemed inexpedient" then at least there should be an examination in mathematics as well as in English literature and history.[24] The Regents were not willing to make the entrance requirements equal to those in the College of Letters and Science, a move that would have mandated proficiency in a foreign language, but they did approve the examination in mathematics. Bryant supported, along with the Board of Visitors, somewhat higher admission standards. "For three years past," he wrote in 1895, "I have recommended to the Regents that the same grade of attainment for admission to the University be applied to the College of Law. But as our school has been for years substantially self-sustaining, they have hesitated lest attendance and revenue be too much reduced." [25] That was certainly a correct assessment.

In a move of potentially greater importance, the Regents in 1895 also transferred the administration of the entrance examination itself from the dean to the general University examining committee. In practice, however, Bryant maintained personal control over the examination process. He claimed that those who entered the law school through examination rather than school certificate received "a reasonably thorough test of their learning and mental capacity." [26] Yet as other officials in the law school viewed it, the examination often was more reasonable than thorough. Associate Dean Charles Gregory wrote to a student applying for admission to the school in 1895 that the examinations are "entirely in the discretion of the Dean, who examines the applicant in matters of general knowledge and intelligence. The examinations are not severe; not unfrequently they consist of little more than asking the applicant to write a letter stating what studies he has pursued and what proficiency he has attained, and if the Dean is satisfied that the man is of sufficient training and intelligence to take the course he sometimes stops at that and admits the man." [27] Gregory's judgment was corroborated by Theodore Woolsey, the dean's secretary. In 1896 Woolsey told an applicant that "the examination is very reasonable, and often very slight if the Dean is satisfied of the intelligence of the applicant." [28] Bryant himself showed a willingness to bend the rules governing admission. In 1897 he wrote to George H. Noyes, a member of the Regent Committee on the Law School, asking if anything could be done to admit a young man who did not meet the stated entrance requirements. Bryant did not want to "ignore rules, but I have been obliged to discourage several applicants, who impressed me as very favorable young men . . . . As we feel the need of being self-supporting we are desirous of a good attendance; and I especially like to have our rolls have the names of the sons of prominent lawyers." [29]

It was not the case, however, that Bryant was lax in his administration of admission requirements. The letter to Noyes exhibited a certain scrupulousness in that regard. Nor should it be thought that Bryant's standards were low. Instead, he viewed formal rules as general guidelines for the personal judgment of the lawyer under whom the student would study. In this sense Bryant acted like the attorney who agreed to take on a student as an apprentice, using the initial interview to form an impression and then acting on that impression until the student proved it inaccurate. Formal standards of admission, if tightly administered, threatened to replace the personal judgment of the lawyer, and that Bryant always resisted. Even though he would not ignore the rules of admission, there were ways to avoid them and still provide young men who "impressed" him with a legal education, if not always a law degree. The 1889 catalog, for example, noted that students who were deficient in subjects for the admission examination "will be permitted during the first year to pursue essential studies in the University course, without charge." [30] There probably were more informal ways to deal with this problem that do not appear in the records but by 1897 a formal solution was devised by creating a category of special student. Any young man could take special studies in the College of Law upon "giving satisfactory evidence that they are prepared to take the desired studies advantageously. If they subsequently desire to become a candidate for a degree or to take a regular course, they must pass the required entrance requirements." [31] At the end of the decade, then, control over entrance to the College of Law still rested firmly in the hands of the dean.

In other ways Bryant resisted rigid administrative rules and interposed his own personal judgment when students were in need of assistance. In 1904 one student recalled how Bryant had silently intervened in a dispute between the student and Associate Dean Charles N. Gregory, a man with the reputation for following administrative regulations to the precise letter.

I had a position from which I should receive pay about the 20th November but entered the law school without the funds for tuition, etc., and attended classes for several days. The associate dean announced to the class two or three times that those whose tuition was unpaid would be excluded from classes after a certain date, and finally all but I had paid. Mr. Gregory called me to his office, (pursuing the rule necessarily enjoined by the Regents) and informed me that though I might have a valid excuse in expecting the money, yet he could not consider it and I must remain from classes till my pay day.[32]

Dean Bryant, sitting in his adjoining office with the door ajar, overheard the conversation and when the dejected student emerged from Gregory's office, intercepted him and wrote his personal check to cover the amount of the tuition. The student was trusted to repay when he was able. That anecdote nicely captures the fatherly role that Bryant adopted in his dealing with students. The law school correspondence from this period contains numerous letters from Bryant informing fathers that their sons were in financial trouble, academic difficulties, or simply wasting their time carousing and gambling.[33] That attitude, which the students perhaps did not always appreciate, was little different from the relationship one might expect between a conscientious lawyer and his apprentice; and it echoed the relationship that had existed among faculty and students in the first decades of the school's existence.

Despite Bryant's efforts to mute the worst effects of administrative rules, his own appointment as full-time dean in 1889, the beginning of fairly regular faculty meetings and the appointment of a secretary to the dean in 1894, and the appointment of an associate dean in 1895, all pointed to the emergence of a more impersonal institutional environment. The relationship between faculty and student was further undermined by the increased use of formal ratings of law students, academic judgments arrived at through regular, written examinations and kept in the faculty files for permanent reference. Bryant, typically, claimed that this trend was simply a way to ensure continued close involvement between student and instructor. "Each students [sic] work is known by each instructor." The student's "oral and written answers to questions and the original work he is required to do, under supervision, give the instructor a very exact gauge of the natural ability and industry of each student." [34]

As the Wisconsin College of Law was drawn more tightly into the orbit of the University proper, and as the law school grew in size, it became more and more difficult to maintain the personal atmosphere that Bryant desired. Symbolic of the closer ties between the University and the Law School was the new building constructed on the campus to house the College of Law. Since its establishment in 1868, the Law Department had been located in various places in downtown Madison and for a number of years in the 1880s classes were held in the state capitol building. Although the Regents' records during this period are filled with complaints about inadequate space and poor ventilation, such inconveniences were endured because the law students were in law offices in the immediate area and because law students were allowed access to the state law library. [35] By the late 1880s, however, when fewer and fewer students were able to combine study in the law school and a law office, overcrowded classrooms and inadequate library facilities became one of the dominant themes of the dean's reports. To solve such problems the legislature, in an 1891 bill increasing the total appropriation to the University, earmarked sixty thousand dollars to construct a building for the College of Law. [36] The Regents voted, nine to one, "to locate and construct the building for the College of Law upon the University grounds." [37] Apparently there were some who still believed that the law school should be located in the downtown district, although the margin by which the resolution was passed was a clear indication that that view was in the minority. Construction was begun in the fall of 1891 and the new structure, constructed of Lake Superior sandstone, was ready for occupancy in September, 1893. [38] The "stray child" had been brought home.

Closer relations with the University, however, did not imply any change in the policy that the law school should be essentially self-supporting. Because of the accounting methods used by the Regents during the first half of the 1890s it is impossible to tell how much subsidy, if any, the law school received during that time. The law school did, of course, benefit from the money appropriated by the state legislature for the construction of a new law building, and in 1890 the school received a bequest of twenty thousand dollars from the will of Judge Mortimer M. Jackson with which to create a professorship of law. [39] But these monies represented outside sources, and they did not contravene the assumption that the law school should pay its own way. The law school budget for the years 1890 to 1895 averaged about eight thousand dollars per year, but it is probable that student fees were then bringing in more than that amount yearly. Two resolutions passed in 1896 indicate that the Regents' practice of placing the law school income from tuition fees into the general university fund and then voting a yearly budget for the school had worked against the College of Law. On January 21, 1896, the Regents approved a resolution which transferred to the Law School the "sum of $5000 arising from the tuition fees paid by the students in the College of Law, and now in the general fund." [40] Four months later the Regents transferred an additional five thousand dollars into the law school budget, stating that "the same [is] to be in adjustment and full settlement and discharge of all claim on the part of the College of Law for receipts or earnings in excess of expenditures at any time heretofore turned into the treasury of the University." [41] While the accounts were more carefully kept after 1895, the basic financial policy did not alter. As late as 1901 the law school brought in an estimated fourteen thousand dollars in student fees while the budget for that year was thirteen thousand five hundred dollars. Similar figures appeared in the estimated budget for 1902, Bryant's last term as dean. [42]

This policy of self-support was unique among the divisions of the University of Wisconsin. In 1896, for example, when the Law School budget was set at seventy-five hundred dollars, the College of Agriculture was allotted over eighty thousand dollars and the College of Mechanics and Engineering was given over thirty-three thousand dollars. Of course, the College of Agriculture and the College of Engineering benefited greatly from federal aid to higher education in this period. The estimated income from the Morrill Grant was twenty-three thousand dollars in 1896 while that from the Hatch Act was fifteen thousand dollars. [43] Even so, this left a substantial amount to be granted from the general fund of the University for the support of the agricultural and engineering schools. It was assumed that legal education was much less expensive than other forms of professional education because the equipment necessary—professors and books—appeared so minimal when compared with the outlays for laboratory equipment and specialized buildings in engineering or medicine. And in the 1890s it was true that faculty salaries constituted the major expense (except for the capital outlay for the law building itself) in legal education. The expense of building and maintaining the law library was as yet small and would not bulk large in the budget until law professors, following the lead of Langdell at Harvard, began to argue that a large library was in essence the "laboratory" of the lawyer.

But legal education was not inexpensive to the student. The College of Law was the only division of the University where substantial student fees were required; indeed, it was the only division where any tuition fees were legally permitted for resident students. Effective with the 1889 school year the fees for the two-year course were one hundred dollars for the full two years and seventy-five dollars for students entering the second year and graduating after one year of study.[44] In addition, nonresidents paid a fee of six dollars per term, a policy that was discontinued in 1890. In 1894, when a three-year law course was announced, fees were set at eighty-five dollars for the first year and sixty dollars for the next two years. The following year these fees were reduced by ten dollars for the first two years and set at twenty-five dollars for the third year, making the total cost of the three-year regular course one hundred and fifty dollars.[45] In the College of Letters and Science, in contrast, students in 1895 paid only a general expense fee of ten dollars. Nonresidents paid an additional tuition fee of fifteen dollars per semester. Even the nonresident's fee in the College of Engineering and in the School of Pharmacy—fifteen dollars each semester and a general expense fee of twenty dollars—was less than that charged to resident students in the College of Law during their first two years.[46]

In spite of the comparatively high tuition charged in the law school, student enrollments continued to climb during the 1890s. When Bryant arrived as dean of the College of Law, the attendance the previous year had been one hundred nineteen. That figure jumped to one hundred sixty-six by 1892 and to two hundred sixty-six in 1894. The two hundred sixty-six students enrolled in the College of Law in 1894 represented the high point of attendance in the nineteenth century, and it occurred at that moment because of the announcement by the Regents in June 1894 that the course leading to the LL.B. would be expanded to three years in the fall. They did, however, allow a one-year grace period so that students who entered in the fall of 1894 could still complete the course in two years;[47] therefore students rushed to enter under the old rules. The establishment of a three-year course brought the Wisconsin College of Law into line with the seven other schools that had by 1890 instituted such programs. Those schools were Harvard, Boston, Hastings, the University of Maryland, Notre Dame, Columbia and the University of Pennsylvania.[48] Even after the three-year course was implemented the attendance continued to be impressive: two hundred twenty-two students in 1895, two hundred sixteen in 1896, one hundred seventy-eight in 1897, and two hundred four in 1898. The attendance for the next four years, beginning with 1899, was two hundred thirty-one, two hundred sixty-six, two hundred sixty, and two hundred twenty-six.[49] The decline in the number of graduates under the new three-year program, however, was substantial: from a high of one hundred twenty-four in 1895 (a figure inflated by the sudden rush by students to graduate under the two-year rule) to forty-three in 1896 and only thirty in 1897. The latter figure was the lowest since 1884.[50] The reason, according to Bryant, was that admission to the bar through the bar examination was relatively easy and "the students who have studied here one year so easily pass the state board examination that many are tempted to enter the profession by that door." [51]

In comparison to some other law schools, the Wisconsin College of Law remained only a medium-size school. In 1889 Columbia was the largest law school in the nation with an enrollment of four hundred fifty-six, followed by Michigan with four hundred five students and Harvard with two hundred sixty-five. Ten years later, in 1899, Michigan had taken the attendance lead with eight hundred eighty-three students enrolled and it was followed by the New York Law School with seven hundred seventy-five students, the New York University Law School with six hundred thirty-four students, Harvard with six hundred sixteen and Minnesota with five hundred twenty-eight.[52] Minnesota's growth had been particularly spectacular with much of the attendance attributed to the popularity of the night school division that attracted part-time students. Nationwide, the 1890s was the first period of substantial growth in law school attendance. In 1870 an estimated one thousand six hundred students were enrolled in American law schools; in 1880 the figure was three thousand one hundred; in 1890, four thousand five hundred; and by 1900 over twelve thousand five hundred students were in law schools across the country.[53]

The Wisconsin College of Law shared in the surge in the law student population during the 1890s, and hence it became more difficult to sustain relationships modeled upon that between the practitioner and his apprentice. In 1901 Associate Dean Gregory wrote: "I am very sorry that I cannot have the pleasure of knowing most of the students. There are now so many that I often find that I do not know even the children of my old friends." [54] Dean Bryant surely shared that regret. However, it was not simply the sheer number of students that made it difficult to maintain the law school in the image of the law office. During the 1890s many university law schools, led by Harvard and Columbia, were moving in an entirely different direction by reducing the amount of practice work in the curriculum and extending the time spent on legal theory. The fact that the Wisconsin College of Law was now considered an integral part of the University, not merely a school hovering on the periphery of the institution, meant that it would face intense pressure from the administration of the University of Wisconsin to follow the lead of the prestigious eastern law schools. Under such pressure, Bryant's ideal law school would become less and less a reality until finally, in the early years of the twentieth century, his vision would be repudiated entirely.

Case Study and the University Law School

The growing popularity of case study in the major university law schools eventually undermined Bryant's plan for a law school modeled upon the ideal law office. Case study was promoted as the key to placing legal education on a scientific basis. As such, it distinguished the university law school from other law schools and from other educational arrangements, like apprenticeship, in which law was taught merely as a craft or a trade. The rhetoric adopted by proponents of case study had powerful appeal at those universities, like Wisconsin, which prided themselves as centers of scientific investigation and teaching. Indeed, the scientific rhetoric that surrounded the introduction of case study served to integrate a new occupational group—career law professors— into the university community. The result, at Wisconsin and elsewhere, would be to reassert even more vigorously the primacy of theory in the law school curriculum.

Law schools, of course, had always emphasized theory rather than practice. Theodore Dwight, dean of the Columbia Law School from 1858 to 1891, put it succinctly: "Principles before practice is the true watchword." [55] Yet, when Dwight asserted that maxim, there existed either formal or informal ties between the law school and the law office. In that context, the neglect of the details of practice in the law school actually became its outstanding attraction for students. By the 1890s, however, the claim that the law school's role was to concentrate on theory alone was put forth in a far different context. Efforts in the 1870s and 1880s to institutionalize the ties between school and office permanently had largely failed. Those efforts took two forms: Some schools added a definite period of preparation to be devoted exclusively to office work while other schools held classes in the late afternoon or evening so that students could work in offices during the day. Neither strategy worked. [56]

The trend away from practical office training reflected in part the growing complexity of American law. At first, according to A. Z. Reed, this complexity "tended merely to force students to supplement their practical office training by theoretical work in a school," a development which helps explain the increasing popularity of law schools after the Civil War. But students did not want to extend the total amount of time spent studying law and so as the difficulty of mastering the theory increased there was a tendency to slight or to give up entirely practical training. [57] Practical details would be picked up in the first few years of actual practice. By the 1890s, however, to slight practical training was no longer merely an understandable, if somewhat regrettable, act of expediency. Now it was viewed by some law professors as a positive virtue. University law school catalogs boasted of their "scientific" approach to legal study and assured the student that he would be trained to think like a lawyer. Underlying this injection of the rhetoric of scientific investigation and methodology into the law school curriculum was the emergence of the full-time law professor, one whose primary commitment was to teaching rather than to practice, to the academic community rather than to the legal profession. In their eagerness to adapt the values of the burgeoning American university to the law school—and thus justify their own place in the academic community—these schoolmen often shunted to one side a concern with the practical application of legal skills.

The rallying point for those law professors, who were beginning to make legal teaching a career rather than a sideline of the active practitioner, was the case method of legal study. Christopher Columbus Langdell developed the case method at Harvard during the early 1870s, and his approach spread to a number of other law schools in varying degrees in the last decades of the nineteenth century. Indeed, by the end of the century the case method had not only come to mean the Harvard type of instruction but it formed the core of the curriculum at many university law schools and was the method against which other approaches to teaching invariably were measured.[58] Christopher Langdell spoke directly to the desire for academic respectability in 1887 when he argued that "if law be not a science, a university will best consult its own dignity in declining to teach it. If it be not a science, it is a species of handicraft, and may best be learned by serving an apprenticeship to one who practices it." [59] In contrast to earlier proponents of a scientific treatment of the law, like Joseph Story, Langdell did not locate the essence of scientific study in the classification and systematization of legal doctrine. Instead, Langdell argued that the law "must be studied in its sources" and that, to him, meant the reports of judicial decisions. "All the available materials" of the science of law, Langdell maintained, "are contained in printed books." These reports, in effect, formed the laboratory of legal study. "We have constantly inculcated the idea that the library is the proper workshop of professors and students alike; that it is to us all what the laboratories of the university are to the chemists and physicists, all that the museum of natural history is to the zoologists, all that the botanical garden is to the botanists." [60]

This was a very narrow conception of legal education and, indeed, a narrow conception of what constituted the law. As Hurst has commented, Langdell's case book method "was in the bad sense, a schoolman's concept." [61] Modern critics have pointed out that Langdell ignored the realities of the law, that by limiting his focus to the few general principles found in selected cases, he squeezed law into a few preconceived and artificial categories. In addition, the case method vastly overemphasized the appellate courts' importance in the legal system. If the essence of law was to be found only in the record of appealed cases, then legislative enactment, statutory law, became of little concern to the university law professor.

But if the weaknesses of the case method were related to the fact that it was a schoolman's concept, its strengths and its rapid adoption by many of the leading law schools of the country were related to that same characteristic. Earlier attempts by American law teachers to place the study of law on a scientific basis had run aground on an unsatisfactory conception of scientific study. As noted earlier, men like Joseph Story assumed that classification of legal doctrine was the essence of scientific treatment. That assumption almost inevitably led to a stress on the gathering of information and the memorization of classificatory schemes. According to the prevailing views of what constituted a science at that time, the early treatise writers were indeed setting the study of law on a scientific basis, but it was exceedingly difficult to see how law schools were a necessary ingredient in their success except, perhaps, as an institutional home for the labors of the law faculty who produced legal treatises. The students in the early law schools did not stay long enough at their studies for anything more than a brief exposure to the scientific treatment of the law. Because these students, with their career preoccupations, could not be expected to spend the long and arduous years attaining a true scientific understanding of the law (a process that Story claimed was the labor of a lifetime), there emerged an uncomfortable chasm between the scientific aspirations of the faculty of the pre-Civil War law schools and the practical, career-oriented studies actually taught in those schools.

Case study, in contrast, replaced content with method. Unlike the early nineteenth-century conception of law, which ultimately judged the lawyer "scientific" in terms of how much law he knew and how systematically he knew that law, the case method placed emphasis on a method of legal study and investigation. Content was by no means unimportant to case lawyers, especially those who used a modified version of Langdell's narrow approach by supplementing cases with more traditional textbook material. But teachers who propounded the virtues of case study were not forced to argue that their students possessed vast amounts of legal knowledge. On the contrary, their students often did not possess as much information as those trained exclusively by the lecture and textbook method, a fact that case teachers themselves often admitted. However, that lack now was turned into a virtue. Students trained in case study, the argument went, acquired a method of analysis by which they could eventually gain as much knowledge as they needed and under whatever new and unforseeable circumstances that might arise. The case method, in other words, made the "scientific" study of law a manageable enterprise. The depth of the law professor's knowledge would be put on exhibit in the increasing flood of casebooks and treatises that appeared after 1870; the professor could, in turn, argue that his students were being given the tools to achieve the same depth of knowledge when the circumstances of their legal practice required it.

The critical question, however, was whether facility in the analysis of leading cases fit the actual circumstances of legal practice. That question was never squarely confronted in the nineteenth century because the proponents of case study were, in many cases, unfamiliar with the actual duties and responsibilities of the active practitioner, particularly the courtroom advocate. Even if these men did enter upon their law school duties after a period of active practice, men like Christopher Langdell of Harvard or William Keener of Columbia viewed themselves more as career academics than active practitioners. This phenomenon—the emergence of career law teachers—was the most important development in legal education of the late nineteenth century.[62]

The model was James Barr Ames who in 1873 received a five-year appointment as an assistant professor of law in the Harvard Law School. Ames was a recent graduate of the Harvard Law School but what was astonishing to contemporaries was that he had had no previous experience in legal practice. Two decades later Harvard's President Charles Eliot recalled that "this school had never done it; no school had ever done it; it was an absolutely new departure in our country in the teaching of law." Eliot was certain that "in due course . . . there will be produced in this country a body of men learned in the law, who have never been on the bench or at the bar, but who nevertheless hold positions of great weight and influence as teachers of the law, as expounders, systematizers, and historians." [63] Eliot's prediction proved correct although it was not until the 1890s that an academic career in the law began to have great appeal; not until after the turn of the century would full-time law professors dominate the faculties of the major university law schools.[64]

One basic difference between law schools like Harvard and Columbia and an institution like Wisconsin in the 1890s was that at the latter there had not yet developed a sense of distinctiveness between law professors and practitioners. Unlike Langdell, Ames, or Keener, most members of the Wisconsin law faculty viewed themselves as practicing lawyers, not as career academics. The vast majority maintained an active practice while teaching only part time, and hence these men did not seek acceptance within the university by closely identifying with its basic values which, by the 1890s, were coming to be dominated by a commitment to scientific rigor. Indeed, not until Edwin E. Bryant was appointed to the faculty in 1889 did any person devote full time to the Wisconsin Law School, and Bryant obviously was closing his career as dean of the school rather than embarking upon a new vocation. It is not surprising, then, to find that under Bryant's leadership the Wisconsin College of Law moved against the waves created by the "new departure" in legal education. Yet there were less visible currents of change at Wisconsin even while Bryant attempted to mold the law school into the ideal apprenticeship experience.

The appointment of Charles N. Gregory as associate dean of the College of Law in 1894 underscores the importance of academic career commitment in the spread of the case method. The circumstances of his appointment demonstrate, as well, that the leadership for such curricular reforms came not from the legal profession but from within the university community. Charles Noble Gregory did not fit precisely the mold of the career academic defined by the example of James Barr Ames of Harvard. When he accepted the position of associate dean and professor in the Wisconsin College of Law Gregory was forty-three years old and had had over twenty years' experience in active practice. He was attracted, however, by bent of personality to the intellectual side of the law and, in fact, to the literary life in general. "In his younger years," one writer commented, "he was regarded as one of the rising poets of the time and frequently styled in reviews as 'the Bryant of the West.' " He was also one of the promoters of the Madison Literary Club. This predilection for literary activities was not in itself unusual (Dean Bryant had earned a similar reputation) but it does suggest the kind of man who would find academic life congenial. And Gregory, unlike Bryant, was still in middle age when he accepted a full-time post in the law school. That fact might have suggested to him the possibility of making a vocation of teaching law.

Certainly that is precisely what Gregory did. After serving in the Wisconsin College of Law from 1894 to 1901, he became dean of the Iowa College of Law. From 1911 to 1914 he was dean of the Department of Law of George Washington University. And during this time Gregory also became increasingly involved in professional activities. He served, for example, as chairman of the meeting which led to the formation of the Association of American Law Schools in 1900 and he was president of that Association in 1909. At the time of his death in 1932 Gregory was one of the editors of the *American Journal of International Law*. In one other respect, however, Gregory's appointment as associate dean in 1894 hardly seemed unusual. Like so many other faculty in the school he had earned the LL.B. from the Wisconsin Law Department (in 1872) and he had the expected connections with previous members of the faculty and the Board of Regents. In fact, his father, Jared C. Gregory, as a member of the Board of Regents during the 1870s, had been one of the more important links among the law school faculty, the university administration and the state legal profession.[65] But in one significant way Gregory's appointment represented a radical break with the past. Although recruited from among that small coterie of lawyers who had dominated the law school since its establishment, he was not recruited by members of that group. Instead, University of Wisconsin President Charles Kendall Adams took the initiative in bringing Gregory into the Wisconsin College of Law.

President Adams brought Gregory into the College of Law specifically to modernize the school along the lines of Harvard. Adams' background, particularly his efforts to make his own teaching more "scientific," indicates why he found the case method such an appealing pedagogical innovation. Charles Kendall Adams had been selected as president of the University of Wisconsin in 1892 after the resignation of Thomas Chamberlin. Previously, Adams had taught history at the University of Michigan from 1862 until 1885 and had served from 1885 until his appointment at Wisconsin as president of Cornell University. While at Michigan Adams was chiefly noted for introducing into the undergraduate curriculum the research seminar, a teaching device that had impressed him during the year and a half that he had spent studying in the universities of Germany and France during the middle 1860s. Although Adams' students at Michigan recalled that his "seminary" was "not wholly research, but rather essay work" and that "there was little discussion and mighty little originality," [66] it is clear that Adams, like other historians at the time who were experimenting with the same pedagogical technique,[67] believed that the seminar, with its radical departure from the reliance upon textbooks and lectures, constituted a significant step in placing the study and teaching of history on a scientific basis. Large amounts of original historical documents and records formed the "seminary library" or, as Adams remarked, "what I have sometimes called the historical laboratory." Such sources, placed in a room by themselves where students could work with them, "were to constitute the furniture of the investigator's workshop." [68] This conception of the proper way in which to organize historical investigation along scientific lines, of course, bore a close resemblance to the justification that Christopher Langdell was setting forth at Harvard for the case method of legal study. Both the history seminar and the case method were attempts to make an area of the university curriculum conform to the methods of inquiry that increasingly characterized the natural sciences.

Given the close resemblance between the seminar and the case method, it is hardly surprising that Charles Kendall Adams became such an enthusiastic proponent of the case method in the Wisconsin College of Law. Shortly after assuming the University presidency, Adams sent for Charles N. Gregory and asked him "to take the place of associate dean in the law school, promising," according to Gregory, "that I should be in line for the deanship; asking me to give up everything else, and to make over the law school without disturbing General Bryant, [and] to introduce the Harvard system of case study, etc." [69] There was only one immediate difficulty with this plan: Gregory had apparently only the vaguest notion of what was meant by case study. A year after joining the Wisconsin law faculty, therefore, Adams sent Gregory east where he "stayed with Dean [James Barr] Ames of Harvard at his country-house, and he and the dean of the Columbia University Law School [William Keener] coached" Gregory in the case system. It was during that summer, Gregory later recalled, that he became "deeply interested" in the possibilities of the case book method.[70] After his return to Wisconsin Gregory continued to correspond with Dean Ames and at least one of those letters suggests that he had not yet drunk deeply of the fountain of Harvard knowledge.

> I write to know if you could kindly favor me with any copies of the lists of questions made use of in examinations in your college of law. I remember an interesting talk that I had with you and Mr. Keener last summer at your house that you spoke of the character of questions assigned being such as to require reasoning on the part of the student and to prevent correct answers as a mere matter of memory or cribbing. I should like much to have the benefit of your type of question if possible in preparing examination papers here. Since my return in September I have been pressing the Harvard method upon the attention of the Dean and faculty to a considerable extent and have been assigned to two classes per week in which I use select cases and seek to [rest?] the teaching upon the methods of which you and Mr. Keener are perhaps the best examples. I am trying it under great disadvantages here, but am more and more impressed with its merit.[71]

The major opposition Gregory faced was the resistance of other faculty members, especially the part-time lecturers, to any movement away from the lecture system. A letter written by Gregory in December 1895 to George H. Noyes, a special lecturer on common carriers, reveals the kind of pressure that was brought to bear upon members of the faculty. Writing in behalf of Dean Bryant, Gregory informed Noyes that "we did not highly value as a means of instruction the lecture written and read without discussion and participation by the students." Gregory pointedly suggested that the course might be given by another professor if Noyes "did not find it convenient or deem it best to give the course further." However, Gregory did attempt to appear sympathetic to Noyes' point of view.

> I feel the difficulties in your giving the course which you speak of. If you could bring the citations up to date, if you could get your lectures either printed or mimeographed to distribute to the men before hand and instead of merely reading them to the students, call on the students for the principles, discussing and emphasizing them from reported cases and from your own large experience. I think you would find that, although it would add to your labors, it would add to your pleasure in the work and give you a sense of lifting the men on in their studies which one can hardly find in reading a lecture however carefully prepared.[72]

Noyes either did not agree with Gregory that his lectures needed revision or else thought that the work of revision would be too much to undertake. He resigned from his post as special lecturer prior to the start of the school year in 1897.

Gregory's criticism of Noyes gives some suggestion of the fertile ground from which case study emerged and indicates why, despite the reservations of many law professors and practicing lawyers, the Langdell approach established roots in so many institutions so quickly. To the nineteenth-century law professor, busy with an extensive practice, teaching "remained a pastime rather than a profession;" [73] the usual preparation for class consisted of dusting off old lecture notes. Unless the part-time lecturer was a naturally gifted teacher, students became bored with the dry and ill-prepared lectures. Even Dean Bryant, who supported Gregory's rebuke of Noyes, recognized that a system of instruction that relied solely upon lectures had serious shortcomings. Bryant believed that the lecture "is by far the most pleasing and satisfactory from the instructor's standpoint" because he "can carefully prepare, analyze, and arrange his subject, garnish it with illustration, [and] deliver it, according to his ability, with force and animation." But Bryant expressed serious doubts about the lecturer's actual effectiveness in teaching students. Even when a lecture was delivered with "force and animation"

> only a small part of a class will take it all in. Few will remember but a small part of it. Lectures upon a topic of law are admirable when delivered to old, trained lawyers. They can take it all in, and per-

ceive the treatment of the subject. The mere beginner, however, but little read in legal principles and untrained in legal methods of thinking, carries away but little from the best and clearest lecture. . . . The lecture system alone is of aid to the reading, thinking, eager student with a habit of perfect attention; but with the majority of law students it is of comparatively small value.[74]

Students, expressing a similar view, complained that "we have found it impossible to grasp and retain more than a very few subjects treated, no matter how excellently treated, when we have not had the opportunity of carefully studying the whole subject over in advance and of being questioned upon it afterward." Without that opportunity "the impressions we receive from the lectures are at best general, vague and fleeting." [75]

The dissatisfaction with the lecture system focused attention on the part-time professors and particularly upon the "special" lecturers who taught one course meeting only once a week. Not only were these lawyers most likely to rely upon the formal lecture, they were also the men who would quickly descend from the podium and rush back to their law practice, leaving students without benefit of their counsel outside the classroom. More typical, however, and less subject to such criticism, were the practitioners who taught at least three hours a week and who arranged their schedule so that they remained on campus after class was completed. Burr W. Jones, for example, lectured during the first semester of the 1896 school year to the junior class on domestic relations for one hour each week and taught evidence to the middle class and the senior class each for one hour a week. A similar schedule, with municipal corporations replacing domestic relations for the junior class, was followed during the second semester. Moreover, the description of Jones' courses in the catalog and Jones' own testimony indicate that he used a mixture of textbook assignments, lectures and analysis of cases,[76] a practice that overcame some of the difficulties that Dean Bryant recognized in the exclusive reliance upon lectures.

Bryant resisted the trend toward full-time law professors because he prized the presence on the faculty of lawyers in active practice. Students, he argued, tended to listen closely to teachers who could spice their lectures with illustrations from recent court actions in which they had played a part. In addition the reputation of these lawyers helped the school in two important ways: First, their fame was such that they attracted more students to the law school; second, these men forged strong links between the state legal profession and the University College of Law. Those "advantages," Bryant told University President Adams in 1898, more than "compensate for the occasional irregularities

Burr W. Jones. (*University of Wisconsin Archives*)

in attendance which their professional engagements renders [sic] inevitable." [77] Yet the advantages did not always outweigh the "occasional irregularities." One serious disruption occurred in 1899 when John M. Olin, who had taught in the school since 1886 and whose academic responsibilities matched those of Burr W. Jones, was absent from the city for two months at the beginning of the school year because of his legal practice. Although Olin made up the missed work by exchanging duties with other teachers, Bryant complained to the president that "it is always a disadvantage and unsatisfactory to students to have class work irregular and schedules uncertain." Olin, in addition to being one of the most prominent lawyers in the state, had been a "forcible, thorough instructor" and a "zealous, helpful worker on the faculty, sparing not himself and infusing energy and studiousness into the student body." Nevertheless, Bryant recommended that the money used to pay Olin and two other part-time instructors would be better applied to hiring a "competent instructor" who would give his entire time to the law school." [78] The Regents quickly approved that recommendation, although after receiving long, bitter letters from Olin and Robert M. Bashford (one of the other instructors affected) the Board rescinded the action, leaving Bryant with the unpleasant task of persuading the embittered lawyers to return to the faculty.[79]

If that episode merely reflected clashes of personality within the faculty or an attempt by the University administration to define more carefully who constituted the "full members of the faculty" (as Bryant later told Olin), then it would be of only minor interest. In fact, the underlying issue, never quite pinpointed in the extended correspondence between Dean Bryant and Olin and Bashford, was the growing tendency to rely upon full-time faculty members in the law school and a corresponding tendency to make sharp distinctions between "professional" law teachers and active practitioners who taught only as a sideline. Bryant, who on balance would always favor the presence of numbers of active practitioners on the faculty, recognized the disruptions caused by an extensive outside law practice and the discontent that resulted from an unwillingness to adjust teaching style to student demands. He came, then, to support the recruitment of full-time professors for reasons that were quite different from those advanced by University President C. K. Adams and Associate Law School Dean Gregory. The latter two men focused not upon the need for instructional regularity—though both believed that to be important—but upon the need to professionalize the law faculty.

This basic difference in perspective between Bryant, on the one hand, and Adams and Gregory, on the other hand, was reflected in the nature of the full-time appointments made to the law faculty after 1895. Some appointments, like those of Lynn Spencer Pease in 1895, William L. Drew in 1896 and Eugene A. Gilmore in 1902, clearly represented an effort to promote the case method and thus to reorient the Wisconsin College of Law along the pattern of eastern law schools like Harvard and Columbia. Other appointments, like those of Andrew A. Bruce in 1898 and Howard L. Smith in 1900, appeared more traditional. These men, though not selected from that small group of Madison lawyers who had dominated the faculty for so long, did have the more usual Wisconsin background and they were not obvious proponents of the case method. The nature of these appointments, then, reveals the shifting fortunes of case study at Wisconsin during the years between 1895 and 1902.

The appointment of Lynn Spencer Pease to the faculty in the fall of 1895 gave the first hint of incipient disagreement over the qualifications proper for full-time law professors. Pease, a Wisconsin native, had graduated from the University of Wisconsin with a B.A. in 1886 and from the Wisconsin College of Law in 1891. While in law school he served as secretary to State Supreme Court Justices Harlow Orton and John Cassoday, both of whom had lectured in the Wisconsin law school. Pease, it appeared, had the usual local connections. But what was unusual about his selection was the virtual absence of any experience in legal practice, a circumstance that recalls the appointment of Ames at Harvard in 1873. Pease, after completing his studies in the Wisconsin law school, became superintendent of the Wisconsin School for the Blind, a position he held until 1895, the year of his appointment to the Wisconsin law faculty. Pease taught in the Wisconsin College of Law for only one year. In 1896 he relocated in Milwaukee where he helped establish a private law school.[80] (That school, the Milwaukee Law School, was eventually sold to Marquette University and was renamed the Marquette University Law School.) Pease's background and subsequent career suggests that he was a compromise candidate for the position on the Wisconsin faculty: His connections were local, yet he probably also had determined to make teaching law a full-time career. The Wisconsin background reassured Bryant and the other experienced faculty while the commitment to a career in teaching held out the potential for development along the lines desired by Adams and Gregory. The only problem was that Pease had little or no experience in using the case method. That probably explains why his tenure at Wisconsin was so brief.

The man chosen to replace Pease, William L. Drew, was skilled in teaching with the case method. Indeed, he was recruited directly by President Adams who wrote to James Barr Ames at Harvard for his recommendation. Ames recommended Drew who had received the LL.B. from the Iowa State University Law School in 1892. During the

1892 school year Drew had attended the Harvard Law School where, he later claimed, a career as a law teacher "was in my mind." [81] After leaving Harvard, Drew went to Omaha, Nebraska, where he practiced law in the firm of Montgomery and Hall. Significantly, his duties with the Omaha firm were "almost wholly in brief work, most of his time . . . having been spent in [the] library." [82] That description would have been high praise to men like Ames and Adams. It indicated skill in searching out precedents, the essential ingredient in the success of the lawyer who taught according to the case method. And, in fact, Drew was listed in the 1896 law school catalog as "Assistant Professor of the Law of Agency, and Study of Cases," a title altered slightly the following year to read "Assistant Professor [of the] Analysis of Cases." [83] Clearly, Drew had been recruited to further promote the use of case study in the law school curriculum.

Drew resigned in June 1898 and the next two full-time appointments, Alexander A. Bruce in 1898 and Howard L. Smith in 1900, suggest a more cautious attitude toward the case method. Both Bruce and Smith were graduates of the University of Wisconsin and of the Wisconsin College of Law. Bruce received the LL.B. in 1892 and Smith was awarded that degree in 1885. Both also had a wider professional experience than had either Pease or Drew. Bruce served after graduation as the chief clerk in the law department of the Wisconsin Central Railway Company's Chicago office for a year and then from 1893 to 1898 practiced law in Chicago in the firm of Bruce and Wickett. Smith practiced law in Madison from 1885 to 1887, in St. Paul, Minnesota from 1887 to 1893 and in Chicago from 1893 to 1900. Once on the law faculty at Wisconsin, neither man taught exclusively according to the case method. While they, like most teachers in the school, used "leading cases" in their classes, they also supplemented the study of cases with assignments in textbooks and with lectures. [84]

By the end of the nineteenth century, then, the "disadvantages" that Gregory labored under as he tried to introduce case study into the curriculum persisted. Despite Gregory's efforts, and those of President Charles Kendall Adams, the Wisconsin College of Law had not been transformed along the lines of Harvard and Columbia. But the school would soon capitulate. In June, 1901 Associate Dean Gregory resigned to accept a position as dean of the Iowa State University Law School. [85] No one was appointed to fill Gregory's position although Bruce was asked to assist Dean Bryant with his administrative duties. The following year Bruce resigned, and the school was forced to look for another professor. The search was carried out by Acting University President E. A. Birge who told the Regents that Bruce's position "should be filled by a teacher of marked ability, so that the faculty of the College of Law may be materially strengthened by the change." [86] After a long search, the Regents in the fall of 1902 appointed Eugene A. Gilmore assistant professor of law. Gilmore had practiced law in Boston for three years before coming to Wisconsin but, more important, he had received his training in that bastion of the case method, the Harvard Law School, where he earned the LL.B. in 1895.[87] Then in June 1903 Bryant himself resigned. Though he retained his position as professor of law, he would not return to the school. He died in the summer of 1903. His successor, recruited by E. A. Gilmore, was Harry S. Richards, another Harvard law graduate (LL.B., 1895).[88] Richards had introduced case study into the Iowa College of Law during the 1890s and he arrived in Wisconsin prepared to transform the Wisconsin College of Law in the same way.

Professional Values in Conflict

The battle over case study at Wisconsin during the 1890s, though not especially dramatic, reflected a clash of professional values. The resistance of Bryant and others to teaching by means of case study was not simply a dispute over teaching methods, nor did that resistance stem primarily from the differing academic perspectives of practitioners who taught part-time and lawyers who sought to make teaching a career. Important though such differences were, they only exacerbated a more profound disagreement. At stake was a conception of the role of the lawyer in the legal system in particular and in national life in general. In Bryant's view the spread of the case system did not represent the triumph of a more scientific approach to legal study; instead it symbolized the demise of what he conceived to be the professional lawyer.

The precise nature of the resistance to case study was clearly articulated only after the arrival of Charles N. Gregory on the Wisconsin law faculty. Shortly after Gregory's appointment Bryant discussed the advantages and disadvantages of the case method in an address before the Wisconsin State Bar Association. Bryant noted that case study "finds great and growing favor in law schools and its friends are most enthusiastic in its praise." He admitted that case study had two great advantages: "It makes the student an investigator, makes him reluctant to take his law at second hand;" and it "tends to make the student, and later the lawyer, a close and accurate critic of legal decisions." But the case method also had important disadvantages.

It must be said that this system teaches *how* to learn law, instead of learning so much of it. It is rather a mental fitting to learn law than the acquirement of a very wide range of general legal knowledge. . . . While it makes the student very orderly and careful in method it is rather apt to make him slow. It well fits him for the profound work of historical and archaic studies, rather than the alertness and nimblemindedness of the active practitioner. It is a very attractive mode of study to those who do not like to be hurried. That it tends to strong vigorous thinking, careful discrimination and self-reliance, I think will be conceded. That it should be adopted as the sole method in a law school, I am not prepared to admit.[89]

Bryant's reservations concerning case study derived partly from his fundamental disagreement with proponents of the method over the purposes of the law school. While Langdell and his followers would have quarantined students in the law library or classroom, directing them to read, study and discuss court decisions, Bryant was attempting through his curricular reforms to retain the flavor of an earlier approach to legal education. That approach combined attention to theoretical work and practical application, and, as it came to be developed by Bryant at Wisconsin during the 1890s, it brought elements of the apprenticeship experience into the confines of the school. When Bryant noted that case study suited the student for the "profound work of historical and archaic studies," he recognized that Langdell's conception of the law was that of a legal scholastic, a schoolman. Bryant, however, operated within the tradition that conceived of the lawyer as essentially an advocate. As described by Bryant, case study might offer adequate training for a lawyer who expected only to write briefs and opinions, for a lawyer like William L. Drew who spent most of his time in the library. But for Bryant the characteristics that he thought the law school ought to cultivate were the "alertness and nimble-mindedness of the active practitioner." These were the characteristics that traditionally had been associated with the legal advocate, the courtroom lawyer who developed his case in the heat of courtroom combat.

There was an even more fundamental difference in outlook between Bryant and proponents of case study. Bryant criticized case study mainly for its narrowness. His own experience in the classroom and his assumptions about the nature of the lawyer's role led Bryant to emphasize a combination of lectures, readings, selected cases and class discussion. He believed that the most important element in legal instruction was "the oral work of the teacher, and that he must use both the text books and selected cases, not according to any rigid and prescribed system, but in such a way that according to his skilled judgment, the principles of law—the end to be sought—can be most easily and thoroughly mastered." [90] Because case study was promoted by those men who sought to give professional dignity to the career of the law professor, it was ironic that Bryant attacked case study because it seemed to him to reduce the importance of the law teacher. There was something mechanistic about the case method (note his description of case study as a "rigid and prescribed system") that Bryant seemed not quite able to put his finger on. Yet it is clear that what Bryant wanted to preserve was the "skilled judgment" of the law professor. Just as he chafed against rigid administrative rules which left too little room for his own personal assessment of students' ability when they presented themselves for admission to the law school, so too did Bryant resist rigid and mechanistic methods of teaching law. He insisted that the professor had a responsibility to make his own decisions about how best to reach students. Indeed, the essence of a professional for Bryant was the ability and the courage to make such judgments, whether in the arena of the courtroom or of the classroom. One who depended upon a mechanistic system to render such judgments could not be, in the most fundamental meaning attached to the word by nineteenth century lawyers, a "professional."

Bryant's insistence that case study was a narrow and debilitating form of legal education echoed a widespread feeling among older lawyers. What Bryant said about the law professor dependent upon the analysis of cases and the search for precedents, practitioners said about the case lawyer: Both operated in a rigid and mechanical manner. The ultimate threat posed by the case method was not that it turned out lawyers who had a superficial knowledge of legal doctrine—though that was a serious problem—but rather that it formed lawyers who assumed that the practice of law consisted only of a search for precedents. Roujet D. Marshall, a justice on the Wisconsin Supreme Court from 1895 to 1918, invoked this theme in his autobiography.

I propose, on every occasion afforded for it, to warn the student against relying on such method [case study] to acquire a thorough, practical knowledge of the law and to warn the young practitioner not to rely on precedents to win his client's cause and, by all means, not to conclude that what his judgment suggests is right is not so in fact because he is unable to find "a case in point." The great mass of our law is grounded on principles found in the unwritten law. Those principles are the embodiment of the experience of the ages and so are older than precedents and much more reliable. Where a plainly established principle and a precedent are clearly antagonistic, the former is to prevail.

Like Bryant, Marshall stressed the importance of the lawyer's "judgment." Precedents might be used "by way of illustration" but they must not be allowed to stand in the way of a lawyer convinced of a "plainly established principle." [91]

Nor were these isolated views. The biographies of lawyers collected in the two volume *History of the Bench and Bar of Wisconsin,* published in 1898, offer a guide to the attributes of the lawyer which the contributors—all prominent attorneys—most highly valued; those descriptions also reveal, by implication, what qualities those lawyers detested. Supreme Court Justice John B. Winslow, for example, was admired because he "followed principles rather than authorities. A rule of law became such on account of its intrinsic reason and justice, rather than because it had been announced by a court in New York or Kansas." [92] Similarly, Justice Byron Paine "had but little idolatry for mere precedents . . . which violated correct principles." [93] And Harlow S. Orton (the second dean of the Wisconsin Law Department) was described as "exceptionally free from the trammels of mere legal technicalities and existing opinion which fell below his high conception of those immutable principles of justice." [94]

This attack on the case method, then, could be formulated in moral terms. Case lawyers, it was implied, elevated reason above the moral sense and pridefully asserted that reason alone could guide judicial decisions. Viewed in this way, the mechanical application of precedents threatened the image of the lawyer as a free moral agent and in so doing threatened to undermine what to many nineteenth-century lawyers was the essence of "professional"conduct. Yet those who were attracted to the case method would have rejected the notion that it was they who should be accused of pride. The "immutable principles of justice" could not always be easily perceived and those who insisted that they could ran the risk of substituting individual moral judgments for more general principles of justice. The reliance upon precedents, in other words, was a way to keep individual prejudices and idiosyncracies within bounds.

The dispute over case study reveals a larger problem: By 1900 the sources of agreed upon principles of justice and fairness had become objects of disagreement. Indeed, the subsequent development of legal doctrine in the twentieth century would be concerned in a fundamental sense with this problem. The older generation of lawyers, trained in the nineteenth century but completing their careers as eminent practitioners in the twentieth century, would continue to rely upon broad moral principles as the basis for justice. Case lawyers, especially those who taught in the major universities, would, in contrast, rely upon a narrow scientific historicism for their source of justice. Still others, like Holmes and Pound who argued for sociological jurisprudence or, later, Karl Llewellyn, who articulated a legal realist position, began to search for principles of justice in the emerging social sciences. Though at first glance dissimilar, all of these approaches to the study and practice of law were preoccupied with a similar problem: the search for agreed-upon principles of justice. Against that background, the battle over the form and purpose of the university law school would continue in the twentieth century.

CHAPTER SIX

Schoolmen Versus Practitioners

Schoolmen, not practitioners, led the movement to establish more stringent admission requirements, a longer and more rigorous course of study, and a concentration on legal theory as the distinguishing features of the university law school. Leaders of major public and private universities actively encouraged career law professors as they attempted to make the university law school an academically selective institution. Law schools in the nineteenth century, of course, had functioned to some extent to select those young men who would become lawyers. But such selectivity operated in the context of other arrangements for training and for certifying professional ability. Increasingly in the twentieth century the law school became the most important guardian of the gates to the legal profession. More important, the basis of selection narrowed to an objective judgment rendered upon the evidence of prior scholastic achievement.

Selectivity based upon academic performance introduced a class dimension into the legal education of the twentieth century that was more rigid than that which characterized the nineteenth century. Academically deficient young men who lacked the opportunity or resources for two or three years of formal schooling beyond high school were no longer encouraged to enter the university law school. Talent would be rewarded but it was intellectual talent, demonstrated by prior academic achievement, that the law schools encouraged. Practitioners, in both urban and rural areas, resisted the trend to select members of the bar solely on the basis of academic achievement;[1] in Wisconsin the practitioners from the smaller towns and cities, simply because they dominated numerically the State Bar Association, were the most effective opponents of the educational reforms promoted by the State University Law School. Those practitioners continued to believe that the legal profession ought to remain open to "poor and worthy" young men who exhibited native talent or unusual perseverance. That belief reflected in large measure an attempt to keep the profession open to men like themselves.

The AALS Package of "Progressive" Reforms

The drive to make legal preparation more selective sharpened the distinctions drawn among American law schools. A small group of university law schools, most of whom were charter members of the Association of American Law Schools (AALS) formed in 1900, energetically promoted such distinctions. The AALS schools identified themselves as the "progressive" element in legal education, and they organized their position around a package of reforms that centered upon adoption of the case method. Their opponents, representing a far greater number of schools and students, continued to give allegiance to a modified version of nineteenth-century arrangements. These schools relied upon active practitioners to staff their faculty, and they encouraged students whenever possible to combine work in a law office with study in a law school. The AALS quickly labeled this approach as anti-progressive, as a defense of low standards, and as a type of legal education that viewed law as a trade rather than as a learned profession.

The dynamics of the process which transformed the nineteenth-century law school into an academically selective institution were clear in Wisconsin during the first decade of the twentieth century. University President Charles R. Van Hise joined with the full-time professors in the law school to select the new dean who would replace the retired E. E. Bryant.[2] The man selected, Harry S. Richards, had been trained at the Harvard Law School, and he rapidly would introduce the reforms recommended by the AALS into the Wisconsin College of Law. The speed with which he moved—the basic changes were completed within five years—suggested that the process of reform was largely imitative. The reforms, institutionalized in their purest form at Harvard, constituted a logically coherent package that simply had to be set in place. It is significant, too, that the leaders of the Wisconsin bar did not press for such reforms. Practitioners were content to rest the statutory standards for admission to the bar at a level much lower than Richards and the law faculty thought desirable.[3] Practitioners, in fact, became interested in the policies of the College of Law only when it became clear that the AALS reforms, when carried to their logical end, threatened to make the law school too theoretical and too restrictive.

The schoolmen who selected Richards were seeking a teacher and an administrator rather than a legal scholar. University President Van Hise and Professor Eugene A. Gilmore, the latter an 1895 Harvard Law School graduate, led the search for the new dean. Richards' background and training had much to recommend him. His midwestern upbringing made it seem less obvious that an outsider was being brought in to make the school over in the Harvard image. Born in Iowa in the fall of 1868 (at the same time that the Wisconsin Law Department opened), Richards had graduated from the University of Iowa in 1892. The follow-ing year he entered the Harvard Law School where, along with classmate Eugene Gilmore, he received the LL.B. in 1895. Richards re-turned to Iowa where he practiced law in Ottumwa from 1895 to 1898. Then in the fall of 1898 he accepted a position as professor of law at the University of Iowa Law School where he remained until, at age thirty-four, he was elected dean at Wisconsin.[4]

The letters received by Van Hise and Gilmore recommending Richards pictured him as a somewhat reserved person, a respected though not inspiring teacher, and a clear though not original thinker. He was, according to one letter, "not extremely cordial," and in the judgment of another writer, only "moderately affable."[5] Yet all the letters remarked on his success as a teacher. One of his colleagues on the Iowa law faculty said: "He knows the law as it is, and is successful in teaching others. His students all regard him highly. He has good control of his classes and they work well."[6] Another colleague said that he had a reputation as "a thoroughly competent man in the law, [he] has a good judicial mind, and is a good, clear thinker." However, Richards proba-bly did not possess "great ability for constructive, original work in law," a judgment that another of his colleagues at Iowa agreed with and that was confirmed subsequently by Richards' scholarly career.[7] But these personal traits—seriousness, thoroughness and persistence—marked the way that Richards introduced the AALS package of reforms at Wisconsin.

The case method was the central element in that reform package, and from that innovation a number of other reforms necessarily followed: a higher standard of pre-legal preparation, a full three-year day cur-riculum, a heavy if not quite exclusive reliance upon full-time law teachers and a large law library. These innovations were expensive, of course, and so it also followed that the sponsoring institution had to make a substantial financial commitment to support the law school. Law schools might adopt these reforms gradually, raising, for example, their entrance standards over a three- or four-year period; because the

Harry S. Richards. (*University of Wisconsin Archives*)

reforms were logically intertwined, however, they could not be introduced piecemeal. It was this fact that made the pressure on the schools who resisted the innovations so unremitting. A law school which introduced the case method while still relying upon practitioners to staff its faculty found itself criticized because only career law professors trained in the approved method could use the case method successfully. A school might adopt the case method and increase its full-time faculty, but even that was not sufficient unless at the same time it upgraded its law library, the "laboratory" of the case lawyer. Finally, a school might do all those things yet still find itself under attack because its entrance standards were too low or its course of study too short. The case method, teachers found, worked best when the students themselves were carefully selected and when they were required to devote full time to their studies. These kinds of criticisms, in fact, could have been leveled at the University of Wisconsin Law School under Dean Bryant's leadership in the 1890s. Although Bryant had introduced all the above innovations into the school, Richards would not have viewed his task as completing that which Bryant had begun. Bryant's innovations had been piecemeal adjustments made to recreate the law school along the lines of the ideal law office. Richards, in contrast, introduced reforms in an effort to obliterate the remaining ties with nineteenth-century educational arrangements.

The central distinguishing characteristic of the modern law school was its commitment to the case method. Richards stated that he was a "strong believer in the inductive, or case method of instruction, as it seems to me it conforms to the modern methods of University instruction, and tends to develop in the student a capacity for analysis and independent thought, which is the end of professional study." [8] The rest of the full-time faculty in the school also believed in the case method, and the shift to almost exclusive use of that approach after Richards' arrival is clearly evident in the Law School catalogs. In 1904, the second year of Richards' term as dean, all the full-time professors used casebooks as the principal means of instruction in their courses. The part-time instructors—Jones, Olin and Bashford—continued to use traditional textbooks but they, too, began to supplement the course work with selected cases. By 1910 even the practitioners had adopted case study in some of their classes. Burr Jones, for example, used Paige's *Cases on Persons* as the sole text in that topic, and John Olin used Gray's *Cases on Property* as the principal text in his course. [9] Richards did not think that the Wisconsin College of Law "could be regarded as an absolute follower" of either "the case system or the textbook method of legal instruction." In a letter written in 1905, he claimed that he made "free use of text books in connection with the instruction, [although] the courses themselves are based upon collections of cases, the text books being used merely by way of reference." [10] But few professors across the nation relied exclusively upon cases in their courses. They found that, especially for first-year students, supplementary textbook materials were absolutely essential to impart general information about legal doctrine and procedure. Indeed, in 1913 when Josef Redlich investigated how the case method was used, he attributed its success to the widespread use of textbooks in conjunction with case study.[11] Still, the analysis of leading cases constituted the distinguishing feature of the modern law school for Richards and all other materials, like textbooks, were of secondary importance.

Although proponents of case study correctly argued that that method was a radical departure from previous teaching practices, in one sense these men merely continued the movement begun by the nineteenth-century treatise writers to "bring wider areas of doctrine within tighter patterns of conceptual order." [12] Case-book authors viewed the law as a relatively fixed body of knowledge capable of being squeezed into a few doctrinal categories but now the impetus was not, as it had been for men like Joseph Story, to organize legal knowledge elegantly into topical categories but instead to reduce sharply the number of categories themselves; within those categories, the intent was to emphasize the method by which the law could be found rather than the content of the law itself. Richards put it succinctly in 1912: "The chief benefit of a course in law is not the large knowledge gained, but the capacity and the habits acquired by systematic, thorough study." [13]

The emphasis upon method rather than content reduced dramatically the number of courses required of students. In 1904 Richards and the law faculty revamped the entire curriculum, grouping fundamental courses in the first year and organizing the second and third years of the course around more specialized and elective offerings. The law school curriculum in 1903, a hold-over from the Bryant years, carried first-year students through thirteen separate courses: elementary law, contracts, domestic relations, commercial paper, real property, public officers, agency, taxation, municipal corporations, common law pleading and practice, courts and jurisdiction (taught with notes and statutes), partnership and bailments. Under the reorganization in 1904 the number of course offerings for first-year students was almost halved. In their initial year students studied contracts, common law pleading, law of persons, real property, personal property, criminal law and procedure and torts. In addition to these seven courses, an optional series of ten lectures on courts and their jurisdiction was offered. After a thorough grounding in legal methodology in these basic courses, students in the middle and senior years were allowed to elect credits from more specialized courses like equity, code pleading, public service companies and insurance.[14] Obviously, the introduction of the elective system into the second- and third-year law curriculum, first done at Harvard in 1886, reflected and in turn contributed to a growing specialization of function within the legal profession. But, like the reliance upon the case method, the introduction of electives also meant that the university law school "no longer professed to give its students a present mastery of judge-made law. It prepared them merely to master judge-made law in the future." [15]

The embrace of the case method led to many of the organizational characteristics—higher entrance standards, a longer course of study, a full-time faculty, and a large law library—of the early twentieth-century university law school. Of greatest importance, the law school became academically selective. The key to the case system, particularly from the professors' point of view, was a group of intellectually agile students. "When I started," one professor noted, "I was told, 'Pick four or five points and keep coming back to them; find the bright students and play them like a piano.' It works." [16] Josef Redlich, in his study of the case method done for the Carnegie foundation in 1913, also recognized that in those classes where the case method was used "for a considerable period only the particularly quick or talented students take part in the debate." [17] In fact, this had been one of the significant criticisms leveled against the case method by law teachers of the nineteenth century. Theodore Dwight of Columbia, for example, opposed case study because it was not suited to the "great and important class of men of average ability" that "exists and always will exist in the profession . . . . These men must be trained as well as those of superior powers." [18] Bryant would have sympathized with that view but not Dean Richards. Characteristically, Richards justified even the elective system mainly on the grounds that it enabled the school to achieve more rigorous academic standards. The elective system allowed "each student, within limits, [to] select as many courses as he demonstrates his ability to carry, and a common measure is not imposed on the able and dull alike. The ambitious student can thus cover more subjects in a given time than would be possible for a less able classmate." [19]

The better solution, however, would be to eliminate the dull student from the school completely, to adapt, in other words, the character of the student body to the imperatives of the case method rather than, as Bryant had done, to adapt the curriculum to the character of the students. Richards quietly began that task soon after his arrival at Wisconsin by placing the administration of the Law School entrance requirements, which at that time demanded a high school education, into the hands of the University registrar. This was done so that "the rules heretofore somewhat laxly administered might be strictly enforced." [20] Bryant, of course, had preferred to use such rules as general guidelines, not as substitutes for his personal judgment. But Richards not only wanted to rely upon clearly written standards, he also wanted to raise those standards even higher because "more uniform attainment of matriculants would make possible more thorough work in the College itself." [21] The law faculty already had reached the same conclusion. They complained in 1902 that "the students at present differ so widely in their scholastic attainments that [we] find it difficult to properly adapt the instruction to all." [22] But higher entrance standards meant that the instruction would not have to be adapted to a diverse group, and therefore in March 1904 the law faculty formally asked the Regents to advance the entrance standards to the College of Law to two years of college training. The Board promptly approved the resolution although the rule itself was implemented gradually. All students entering the Law College in 1905 were required to present credits equivalent to the freshman year of college; and students entering the following year, 1906, were required to present the equivalent of two years' college training. [23]

This stress on academic excellence was reflected in a number of other areas as well. The faculty, for example, raised the standard of attainment expected of students enrolled in the school. Richards told the Regents in 1904 that "students who fail to obtain a passing grade in a major part of their studies are dropped and others whose work is of a low order are advised to withdraw. The result has been to restrict the upper classes to men of proven ability." [24] The regulations governing special students were also tightened in the first decade of Richards' deanship. Under Bryant students twenty-three years of age or older were admitted to the College of Law as special students if they could not meet the minimum admission requirements. If such students subsequently decided they wanted a degree, they had to pass the entrance examination required of regular students. In January 1904 the University Regents rescinded this provision and adopted in its place a policy that required even special students to pass an examination for entrance into the freshman class of the University. These students were allowed all the privileges of regular law students but only in order to prepare for the bar examination. However, those special students who displayed "unusual ability in their work, by special action of the faculty, [would] be recommended for a degree." In this way, Richards argued, "worthy students may still be honored by a degree, when for any reason they are unable to meet the maximum entrance requirement." [25] For a short time this regulation cut down on the number of special students enrolled in the school—only four students entered under this status in 1905 and only three in 1906—but thereafter the number rose sharply with as many as forty-eight special students enrolled in 1909 and an average attendance in this group between 1908 and 1928 of twenty-four students. But the rule was extremely effective in reducing the number of special students granted the degree: a total of four hundred forty-eight specials were enrolled in the Wisconsin College of Law from 1908 to 1928 but only eighteen were awarded the LL.B.[26]

Richards also made the rules governing admission to advanced standing more stringent. Under Bryant students were allowed to take examinations that admitted them to either the middle or senior year of the law course, and it made no difference whether they had picked up the requisite legal knowledge in a law school or in a law office. In 1904 this was changed to require of the student not only an examination but also a certificate "signed by the executive officer of a law school of good standing having a three years' course, showing at least one year's study as a regularly enrolled student." At the same time the graduation requirements for regular students in the College of Law were advanced to require at least two years in a law school before the LL.B. was granted. Three years later the graduation requirements were again advanced. The 1907 Law School catalog announced that candidates for the degree must complete "residence of at least three years in a law school of good standing, having a three year course, one year of which must have been in this college." [27] Thus, by 1907 the Wisconsin law degree signified, for the first time, three full years of law school training.

The alignment of the Wisconsin College of Law with the ideals of legal training supported by the AALS also meant that the library had to be enlarged and that greater reliance had to be placed on full-time law teachers. In what had come to be a commonplace observation, Richards pointed out that "under modern methods of instruction the law library bears the same relation to the work of the law school that the laboratories do to the work in natural science." Not only did an "effective working library" need an incredible number of state and national reports and statutes, it also needed those reports in duplicate because "an entire class is referred to a particular case, and unless it can be found in duplicate it will be inaccessible to a large number, at the time needed." Under the pressure of Richards' prodding, the Wisconsin legislature in 1905 provided the school with ten additional sets of *Wisconsin Reports,* and in that same year the Regents appropriated fifteen thousand dollars for the purchase of books. Together with an increased annual expenditure for books and journals, this enabled the faculty to enlarge considerably the holdings of the law library from the seventy-four hundred volumes it contained when Richards arrived. By 1910 the library held eighteen thousand volumes and by 1920 Richards reported that the library contained over thirty thousand volumes.[28]

The impression that instruction in the law school ought to be less expensive than instruction in other departments of the university also

University of Wisconsin Law School Library, 1914. (*University of Wisconsin Archives*)

had to be countered by Richards and the law faculty. That impression, according to Professor Howard L. Smith, was "a survival of the days when legal instruction was given by practicing lawyers, who snatched a hour from a busy day to read a 'lecture' to law students." But, Smith contended,

> cut-and-dried lectures, as an exclusive or even principal method of instruction, are as obsolete in law as in all other branches of university instruction. The methods in vogue in all progressive law schools are now the methods of conference of some sort, over either cases or texts, or statutes, or in moot courts, involving the co-operation of student and professor.[29]

That kind of teaching required specialists in legal education, and specialists were expensive. "To obtain and retain the services of competent teachers of law," Richards maintained, "the salary paid must have some relation to the income which a lawyer of like ability would be able to command as a practitioner." [30]

The salaries paid in the Wisconsin College of Law, however, were somewhat lower than at other major university law schools and in many cases were not sufficient to keep promising young men on the faculty. In 1905 Professor Howard L. Smith threatened to resign and take up private practice unless his salary was increased to thirty-five hundred dollars. Richards suggested that his salary be increased to three thousand dollars the following year and to thirty-five hundred dollars thereafter, an increase that kept Smith on the faculty but which still represented about a thousand dollars less than the salary paid at some other law schools.[31] In 1909 Smith was still receiving thirty-five hundred dollars a year while two other full-time professors, Eugene Gilmore and Walter Wheeler Cook, received three thousand dollars. Having discovered the previous year that he could not fill a vacancy on the staff for less than thirty-five hundred dollars, Richards recommended that the salaries of Gilmore and Cook be advanced to that amount.[32] A year later Gilmore was offered a job at the University of Illinois Law School which paid forty-five hundred dollars, a fact that prompted Richards to recommend that Gilmore's salary be increased to four thousand dollars.[33] But many of the younger members of the Wisconsin faculty did resign because of low salaries. In 1914, after three members had left for better-paying positions in other universities, Richards complained to the University Board of Regents that the school had been forced to give up good men "just when they had reached the full measure of their efficiency and usefulness." The Law School, Richards warned, "can not go ahead as it should if it is forced to be a training school for teachers for other schools." [34] Two years later, after Henry Ballantine resigned to become dean of the University of Illinois Law School, Richards again complained about the low salaries paid professors at Wisconsin. He noted that from 1902 to 1916 thirteen men had held full-time positions on the faculty. One, Edwin Bryant, had died, while seven others had resigned. "All the resignations were due to higher salaries elsewhere." [35]

Yet the problem was not easily resolved because the school was also competing with industry and with lawyers in private practice. Reliable figures on lawyers' incomes during this period are difficult to find although a salary of four thousand dollars for a law professor probably was competitive with the income of most private practitioners. According to Hurst, in Boston during the 1890s probably no more than half a dozen men made over twenty-thousand dollars a year, another dozen made ten thousand and no more than a quarter of the bar had incomes in excess of five thousand dollars. [36] A careful study of the earnings of Wisconsin lawyers based on income tax returns and covering the years 1927 to 1932 indicated that in 1927 the majority of lawyers (almost seventy-four percent) had a net professional income of under five thousand dollars, while 15.8 percent earned between five and nine thousand dollars, and only ten percent earned more than nine thousand. [37] While hardly conclusive, this does suggest that the salaries for law professors in the top universities in the early twentieth century were competitive with all but the elite practitioners. Still, a problem existed as the example of Professor R. B. Scott indicated. He resigned in February, 1911 to take a position with the Burlington Railroad at an annual salary of ten thousand dollars. Clearly, the University, which paid President Van Hise only seven thousand dollars, could not compete on that scale. [38]

A modern law school obviously was expensive. In contrast to the nineteenth-century law department, the expenditures for the faculty and the library alone were enormous. Less obvious but equally important, the law school could no longer depend upon the fees from students to cover these expenses. In fact, both the number of students attending the school and the number of graduates declined during the first two decades of Richard's term, a drop that can be attributed in part to the ever-more stringent admission and degree requirements that he instituted. Between 1895 and 1903 the attendance fluctuated between two hundred and two hundred sixty-two students and in Bryant's last year as dean two hundred twenty-six students attended the school. In the first decade of Richards' term as dean the school averaged an annual attendance of about one hundred sixty-five students; and in his second decade, from 1913 to 1923, the school attracted over one hundred seventy-one students a year (a figure artificially lowered by the severe drop in attendance during World War I when the school almost closed its doors). During Bryant's last five years as dean, the school graduated over sixty students each year. From 1903 to 1913 that figure dropped to an average of thirty-eight students a year and in the next decade to thirty-one students a year. In 1929, Richards' last year as dean, the school awarded the LL.B. to ninety-three students. Not until the 1930s would the Wisconsin Law School begin to award law degrees to over one hundred students each year.[39]

The reforms introduced into the Wisconsin Law School after Richards' arrival were made possible only because the University increased the amount of money given the school in addition to the income from student fees. The law school budget for the year 1903 and 1904 was estimated at about five thousand dollars more than the student fees were expected to bring in, and in 1906 Richards reported that the biennial budget for the school had been increased an additional $5,950 over that for the years between 1902 and 1904. Finally, beginning with the academic year 1908 the University assumed practically the entire responsibility for funding the operations of the College of Law. In 1907 the state legislature had repealed the provision in the statutes permitting tuition fees in the College of Law, and the Regents then applied to law students the same schedule of fees charged to students in the College of Letters and Science. Thereafter Wisconsin residents paid no tuition fee at all, nonresidents paid a tuition fee of fifteen dollars per semester and all law students paid an incidental fee of ten dollars each semester.[40]

The speed with which Richards introduced the AALS package of reforms at Wisconsin concealed their long-range impact. In many cases the basic changes were in place before the legal profession could react. Moreover, Richards softened the impact of those reforms by implementing them gradually. He advanced, for example, the Law School entrance requirements from a high school education to two years of college attendance only one year after arriving at the University of Wisconsin. The rule itself, however, went into effect over a three-year period, and its impact was softened even more by allowing young men without sufficient preparation to enroll in the school as special students. But as Richards pressed his reforms even further, leaders of the legal profession began to resist. They did not realize that wholesale commitment to the case method meant, as it did for Richards, that the Law School eventually would delete from the curriculum the traditional courses in legal practice. Nor did leaders of the legal profession forsee that the commitment to case study also meant a decreasing reliance upon part-time practitioners on the faculty. Practitioners could not accept either trend. At first they expressed their criticism privately in correspondence between Richards and some members of the Board of Regents. But gradually practitioners discovered a specific institutional alternative to the state university law program. That alternative was the Marquette University Law School established in 1908. The Marquette school advertised an intensely practical curriculum taught by lawyers still active in legal practice. That model of legal education, which in some respects recalled the University of Wisconsin Law School under Dean Bryant, still commanded the allegiance of many of the state's lawyers.

A School for Practitioners

The ideal of legal preparation that combined law school lectures with office experience survived well into the twentieth century. That ideal, however, was blurred and then became indistinct as the growth in the number of American law schools (sixty-one in 1890, one hundred two in 1900, and one hundred twenty-four in 1910)[41] spawned a variety of institutions. There were almost endless ways to categorize such schools. One basic category distinguished among schools according to when (or, in one case, how) they held their sessions. Thus, there were night schools, "mixed" schools offering both day and night sessions, day schools (the "better" ones held classes in the morning and early afternoon) and even correspondence schools. Schools could also be typed according to entrance standards, length of the course, the kind of teacher hired, whether students were full- or part-time and, of course, the teaching methods adopted. Such categories were academic categories and they represented the AALS view that these were the significant characteristics of the first-class law school. This view still dominates the historiography of legal education.[42] The tendency has been to lump all the schools that opposed or resisted the AALS standards into one general category and then to view that category in terms of the worst schools within that group. And there were bad law schools. Some of the schools did become diploma mills or cram schools for the state bar examinations. Yet there were other schools within that category whose history and significance have been obscured. They attempted to carry forward into the twentieth century the vision of the law school set forth by Bryant at Wisconsin in the 1890s and Dwight at Columbia in the 1880s. Unfortunately, certainly for our understanding of legal education and perhaps for legal education itself, these schools were unable to translate their practices into theory and, in particular, they were unable to provide a theoretical justification that was acceptable to the culture of the universities. That ground was already occupied by the AALS schools.

In 1909, however, the command of that ground did not seem secure to

AALS members. When the AALS president, Charles N. Gregory, formerly the associate dean of the Wisconsin Law School and at that time dean of the Iowa Law School, reviewed the progress of legal education in the past decade, he found the facts disturbing. In 1899 there were ninety-six law schools in the United States, and thirty-five of those schools were represented at the initial meeting of the AALS. More important, those thirty-five schools represented about two thirds of all law school students in the country (approximately eight thousand of a total of twelve thousand five hundred law school students). In 1908, Gregory discovered, there were one hundred eight law schools in America with a total enrollment of 18,609 students; but the increase in the number of students in law schools represented in the AALS was only 1,429 while the increase in students at schools not members of the Association was 4,124.[43] Although that trend would begin to reverse itself in the next decade, members of the AALS and the leaders of the American Bar Association would remain disturbed at what they regarded as the unnecessary proliferation of law schools in the country. They were especially impressed with what their counterparts in the medical profession were doing to root out inferior medical schools. In 1900 there were one hundred sixty medical schools in the country with 25,213 students; by 1910 that number had dropped to one hundred thirty-one schools with 21,394 students; and by 1920 there were only eighty-five medical schools with 13,798 students. In that same year there were one hundred forty-six American law schools with 24,503 students.[44] American law schools continued to proliferate in the first decades of the twentieth century because practitioners did not agree with the AALS schools that higher, and different, standards of legal education were immediately necessary. Eventually, for reasons to be examined later, the practitioners would draw closer to the schoolmen's position. In the meantime, however, many members of the bar continued to give support to that form of legal education with which they were most familiar.

In Wisconsin the Marquette University Law School represented the customary mode of legal training. Indeed, in some respects its early history resembled that of the Wisconsin Law Department. In 1892 a group of Milwaukee law students who were preparing for the state bar examination began to meet together for additional study. These young men, like the students in the Madison law club in the mid-1860s, occasionally invited practitioners in Milwaukee to deliver lectures on some legal topic. One of the students, W. H. Churchill, a recent graduate of the University of Michigan Law School, attended the meetings in order to learn more about Wisconsin law; because of his background, Churchill was often called upon to lead classes and deliver lectures when a scheduled speaker was unable to appear. Out of these sessions emerged the Milwaukee Law School. Churchill became a regular lecturer on torts, and he was assisted by Frank Spies and Frank Van Valkenburgh, Jr. This arrangement continued until 1895 when Edward W. Spencer joined Churchill as a lecturer. A year later Lynn S. Pease, who had taught the previous year in Madison at the University of Wisconsin Law School, joined the group. These three men—Churchill, Spencer and Pease—constituted the faculty of the school until its merger with Marquette University in 1908.[45]

Marquette University desired affiliation with the Milwaukee Law School in order to publicize its new status as a university. Its name had been changed from Marquette College to Marquette University in 1906. In the spring of that year Marquette President Burrowes indicated that Milwaukee needed "an educational institution of the scope of a university . . . with technical and professional schools attached." He also indicated that it would not be long before the school would have a law department. "We have twenty alumni who are practicing law in Milwaukee [and] we expect to get considerable encouragement from the alumni when we present this proposition." Burrowes believed that a Marquette law department "probably will be established within five years," even before other technical and professional schools. "You see," Burrowes said, "to establish a law department does not require the large outlay of money for equipment that would be necessary to establish a medical school or an engineering school."[46] Although the faculty in the Law School at Madison would have objected vehemently to that statement, Burrowes was essentially correct except in his predictions about the timing. Marquette succeeded in attaching (in 1907) an existing medical school prior to the organization of a law department. They bought the Milwaukee Law School in 1908 for six thousand dollars. Actually, they bought the school's name because it had no property and no library. Churchill, Spencer and Pease agreed not to teach in another school for a period of five years so that they would not siphon off students from the Marquette Law Department. Marquette also stipulated that the second installment of three thousand dollars would not be paid until the number of students in the school reached fifty. With the transfer arranged, the students were brought to the Marquette campus in May 1908 to get them used to the new arrangement. Marquette also offered to give the LL.B. to all previous graduates of the school who had passed the state bar examination. Eighty-seven such degrees were given out at the commencement exercises in June 1908.[47]

The circumstances that surrounded the attachment of the Milwaukee Law School to Marquette University made the law school a target for the University of Wisconsin law faculty when Marquette applied for admission to the AALS in 1911 and when the battle over the diploma privilege began in 1913. Yet the purchase of an already existing private law school had been a normal practice of universities in the nineteenth century, and often a law school was either attached or begun as an announcement to the public that a liberal arts college was really a university. When Marquette awarded the LL.B. to lawyers who had attended the proprietary Milwaukee Law School, an act that provided them with an instant body of alumni, that, too, could be viewed as reflecting the older attitude that the law degree was merely symbolic of a short period of attendance at a law school rather than evidence that one was qualified to practice law. Indeed, because Marquette awarded the degree in June, 1908, only to those who already had passed the bar examination, it could be argued that it represented more than the University of Wisconsin Law Department's LL.B. in the 1870s which was granted for as little as a term's work and which admitted directly to the bar.

Marquette, in fact, was an old-fashioned law school, not only in conception but also in its development for at least a decade after 1908. The faculty consisted of nineteen active practitioners from Milwaukee and a dean who gave full time to the school. Case study did not appear to any marked extent until after 1917 (though it was used along with other "approved methods" by some of the faculty), and the school always advertised that the presence of the practitioners on the faculty made the "atmosphere more practical and less academic than is found in most law schools." The Milwaukee Law School had offered instruction only at night and even after merger the Marquette school continued to operate a night school until 1924. The night-school course, increased from three years to four years in 1915, offered no degree and served the "poor and worthy student" who worked during the day. According to the dean of the school, "some clerked at the post office; some were ushers at the Milwaukee Auditorium; others got part time work keeping books; some were street car conductors, and others motormen; some worked in law offices and others worked as clerks in stores." The attendance in the night school division averaged seventy-five students during the decade from 1908 to 1918 and from 1918 until February, 1924, when the night school was closed, the attendance averaged one hundred seven students a year.[48]

Marquette's day division, a three-year course leading to the LL.B., opened in 1908 with twenty-four freshman in the first class. During its first decade of operation the day school attracted an average of seventy students each year (and awarded the degree to about eleven students each year). In its second decade, from 1919 to 1929, the average attendance was two hundred eight, a figure that surpassed that in the University of Wisconsin Law School, and the LL.B. was awarded to an average of forty-three students a year. The day school course, like that

Marquette University Law School Building (the Mackie Home) prior to 1923. (*Marquette University Archives*)

offered at night, was practical and not only because it was taught by practitioners. Because classes were held in the morning, the students were free to "work and study in the afternoon" and they were also "anxious to secure work in law offices, where they will acquire familiarity with the practical part of law." [49] It was an arrangement that Dean Bryant would have admired.

Dean Richards, however, believed that the Marquette University Law School represented a retrogression in legal education. According to Richards' standards, the Marquette School could not be considered truly a university law school because its outlook was so severely "practical" and because it did not stress in its curriculum the techniques of legal reasoning. At Wisconsin, the trend was precisely the opposite. As the University of Wisconsin College of Law began to stress in its curriculum the techniques of case analysis, Richards dropped the emphasis upon practical work that had been the distinguishing characteristic of the school under Bryant, and which the State Bar Association had formally approved in 1895.

The decreased emphasis on practical work was deliberate and it parallelled the trend at many other AALS law schools. In 1911 Richards told Henry Bates, dean of the Michigan Law School, that "I have always been a little bit skeptical as to the extent to which practice can be taught in a law school, and as a result of my skepticism and that of the other members of the faculty, we have done very little here, confining our work to the volunteer practice courts of the students, and offering our practice courses as class work, and not through the medium of Moot Courts." [50] In fact, even the student practice courts were being allowed to wither. Five such clubs were prominently listed in the last catalog prepared under Bryant's direction but by 1906 the Law School bulletin noted only that "the practice court is supplemented by a number of club courts, voluntary student organizations, where legal questions are argued and debated." [51] The following year the catalog dropped entirely the reference to the voluntary student organizations.

Such developments did not go unnoticed. G. D. Jones, a conservative Republican lawyer, and probably the most influential member of the Board of Regents during his term from 1909 to 1922, soon began to question the law school's policies on practical training. Richards did not believe that the majority of the lawyers in the state agreed with Jones but because he was "a rather forcible man among the Regents," Richards was afraid that he "may be able to impress the [Regent] law committee" with his opinions. [52] In fact, Richards may have been correct in asserting that the majority of lawyers did not support Jones' position but the corollary—that the majority supported Richards—

could not be drawn. Most lawyers were simply indifferent to these matters. But among the minority of lawyers who belonged to the State Bar Association and whose opinions carried weight in the state legislature, Jones' position was popular. The best evidence is the extent to which Richards, "skeptical" of the extent to which practice could be taught in a law school, altered the school's policies after 1910.

In April, 1910, Richards wrote to Howard L. Smith, then on leave at the Stanford University Law School, telling him that "it would please Mr. Jones very much, and it would serve as an advertisement if we would devote more attention to the practice side of our work." Richards was still not convinced that it was "a wise economy of the student's time to do so," [53] but he capitulated to Jones' demands. He wrote Jones in July 1910 proposing extensive additions to the school's program in practical training. In addition to a new course in wills and probate law, taught by a local practitioner, Richards proposed

> to introduce a course in the drafting of legal documents. This work would consist in exercises in drawing the more common legal documents such as wills, contracts, deeds, examination of abstracts, running down titles on records, etc. I think this will be a very practical course, and will compel the student to apply the principles of law in a concrete way that he has picked up in the various other courses in the School.[54]

Richards also indicated that the practice work for the third year would be increased by reestablishing the practice court. "For the past two years," he claimed, "we have been experimenting as to the best way of presenting practice courses, and have concluded that in addition to the course in code practice, which is now offered, it would be desirable to institute the practice court." [55] There is reason to doubt Richards' statement that the law faculty had engaged in extensive debates over the best way to organize the practice court. There is no record of any such discussion in the faculty minutes during that period and in view of Richards' skepticism about practice work itself, it is more likely that any debate concerned how best to rid the curriculum of such courses. To make certain that Jones knew the law school had changed direction, Richards not only listed the new courses in the 1911 catalog, he also reinstated the notice about the importance of the voluntary student law clubs in the school's curriculum. By 1914 Richards could claim that the school offered "19 hours of instruction in adjective law, and with the exception of the University of Michigan, I think we are devoting more attention to this subject than any other school I know of. We give: 4

hours of Common Law Pleading; 4 hours of Evidence; 4 hours of Code Pleading; 1 hour of Briefmaking; and 2 hours in Office Practice." [56]

Richards' rapid adoption of Jones' suggestions was not simply an attempt to appease the practitioners in the state. The argument against practical training in the law school also became increasingly difficult to defend after Abraham Flexner published his report on medical education in 1910. According to Flexner, extensive clinical education was one of the distinguishing features of the first-class medical school. Lawyers and law professors alike, impressed with the manner in which the American Medical Association was beginning to drive marginal, low-standard medical schools out of business and with its success in limiting access to the medical profession itself, naturally looked to medicine as an example to follow. One result was that law professors began to talk about legal clinics associated with law schools in a fashion analogous to the medical clinics connected to medical schools. [57] Yet legal aid clinics would not prove to be the answer to providing the desired practical dimension of legal practice. Because the clinics were limited basically to the crisis needs of the very poor, it had "only a relatively narrow role as a teaching institution." [58]

Some law professors recognized immediately that the analogy between the medical clinic and the law clinic was a poor one. O. L. McCaskill of the Cornell Law School, for example, criticized the legal aid program at Minnesota for giving the student work that was "not really legal in character." He noted that "a total of 72 percent of the work is devoted to petty wage claims, domestic troubles, collections, and advice on everything that comes." In only one instance did a law student actually go into a court room or attend a judicial proceeding and "that was on a garnishment proceeding." And not only was the work centered outside the courts, it was office work that mainly "consisted in running errands, riding five miles on a street car to serve a summons, making collections, writing down statements of clients, and making settlements." This work, McCaskill concluded, "does little more than supply the opportunity to study character." [59]

The faculty of the Wisconsin Law School did not experiment with the legal aid clinic because they needed a more dramatic manifestation of a renewed commitment to practical training. Regent G. D. Jones told Richards quite directly that the Wisconsin College of Law would do well to follow the example set by Marquette. According to Richards, Jones thought that "the law school ought to have more men who are eminent at the bar or on the bench as members of the faculty, saying that the law school as now run was not favorably regarded by the bar, and intimating that a school run along the lines of Marquette was much more desirable." Richards believed that that policy was "some twenty years behind the times." [60] Nevertheless, the pressure exerted by Jones forced Richards to align once again the University College of Law with the law offices in the state.

Richards and the faculty decided to formalize the sort of relation between the law school and the law office that had existed prior to Bryant's deanship. The law school would not become the ideal law office, but the faculty could insist that students spend time in a law office before receiving the LL.B. Consequently, in December, 1913, the faculty passed a resolution that required all graduates of the Wisconsin Law School to serve a clerkship in a law office of at least six months. This requirement, which took effect July 1, 1916, could be met by study for two periods of three months each during the summer or after the student had completed the residence requirements in the law school.[61] Richards, explaining that "a great many of our better students do that now," told President Van Hise that the faculty was also "influenced by the fact that our degree admits to the bar, and we all felt it was desirable that the law graduates should serve apprenticeship in a law office before undertaking the responsibilities of the practice." Richards also believed that an apprenticeship requirement "would serve to bring us in closer touch with the bar of the state, since we can ultimately make arrangements with the better offices of the state to receive our students." [62] Richards surely was genuinely concerned with his students' future placement but, as the phrasing should indicate, that was not his primary concern. His immediate aim was to bring the College of Law into "closer touch" with the bar by cultivating contacts with the "better offices" of the state. Those contacts, he hoped, would counter the emerging alliance between rural and small town practitioners, on the one hand, and the urban-based supporters of the Marquette Law School, on the other hand. That alliance, based upon a shared perception that poor and worthy young men were being excluded from the legal profession by stringent academic requirements, threatened the further development of Richards' ideal of the university law school.

Professional Standards and the Diploma Privilege Controversy

The differences in educational philosophy between the University of Wisconsin Law School and the Marquette University Law School were, at the core, differences over the kind of student each school sought to attract. Marquette early gained a reputation as a school where ambitious sons of immigrants, with minimal formal schooling and limited financial resources, could better their future by studying law at night. The University of Wisconsin Law School, in contrast, attempted to recruit students with some college training and with financial resources that would permit full-time study. Although these differences can be exaggerated, supporters of the two schools viewed them as absolutely fundamental. Marquette men argued that their school operated in the finest democratic tradition of keeping the legal profession open to talent from all economic strata and ethnic backgrounds. University of Wisconsin supporters, in contrast, asserted that the primary concern must be the quality of men entering the legal profession.

Richards continued to press for higher academic standards governing admission to the bar as a device to exclude "untrained and ignorant" men from the legal profession. He appealed to the prejudices of practitioners against "Emigrants," those "shrewd young men, imperfectly educated," whom Richards believed filled the night school of the Marquette University Law School. Yet that appeal, designed to convince lawyers that the model of legal education promoted by the state university law school was superior to the model adopted by Marquette, not only did not work, it actually backfired. Members of the State Bar Association, who were mainly practitioners from small cities and towns, had little direct experience with the evils that their urban brethren associated with the changing ethnic composition of the bar. Richards' demand for higher standards to exclude immigrants from the profession was interpreted by rural lawyers as a threat to close the profession to "poor and worthy" young men from the small towns and cities, from the farms, and from the lumbering areas of the state. Unacknowledged and perhaps even unrecognized, the alliance between the rural and small-town practitioners and the supporters of the Marquette University Law School forced the University of Wisconsin Law School into a defensive posture after 1910.

Marquette strengthened its position immensely when it became a member of the Association of American Law Schools in 1912. Richards worked hard, though unsuccessfully, to bar the school from the Association. When Marquette submitted its application for membership in 1911, Richards wrote to a member of the Association that "it would be an unfortunate thing for the Law School Association to admit a school like Marquette."

I have had some opportunity to know through persons who have actually observed the school, the sort of work they are doing there, and it is of such an order that I should think the school ought not to be entitled for admission. I don't believe they observe their paper standards in conferring degrees. Indeed, the inducements they have offered to some of our lame students to come there and take a degree would indicate that they are not very particular. No doubt we have some schools in the Association that are no better than Marquette, but I don't see that this is any reason for adding another lame duck to the collection.[63]

Richards did not openly oppose the application of Marquette at the AALS meeting out of a belief that such opposition would appear self-serving, as indeed it would have. The AALS members voted favorably on Marquette's application and admitted the school to membership in 1912. Although it certainly did not hurt Marquette's cause that the school had invited the AALS to hold their annual meeting for that year in Milwaukee, where the hospitality of the school and the bar could be opened to the Association, the Marquette Law School did meet most of the AALS membership requirements and appeared to be moving in the direction of fulfilling others. AALS member schools could award the LL.B. only to students who had studied law during the day for a period of three years of thirty weeks each or, in the case of night schools, for a period of four years of thirty-week sessions. It also required member schools to enforce an admission requirement of at least a high school education and to own and maintain a law library of at least five thousand volumes. Marquette's day school did have a three-year course leading to the degree and its night school, while it did not at the time of admission to the AALS offer a four-year course, offered no degree. Marquette allowed transfer from the night course to the day course, a practice that the AALS would later question. Its library did not meet AALS standards, a fact that the Marquette faculty admitted but which it claimed was being corrected. Finally, Marquette required a high school education "or its equivalent" for admission to the day course although, again, the AALS would later raise questions about whether that standard actually was being followed.[64]

The principal investigation of Marquette by the AALS was made in 1916, and it is now impossible to determine whether or not the charges of noncompliance with Association regulations were true although the AALS executive committee finally recommended, after "assurances" of compliance from Marquette, that no action be taken. The significance of the investigation, however, lies in the way that it reveals the conflict between a school whose administration depended upon personal judgment by the faculty, on the one hand, and a group of schools, represented by the University of Wisconsin, on the other hand, that relied upon stringent application of formal academic rules. The AALS representative who visited Marquette, found, for example, that the records of the school "were in such condition as to make it difficult if not impossible" to ascertain whether the school required its students to have a high school education prior to admission. The AALS suspected, but could not prove, that some students were admitted without such an education and were later allowed to make up the deficiency.[65] The issue, as Marquette's defense of the charges showed, really hinged on a personal judgment of a high school education or its equivalent. In the case of one student, it was clear that he did not have a high school degree. He had completed eight grades in various parochial and public schools in Wisconsin, then graduated from a teacher training school, the diploma from which entitled him to teach in the common schools. He then graduated from the state normal school, again with a certificate that entitled him to teach the elementary grades. He immediately accepted a position as principal in a school which had ten grades where he taught for two years. He applied for admission to Marquette in 1910 and was accepted. That kind of educational background and probably as important, the persistence it showed, was judged sufficient by the Marquette faculty.[66] It is not clear if the AALS investigating team disagreed with the judgment or if the records themselves were incomplete and ambiguous. The latter is surely a possibility since the dean of the school, Judge James G. Jenkins, appears to have followed rather loose administrative procedures. One of the main tasks of his replacement, Max Schoetz, Jr. in 1916 was to put the school records in order. Nevertheless, what appeared to the AALS as administrative looseness reflected in the mind of Jenkins and, later, Schoetz simply a determination to use personal judgment in assessing the qualifications of applicants to the school. And it reflected, too, a determination to keep the law school open to poor and worthy young men who had not had the benefit of an academic education. It is revealing that one of Dean Schoetz' first acts was to raise the preliminary education required of applicants from a high school education to one year of college but at the same time institute a "four year [day] course" expressly designed to give high school graduates a year of college training while studying law. Thus, Schoetz continued to guard against what he would later imply was the "aristocratic" tone of the AALS and, in particular, the University of Wisconsin Law School.[67]

The 1916 AALS investigation of Marquette (along with six other schools) inflamed already badly strained relations between Marquette and Wisconsin. Because the five-man Executive Committee that carried out the investigation had as two of its members Dean Richards and E. A. Gilmore of the Wisconsin Law School and a third, Walter Wheeler Cook, who had previously served on the Wisconsin faculty, the Marquette faculty believed that the state university law school had led the movement for the investigation. That was probably not true because the investigation had been ordered in 1912 when the AALS Executive Committee was composed of Professors Bates of Michigan, McGovney of Tulane, Lewis of Pennsylvania, and Pound and Cook of Chicago.[68] Nevertheless, men at Marquette remained unconvinced that the investigation was not simply an attempt to embarrass the Marquette Law School because of its attack, begun in 1913, on the University of Wisconsin's diploma privilege. That attack raised, in a different context, the issue of the standards of legal education at Marquette and Wisconsin.

The University of Wisconsin Law School had been granted the diploma privilege in 1870, two years after it had opened. The purpose of the law was to attract students to the new institution by granting them a professional payoff at the end of the law school course. Other schools had used this device with marked success and it worked well in Wisconsin, particularly as long as the students continued to combine law school work with office training and as long as regulation of the bar occurred after admission to practice had taken place. But when the older nineteenth-century arrangements for training and regulation began to break down, the diploma privilege was subject to great abuses, especially when the school that obtained the right to admit its graduates to the bar was a proprietary school concerned with financial profits. Because the diploma privilege was often abused in the late nineteenth century and because it represented an obstacle to uniform requirements for entry to the bar, by the turn of the century the almost unanimous opinion of the bench and bar decreed that this privilege ought to be abolished. One of the first arguments against the privilege was made in 1881 by Francis Wellman in *The American Law Review*. His article was widely reprinted and had appeared in the *Annual Report* of the Wisconsin State Bar Association in 1881. The American Bar Association declared against the diploma privilege in 1892 and again in 1908.[69] Even faculty members of the University of Wisconsin Law School were reluctant to defend their favored position, although their doubts were always expressed privately. Associate Dean Gregory wrote in 1898:

Of course it is a certain advantage to our School . . . to be able to grant a diploma which admits to the Bar although I think the best opinion is that no school ought to have that privilege. I find it is much prized by our students and tends probably to stimulate attendance at our school. For that reason I should feel a little sorry to see it done away with although I do not think I could very vigorously defend it.[70]

In 1907 Dean Richards remarked that he was "heartily" in favor of requiring state bar examinations for all students although he did not favor giving up the Wisconsin diploma privilege until all other schools in that section of the country had done likewise.[71]

The attack on the Wisconsin diploma privilege began in 1913. The bill introduced in the legislature had the enthusiastic support of the Marquette faculty and it was, at least on the surface, unexceptionable. It embodied in the main the requirements suggested by the Section on Legal Education of the American Bar Association. The bill required that all students register with the board of law examiners at the beginning of their legal study; that all students have at least a high school education before beginning such study; and that the term of legal preparation must be three years' study in a law school having a day course, four years' study in an evening law school, or a four-year apprenticeship in a law office. The bill also provided for a paid secretary for the board of law examiners and more stringent requirements for determining the moral fitness of candidates for the examination. Finally, the bill provided for the abolition of the diploma privilege.[72]

A member of the Marquette law faculty would later, and correctly, claim that this last provision "wrecked" the chances of the bill. In a scathing attack on the University of Wisconsin Law School published in *The American Law School Review* in 1914, Professor A. W. Richter of Marquette charged that

> The University of Wisconsin mustered all its forces in defense of its vicious privilege, and by the tremendous influence which it has and through the blind allegiance of many of its alumni (especially the younger men in the legislature—it was a refreshing sign that many of the older graduates did not support their University in its wrong stand) it was able to defeat the bill . . . . Verily, there seems to be room for some proselyting [sic] within the Association of American Law Schools, when one of its old and prominent members bends all its efforts toward defeating legislation which would establish higher standards.[73]

In its defense of the diploma privilege, the University of Wisconsin Law School agreed with Marquette that the state university school maintained an advantage in the competition for students but, they argued, the effect of this favorable position was to raise the standards of legal education in the state. This was a plausible argument. With the exception of a few years in the early 1870s, the Wisconsin LL.B. had always represented a higher standard of preparation than that required by the formal rules governing admission to the Wisconsin bar. "In the efforts which the law school has been making during the past ten years to improve conditions of legal education in this state," the law faculty claimed, "the possession of the diploma privilege has been of great assistance."

It has enabled the school to raise the standards and hold students up to stricter requirements. Instead of being a source of danger to the best interests of legal education, or of interfering with the creation of better standards for the Bar, the enjoyment of this privilege by the law school has been a very potent factor in accomplishing desirable reforms.

Moreover, the law faculty argued, the Law School is a state institution and therefore should be treated "on a different basis from private institutions." The members of the law faculty "are in a sense state officials and constitute a specially appointed and well equipped state board to train and examine applicants for admission to the bar." Because the "school is not dependent upon the fees derived from the students" and because the faculty have no financial interest in securing large numbers of students, and therefore are under no temptation to lower standards or to be lax in administration, the position of the University law faculty "is as impartial as that of the state board of bar examiners." [74] Finally, a third argument was developed in the battle over the same issue that occurred in the next legislative session. This position maintained that if the diploma privilege were taken away from the University, then the institution would be under severe pressure to "train for ability to pass the bar examination rather than to practice in fact." According to C. B. Bird, a lawyer who was asked to present the law school's position to the assembly judiciary committee, to strip the law school of the diploma privilege would accentuate the "whole vice of studying to pass examinations rather than for the knowledge and ability itself which the studying is designed to furnish." Dean Richards agreed that this was the "weightiest argument against the bill from the point of view of the law school." [75]

All of these arguments, it is important to note, were couched so that they contained an implicit criticism of the Marquette school. It had low standards, it was a private institution (and its Catholicism was also occasionally mentioned), it was dependent upon fees from students (and its faculty were therefore likely to relax their standards in order to secure a large enrollment) and it was a cram school for the state bar examination. If observers of the debate missed the implications, the article by University Law Professor Howard L. Smith, printed in the *American Law School Review* as a rebuttal to Richter's article, left no doubt about the position of the Wisconsin Law School. Together with Richter's article, Smith's attack on Marquette illustrated how bitter and rancorous the dispute between the two schools had become. Smith first noted that Marquette's strong stand against the diploma privilege was difficult to square with the fact that only a short time before, Marquette had introduced another bill (not mentioned by Richter in his article) which would have extended the diploma privilege to its own law school. (It is not certain that the Marquette Law School either introduced or supported this bill although it is probable that Marquette alumni were in favor of extending the diploma privilege to the Marquette Law School.) [76] Smith then went on to comment sarcastically on the "practical" nature of the Marquette curriculum, mentioning in passing that the atmosphere at the school "nevertheless has a flavor of intellectuality, for the school possesses a library supplied with the English Common Law Reports, the Federal Reports, and the reports of all but forty-three states." Smith charged that the Marquette school was

One of those institutions that seem inevitably to spring up in our large cities, which owe the possibility of continued existence to the indifferent and good-natured complaisance of a bench and bar who permit themselves to be used as the unwitting and entirely unintentional instruments for the degradation of legal instruction. Any young lawyer can start a "law school" in any of our big cities, and in two weeks time announce to the world a "faculty" that shall absolutely blaze with legal luminaries from judges of the highest courts down. Their connection with the school may be so tenuous as to be little more than nominal, but that does not prevent them from figuring as corner stones of the temple in the advertising literature scattered by the promoters.

Smith concluded with the suggestion that if the supporters of the Marquette Law School were really interested in the improvement of legal education, then they should raise an endowment of a million dollars, supply themselves with a good law library and maintain an adequate faculty. [77] The opening salvos in the battle over the diploma privilege were thus marked by a great deal of animosity. At one point Marquette even threatened the editor of *The American Law School Review* with a libel suit for printing the "scurrilous lies" of Professor Smith. [78] While the heat of the argument cooled somewhat in the following years, the bitterness never entirely disappeared so long as Richards and Schoetz remained as deans of the two schools. [79]

Academic Training and Professional Ethics

Even as Marquette pressed its case, nationally in the councils of the AALS and, locally in the Wisconsin legislature, its position slowly was being undercut by changes in the composition of the bar. Those changes stemmed from the influx of the foreign-born and the children of the foreign-born into the legal profession in urban areas. Dean

Marquette University Law School Dean Max Schoetz. (*Marquette University Archives*)

Richards seized upon that fact to buttress his argument that there existed an important link between high academic standards governing admission to the bar and the maintenance of high ethical standards among members of the legal profession. But his strategy would have little effect in Wisconsin prior to the 1920s because practitioners in the small towns and cities were not threatened directly by those changes.

Jerold S. Auerbach has analyzed carefully the response of elite practitioners to the emergence of an ethnic bar in the first decades of the twentieth century. According to Auerbach, "the percentage of new lawyers born abroad or with foreign-born parents greatly exceeded the general rate of professional growth" in city after city between 1900 and 1920. In Boston between 1900 and 1910 the number of lawyers increased by thirty-five percent but the number of foreign-born lawyers increased by seventy-seven percent and the number with foreign-born parents increased by seventy-five percent. In New York City the number of lawyers also increased by thirty-five percent but the number of foreign-born lawyers expanded by sixty-six percent and the number with foreign-born parents jumped by eighty-four percent. The same trend developed in Chicago, Philadelphia and St. Louis in the following decade.[80] The foreign-born, grouped in urban areas and swarming into the night law schools in those cities, were perceived as a distinct threat to professional values based upon Anglo-Saxon Protestant culture. Wisconsin Law School Dean Richards warned his colleagues at the AALS annual meeting in 1915 that night law schools enrolled "a very large proportion of foreign names. Emigrants [sic] . . . covet the title [of attorney] as a badge of distinction. The result is a host of shrewd young men, imperfectly educated, . . . all deeply impressed with the philosophy of getting on, but viewing the Code of Ethics with uncomprehending eyes." [81] More important, practitioners also were becoming concerned with the waves of foreign elements inundating the bar. A Pennsylvania attorney observed that the Jews coming to the bar in his state, although intellectually gifted and persevering, were "without the incalculable advantage of having been brought up in the American family life," and therefore they "can hardly be taught the ethics of the profession as adequately as we desire." [82]

The influx of immigrants into the legal profession undercut the balance, forged in the nineteenth century, between two competing models of the lawyer. On the one hand was Tocqueville's lawyer-aristocrat; on the other hand stood the model of Abraham Lincoln, the country lawyer without formal training but endowed with strength of will and character. "These models," Auerbach argues, "were compatible, and indeed mutually reinforcing, as long as the profession recruited primarily from a homogeneous Anglo-Saxon Protestant Society."

But immigrants, Jews, aliens, city-dwellers—the "unfit"—threatened to sabotage both of them. Notions of the profession as an accessible democratizing institution which fostered social mobility became suspect once the social composition of its newest members changed. Tenement dwellers from Manhattan's Lower East Side were not permitted to usurp the places reserved for Kentuckians who studied Blackstone by candlelight. Furthermore, the "privileged body" described by Tocqueville, which occupied a "separate station" in society, could hardly survive inundation by the masses. The legal profession would no longer be "the most powerful, if not the only counterpoise to the democratic element," once the demos poured into its ranks.[83]

Although fear of an immigrant-dominated bar received less overt expression in Wisconsin than in the eastern states analyzed by Auerbach, the concern with the ethical conduct of some lawyers which began to preoccupy members of the State Bar Association after 1914 suggests that ethnic and racial hostility did play a role in aligning some practitioners on the side of higher academic standards. The problem involved lawyers, mainly in the city of Milwaukee, who were accused of "ambulance chasing," splitting fees with doctors, and in other ways openly soliciting for business. One attorney asserted that "there are three branches of the law almost controlled in this way in the city of Milwaukee today, the criminal business, the accident business, and, I am told, without personal knowledge of the subject, the divorce business is joined in the procession." What is to keep the probate business, he asked, from the same "gang of plunderers?" [84] The following year Association President Christian Doerfler, a prominent Milwaukee lawyer, complained in his presidential address about the practice of ambulance chasing. The Committee on the Amendment of the Law reported that a bill to outlaw that practice had been defeated in the legislature by Milwaukee lawyers who claimed that it was a necessary outgrowth of the "corporation practice of denying accident victims of their proper rights." [85] Much of the discussion at the three-day meeting centered on this spreading problem and what could be done about it. Although the members' concern clearly had an economic dimension, the problem itself was conceived in ethical terms. Judge C. Smith introduced a resolution which recommended that the Association "go to the foundations" of the problem by striking "as hard as we can at the students in our University, and make it a specialty to exhibit the ideals of the lawyer." This resolution urged the Chief Justice of the Supreme Court to "superintend," in an unspecified way, "the ethical culture of the law students of the State University." That resolution was referred to the Committee on Legal Education, chaired by Dean Richards, where, predictably, it was ignored.[86]

Richards agreed that the problem was one of ethics but he did not locate the source of the problem in the students graduating from his school. Instead, Richards wanted to "diminish the steady stream of incompetent and badly educated young men, who yearly throng the bar." He therefore recommended that all prospective lawyers be required to have two years of college education and three years' study in a law school followed by a one-year period of apprenticeship. These were the standards recently implemented by the University Law School. American law schools, Richards noted, had become the "principal medium" for preparation for the bar and thus it was of the utmost importance that the three years of legal study be in a certain type of law school. What Richards meant by the "American" law school was that type endorsed by Josef Redlich as "superior to any other institution in the world as a medium of preparation for the bar." Redlich, of course, had visited only those schools which were leading proponents of the case method; hence Richards' recommendation for "prolonged" study at a "reputable" law school really constituted a thinly veiled strike at the Marquette University Law School.[87] Richards here was necessarily circumspect because his recommendations for more stringent admission standards in 1915 came only two years after he had led the movement to defeat the legislation sponsored by Marquette supporters that would have stripped the University of Wisconsin of its diploma privilege and only one year after Richter and Smith had so hotly debated the merits of the Marquette school in *The American Law School Review*.

The problem that confronted Richards was to convince the practitioners from smaller towns and cities that his analysis of the situation was correct and that the solutions he proposed would solve the problem. For some members, the problem itself seemed remote. When Richards introduced a similar set of proposals in 1916, Bernard R. Goggins of Grand Rapids said: "We are not troubled up in the country very much from this evil [of ambulance chasing]. The only place we run up against that proposition . . . is when somebody from Milwaukee, or . . . Minneapolis or St. Paul runs down in our territory just as soon as the papers announce that somebody has been injured."[88] Other practitioners were not convinced that higher educational standards would automatically lead to higher ethical standards. E. E. Brossard of the Madison bar asked: "Is it a fact that the moral character of those who have come to the profession by way of the bar examination is any lower or worse than of those coming to the bar through the law school?" Brossard, who said that twenty-five years ago he had gone to the law school and then took the bar examination, believed "that the bar examination is far harder than it is to take the course at the law school." That line of reasoning was picked up by other lawyers and elaborated into a defense of those "poor and worthy" young men who could not afford to go to college or to the law school. P. H. Martin of Green Bay was not willing to "say to the great mass of young men who are not fortunate enough to be able to go to the law school, and perhaps have had to do a kind of work that was just as valuable to society, that precluded their graduating from a high school," that they must take a general examination covering cultural subjects before embarking upon law study in an office. C. E. Buell of Madison agreed: "I would as lief take my chances on the man who has the force of character, the ability, the initiative to go ahead and acquire a legal education which is sufficient to pass the bar examination, as the one who has chosen the route of taking a college course and also the law course." Behind these comments, of course, lay a conception of character that drew upon the image of Abraham Lincoln, not Tocqueville's aristocratic lawyer. Martin of Green Bay argued "that the boy who struggles on the farm, or struggles in the lumber woods and aspires to become a lawyer, and studies with sufficient persistence and diligence . . . ought not to have any more barriers thrown in his way." [89] Evidence of diligence and persistence, along with the ability to pass the bar examination, was enough to ensure the morality of the profession in the future.

As long as the image of Lincoln remained vivid in the minds of practitioners from outside the Milwaukee area, supporters of the Marquette University Law School did not even find it necessary to defend their position at the meetings of the Wisconsin State Bar Association. Richards continued to press the Association to approve standards of legal preparation that would mandate two years of college training and three years of study in a "reputable" law school but Association members consistently refused to accept his recommendations. In 1915 Richards' report as chairman of the Committee on Legal Education was "received and placed on file." In 1916 the report was referred back to the Committee. In 1917 and again in 1918 the report was tabled. By that time the American Bar Association had under consideration a similar series of recommendations, and so the Wisconsin Bar Association delayed any further action until the ABA recommendations were published. When, in 1921, the ABA Committee finally did report, it recommended that every candidate for admission to the bar should graduate from a law school and that all law schools should require two years of college as a prerequisite for admission. [90] Still the Wisconsin Bar Association refused to act. Members would not approve such stringent academic standards governing admission to the profession until the late 1920s. They would do so only when they began to perceive a significant economic dimension to the complaints of ethical decline.

CHAPTER SEVEN

Schooling Triumphant: The Emergence of a Private Profession

By 1930 legal education centered in the law schools and, in spite of the initial opposition of many practitioners, a single type of law school increasingly dominated professional preparation. The ideal law school, against which all other institutions were measured, demanded three and in some cases four years of prior college training and it inducted students into the study of legal science through a three-year course of largely theoretical instruction. The practitioners' opposition to that model withered in the face of ethical and economic considerations. From their point of view, the key was the stringent barrier to entry into the legal profession that a combination of college and law school training posed. A minimum of five years of formal academic preparation beyond high school was a device intended to regulate both the character and the number of persons entering the bar.

Ironically, as legal education throughout the country became more homogeneous, the intellectual foundations of the law splintered. Many law professors first questioned and then rejected the narrow scientific historicism of Langdell's case method. Using the insights and the methods of the social sciences, they sought to study law as it actually functioned in society. But for all the intellectual excitement generated by the advocates of sociological jurisprudence or, later, the legal realists, it cannot be said that these men succeeded in imposing a clear scientific framework upon the law. However, they did implant in the mind of the profession and the public the view that the law indeed was a science. And if law was a science, then it logically followed that the law was too specialized and too complicated for laymen to understand, much less master. That represented a profound shift in professional consciousness. After 1930 lawyers now viewed law as a private profession whose intellectual boundaries had to be sharply defined and defended.

Ethics, Economics and Professional Solidarity

Practitioners accepted the AALS package of educational reforms during the decade of the 1920s in an attempt to purge the bar of immigrants and in an effort to mute economic competition. For leaders of the profession in metropolitan areas the need to control, if not eradicate, the entry of immigrants to the bar constituted the primary motive underlying their support for increased educational standards. But in states like Wisconsin, where the bar association was dominated by practitioners from the smaller towns and cities, most lawyers came to support higher entrance standards to the bar because they began to perceive the bar as overcrowded. They aimed to control the number of people entering the profession rather than to regulate the character of the bar.

Because control over entry to the bar was the primary concern of lawyers, they were concerned hardly at all in this period with the precise nature of legal education. Instead, practitioners saw a desperate need for more prelegal, cultural training. Two, three or even four years of college attendance prior to entry into a law school became of much greater importance than what went on in the law school itself. It cannot be said, then, that the schoolmen convinced the practitioners of the wisdom of the AALS reform package. The practitioners, acting through state and national bar associations, bought only a piece of that package: more stringent and selective academic standards for those who aspired to become lawyers. But the package itself remained intact (even as its content was altered) because the practitioners left it to the law schools to enforce those new standards of admission to the bar. The effect was to enshrine academic training as a measure and in some sense the creator of moral character.

Practitioners from small towns and from rural areas played a critical role as the legal profession moved toward more stringent requirements governing admission to the bar. At first country practitioners opposed increased general education requirements because they believed that such requirements would exclude "poor and worthy" young men from the profession. Their opposition to higher and more formal education requirements explains why in Wisconsin supporters of the Marquette University Law School were so little in evidence during the debates over educational standards carried on in the State Bar Association prior to 1923. During that time there had existed an unacknowledged alliance between Marquette supporters and country practitioners. In 1923, however, Marquette attempted to cement that alliance formally. That move suggested that they no longer could count upon automatic support for their position from practitioners in the Association.

Max Schoetz, Jr., the dean of the Marquette Law School, and E. E. Brossard, the Madison attorney who earlier had persistently challenged Dean Harry S. Richards' recommendations on legal education, were named to the Bar Association Committee on Legal Education in 1923. When Richards, still the chairman of that Committee, submitted a report to the Association that embodied the recently proposed ABA standards, Schoetz and Brossard moved to substitute a report of their own. That report applied the model of Lincoln to urban students. "In the large cities of this country an evening law school is a necessity to furnish instruction to a large number of desirable law students whose circumstances prevent them from attending the day school." Although such work should not lead to a degree, Schoetz and Brossard maintained that "it should serve as a preparation for the bar examination for the poor and worthy student who by force of his circumstances cannot get a legal education otherwise." Their report also opposed the requirement of "actual attendance" at a college, recommending instead that the "equivalent" of such experience be allowed.[1]

In an obvious attempt to gain the support of practitioners outside Milwaukee, Brossard and Schoetz argued that forced attendance at a college or law school "tends strongly to restrict the profession to dwellers in cities" where such schools are located. It tends therefore "towards an aristocratic bar, and to monopolize the practice in those who have command of the requisite means to spend three years at such a law school." Finally, compulsory college and law school attendance threatened to destroy the influence of the bar in the local community because it "tears the candidate from his home . . . for five years."[2] Although this report succeeded only in delaying the implementation of the ABA rules in Wisconsin—in June 1926 the State Supreme Court ordered the ABA rules to take effect in January, 1928—the arguments made by Marquette supporters had merit.

Alfred Z. Reed in a report on legal education funded by the Carnegie Foundation and released in late 1920 had recognized the dangers inherent in establishing rigid formal educational requirements to govern admission to the bar. Reed argued that the law was a public profession inextricably a part of the democratic process of government. Therefore the administration of law must not become a class privilege. Although he was highly critical of the achievements of the night law schools and wanted them upgraded, Reed did sympathize with their objectives. Night schools served the broad interests of the community by assuring "that participation in the making and administration of the law shall be kept accessible to Lincoln's plain people." Reed proposed that the bar recognize that it already was organized around functional lines and that it move to formalize that differentiation through a hierarchy of schools. The night schools, upgraded and improved, would train lawyers for local practice, and especially the fields of probate law, criminal law and trial practice. The university law schools would become the "nursery for judges" destined "to produce a minority of our actual legal practitioners, but textbooks for all." Graduates of these schools would also dominate the more prestigious and lucrative work in corporate and government law. Although Reed recognized that lawyers then would be differentiated "by the economic status of the client rather than by the nature of the service rendered," this left him untroubled since "the general principle of a differentiated profession is something we already have, and could not abolish it if we would." [3]

A differentiated profession did not prove to be a view at all congenial to the leaders of the bar. Elite practitioners, as Auerbach has argued, wanted to use higher and more uniform standards "to preserve an Anglo-Saxon professional elite." However, the elite practitioners, mainly from metropolitan areas, were not notably successful in getting higher standards enacted into law. Measured by state statutes, "the fight for higher standards was mostly sound and fury." In 1922 fifteen states had no general education requirements for admission to the bar while twenty-three states, including Wisconsin, required nothing more than graduation from a high school. By 1926 not a single state had adopted the ABA recommendations for two years of college and a law degree. [4]

The explanation, as the Wisconsin experience suggests, is that the average practitioner in the state bar associations and in the state legislatures, without extensive or direct experience with problems of unethical practice in urban centers, was not disturbed enough to support increased educational standards that might exclude the "poor and worthy" from the profession. Yet beginning in the late 1920s state bar associations began to take positions in favor of the ABA standards. They did so not because the elite practitioners, representing the upper echelons of the metropolitan bar in cities like New York, Chicago and Philadelphia, convinced them of an ethnic and racial menace to the profession, but because the practitioners in small towns and cities began to see an important economic dimension to the complaints of unethical practice. To the average Wisconsin lawyer the major source of unethical practice was the practice of law by nonlawyers.

Dean Richards of the Wisconsin Law School previously had used this argument in support of higher admission standards. As early as 1910 he had argued that "the increase in legal business in the last ten years has not been sufficient to justify this very large increase of persons preparing for the bar." [5] Prior to the mid-1920s, however, most members of the state bar were little concerned about overcrowding in the profession. The only exceptions were those members of the Milwaukee bar who complained about the tendency of poorly educated lawyers to monopolize the "criminal business, the accident business, and the divorce business." By 1928, though, the central topic at the Wisconsin State Bar Association annual meeting (and at meetings in the future) was "The Practice of Law by Non-Lawyers," the subject of addresses by Jerome J. Foley of Racine and Charles Aarons of Milwaukee. Aarons' speech, reflecting the urban point of view, focused on ambulance chasers and claims adjusters. Foley's speech was the more significant because it located the problem of unethical practice in rural areas. Foley had in mind bankers "who continued to draw wills, contracts, and conveyances" and those who were engaged in the "real estate business, the buying and selling of lands and the writing of insurance." There even was evidence that the problems associated with ethnicity were beginning to spread to the countryside. Foley noted that "in the countries of Europe a notary public is a man of considerable standing. Many of these shrewd people," he complained, "have come to this country, secured a commission as a notary public, and then take advantage of people by advising them of their legal rights." [6] Such problems pervaded even the smallest hamlets. Claude D. Stout recalled that when he set up practice in 1930, "the local bankers at Eagle, Palmyra and Milton were drawing mortgages, deeds and most of all wills, and advising their depositors on legal matters." [7]

The concern with the practice of law by nonlawyers was of a piece with the proposals, appearing in Wisconsin first in 1915 and then with increasing frequency in the 1920s and 1930s, for an integrated or incorporated bar. The movement for an integrated bar sought to substitute compulsory membership in bar associations for the traditional voluntary membership. It was viewed as a device to enforce discipline among lawyers and, by increasing the total membership of the bar, strengthening the influence of the legal profession as a lobbying force. But it also should be observed that it reflected an attempt to define more consciously and precisely the limits of the profession itself. If lawyers were required by law to join the state bar association, then it logically followed that those who did not belong to the association were not lawyers. The preoccupation with professional identity was most obvious in 1931 when the Wisconsin State Bar Association succeeded in getting through the state legislature a bill which defined those activities that constituted the practice of law. That bill was necessary, according to the Association, to stop "the encroachment of corporations and laymen" into professional territory. If such encroachment were allowed to continue, it would "ultimately destroy the profession and make it a commercial business." [8] Economics joined ethics, then, as practitioners allied with professors in support of new regulations governing entry to the profession.

The various methods—higher entrance standards, the integrated bar, the definition of legal practice in the statutes—that the state legal profession considered in their attempt to regulate the profession did not, however, attack the basic problem. The character of the bar and the apparent inability of the profession to control the conduct of its members remained a problem. In 1930 the WSBA Committee on Qualifications for the Bar complained that the "young men who go wrong are very apt to do so in the early years of their practice." The problem was in the professional environment which failed to nurture correct conduct in the early years of practice. "A young man goes out and enters a bank, he is there, he grows up, he is developed in a proper environment and in a proper atmosphere. But in our profession we turn a young man out, he puts his name on a window over the word 'Lawyer' and he starts to practice, and we don't pay any attention to him. He has no one to advise him. He has no one to guide him." [9] That was precisely the problem. The convivial life of the nineteenth-century bar, a life style that had peaked in the frontier years but which had persisted so long as the law office and the law school had been viewed as complementary rather than competitive educational arrangements, had disappeared. And with the disappearance of that professional life style had gone opportunities for personal initiation and voluntary regulation of the members of the profession.

The Homogenization of Legal Education

The problem facing the profession—and many law students—was not simply that the early years of legal practice failed to provide for companionship which nurtured professional values. Some students were doubly isolated by a law school experience that ignored the practical realities of the beginning lawyer's job. The emphasis on theory and on methods of legal reasoning emphasized in the law school curriculum was, of course, a practical kind of knowledge. The ability to grasp the essential facts in a complicated situation, to sort out the legal issues involved, and to work through tangled affairs toward a realistic definition of the ends to be sought and the means by which to pursue those ends constituted a large part of the lawyer's business in the twentieth

century. Those skills were especially valuable for lawyers who entered
large law firms. Indeed, for such lawyers the law firm itself formed an
institutional nexus through which they were introduced to a set of
professional values and norms. But not all law students entered large
law firms. For those who did not, and especially for those who became
solo practitioners, the law school often failed to provide adequate training in the everyday matters of legal practice. That sort of practical training became the "missing link" in legal education.

The gradual homogenization of legal education became evident in
Wisconsin in 1933 when the state legislature passed a bill that extended
the diploma privilege to Marquette graduates. That law simply recognized that the Marquette University Law School now resembled other
university-sponsored law schools in the country. The gradual transformation of law schools like Marquette into the model of legal education
promoted by the AALS meant that no significant alternative to that
model would be developed, tested, or even articulated in the twentieth
century. That was perhaps the price paid for having a school staffed by
practitioners. Too often they were involved with the details of an extensive legal practice to devote attention to developing a theory of legal
education. Their failure to do so, however, reflected more than a lack of
time. Even those who gave all their energies to the law school, like
Bryant at Wisconsin in the 1890s and Jenkins and Schoetz at Marquette
in the first decades of the twentieth century, showed little interest in a
theory of legal education. Just as they chose to teach students by example in a kind of idealized apprenticeship arrangement within the law
school, so too did they view their law schools as exemplary, in little
need of defense, only institutional elaboration. Their descriptions of the
law school—and they were simply descriptions—had enormous appeal
to the practitioners of the same generation. But because the model was
so familiar, practitioners were content to applaud rather than promote
the plan vigorously.

The Marquette night school was one victim of the homogenization of
legal education. Marquette had granted degrees to night course students since 1916 but only to those who had had one year of college
attendance. Others, students who wanted to learn law not with a view
to practice but for the needs of business or general information, "were
granted admission to the school at the discretion of the officers." [10] In
1919 the AALS ruled that no member school could grant degrees for
night work and Marquette thereafter phased out its night school degree.
The school also stopped the practice of permitting transfer from the
night to the day course and began to conduct the night school "as a sort
of extension department of the University." [11] What finally killed the
evening law division, however, was the series of resolutions passed by

the American Bar Association in August, 1921. The ABA recommended that every candidate for admission to the bar should give evidence of graduation from a law school which complied with a certain set of standards. Among those standards were the following: The admission requirements to the school should be two years of college training; the law course should be three years in length for full-time students and for part-time students the course must be the equivalent in hours of the day course; the school must have an adequate library and a sufficient number of full-time teachers to assure close contact with the students. Finally, the ABA's Council on Legal Education and Admission to the Bar was directed to publish the names of those schools which met the recommended standards. Although the ABA standards did not outlaw night schools, the Council's decision that law schools "which maintain a part time school along with a full time day school [would] be classified according to the standards of the lower of these two" meant that Marquette could not gain ABA recognition for its day school as long as it continued the night school along traditional lines.[12] Marquette had raised the standards of admission to its day course to one year of college in 1916 (providing a four-year day course for those without the college background) and then in 1923 announced that it would require two years of college training for admission beginning in the fall of 1925. But when the ABA published its first list of approved law schools, Marquette was not only omitted from the Class A law schools (those which had accepted the ABA standard) but also from the Class B listing (those which had announced their intention to comply). The reason given to Marquette President Fox was that Marquette's night school did not require two years of college preparation. Marquette thus decided to discontinue the night school completely and accepted no more students in the evening division after February 1924. It did for a time consider reopening the school with standards the same as those in the day school but because only eight students asked for applications for registration, the faculty postponed the move indefinitely and, as it turned out, permanently.[13]

The day school, which gradually raised its requirements to correspond to ABA standards, also altered its approach in other fundamental ways. After 1917 the method of instruction was the case method, an approach that Schoetz now maintained "develops the student's power of legal analysis and inculcates habits of accurate reasoning."[14] The faculty also made efforts to eliminate the school's reputation (at least among University of Wisconsin supporters) as something of a cram school for the state bar examination. In 1925 the faculty decided "that the better policy . . . would be to have the students conduct their own review classes as their own voluntary act; that the faculty is busily engaged in the regular courses and there should be no interference with Bar reviews during the year." In 1935 the practice of faculty coaching students for the bar examination was halted entirely upon order of Marquette's president.[15]

By that time, however, such coaching was no longer useful to Marquette students because in 1933 the diploma privilege was extended to Marquette University Law School graduates. Although Marquette University consistently took the official position that all graduates of a law school, including the University of Wisconsin Law School, ought to take the bar examination, many of its alumni did not take the same view nor did the students in the Marquette Law School. In 1931 a law passed the legislature which authorized a graduate of any law school in the state to gain admission to the bar through the diploma if the Supreme Court should find that the school had standards as high as those of the University of Wisconsin College of Law. Marquette, however, refused to apply for the privilege, much to the consternation of its students. In taking that stand, Marquette pointed to its long record of opposition to the diploma privilege, an opposition consistent with the attitude of the AALS and the ABA. What the students and some of the public did not apparently recognize was that shortly before that law was passed the University of Wisconsin had raised its requirements for admission from two to three years of college training. Had Marquette applied for the diploma privilege under the 1931 law, it is possible the Supreme Court would have turned them down on the grounds that their standards were not equal to the University of Wisconsin Law School. In 1933, finally, a law which had the approval of the State Bar Association, the new dean at the University of Wisconsin Law School, Lloyd Garrison, and Marquette supporters, granted all ABA approved law schools in the state the diploma privilege. The bill was signed into law on April 7, 1933, and took effect on January 1, 1934.[16]

The transformation of the Marquette Law School into the model approved by the AALS and the ABA had its price. Acceptance of that model threatened relations with practitioners, and it began to sever the traditional ties that had existed between the law school and the law office. In the 1930s both Marquette and Wisconsin struggled to find ways to introduce their students to the elements of legal practice. Toward the end of that decade a group of fourteen Milwaukee lawyers announced that they would each take one Marquette law student into their professional lives for at least one afternoon a week. "If the lawyer has an interesting case he will take the student to court with him or perhaps he will let him sit in on a conference with a client." This contact with practicing attorneys was expected to provide the students with the "missing link" of legal education, "practical experience." [17] Marquette

University of Wisconsin Law School faculty, circa 1924. Back row: William Gorham Rice, William Herbert Page, John Sanborn, Raymond Brown. Front row: Frank Boesel, Harry S. Richards, Howard L. Smith, John D. Wickhem, Oliver S. Rundell. (*University of Wisconsin Archives*)

did not adopt, as had Wisconsin, a period of apprenticeship to solve the problem of reintroducing knowledge of legal practice into the curriculum but even the Wisconsin experiment did not always provide students with the kind of practical experience they felt they needed. In 1930 a recent graduate of the school drove home that point to Acting Dean Oliver Rundell.

> It is rather embarrassing to have a client ask one to put through a land deal requiring an abstract, conveying the interests of several minor heirs, and assigning or paying off three mortgages before the varnish on the second hand office furniture is dry, as well as before the practical way of handling these confusing transactions has been learned. That was my first law business. I told them I would have everything ready the next day at eleven, and by dint of no less than seven hours of night work, I kept my word.
>
> The theory is relatively simple, but what the Court may think the proper wording, and where to get the forms, if any, is a harder matter . . . .
>
> If I could go back for just one semester, I should spend less time on the books and hours more in the courts, and in studying form books; the law is easy to find once you get the hang of it, but God help you if you don't know how to address the Court.[18]

The Wisconsin faculty, like the faculty at Marquette, continued to experiment with ways to make practical training more effective. In 1930 Rundell helped establish a Legal Aid Society in which selected second- and third-year students provided legal advice for indigents. And under Dean Lloyd Garrison in the 1930s the practice courts were invigorated and practitioners brought back into the school to aid with both the moot court work and the course in office work. But Garrison finally concluded that "experience could not be taught; it can only be lived."[19]

Legal Sciences and Social Reform

The emerging homogeneity among university law schools masked a growing turbulence in the intellectual foundations of the law during the first three decades of the twentieth century. In order to justify the study of law and the preparation of the lawyer as a proper function of the university, law professors had developed a vision of the professional lawyer which rested upon the assumption that law was a science. But that vision splintered over differing conceptions of science. Some lawyers (like Richards at Wisconsin or Joseph Beale at Harvard) adhered to a narrow view of legal science; the case method, with its emphasis upon dissecting the legal reasoning used in appellate court cases, formed their limited horizons. Other law professors (like Roscoe Pound at Harvard) found a scientific approach to the law in the ideas of sociological jurisprudence. The insights of the emerging social sciences, like economics or sociology, could be used to guide lawyers in their search for principles of justice. Later, still other law professors (like those at Columbia in the 1920s) articulated a legal realist position. Legal realists, using methods of investigation developed in the physical and social sciences, attempted to determine what was law by studying what courts and other law-related agencies actually did. The aphorism of Oliver Wendell Holmes, Jr. struck to the heart of the realist stance (even as it vastly oversimplified the realists' positions): "The prophecies of what the courts will do in fact . . . are what I mean by the law." [20]

The adoption of the scientific viewpoint as the hub of professional consciousness did not necessarily lead, as Auerbach has argued, to a conception of the law professor as reformer or to a perception of law "as an instrument of social change." [21] Some law professors were involved in reform; many more were not. What linked all career law professors together in professional brotherhood was a commitment to science, not a commitment to reform. Those professors who were drawn toward reform activities tended to be those who had rejected the narrow scientific historicism of the case method and who found congenial the perspectives of sociological jurisprudence or legal realism. Moreover, attitudes toward law as a science and, ultimately, toward law as an instrument of reform was linked, in turn, to institutional affiliation. The view that law could be an instrument of social change was centered prior to 1930 almost exclusively in the major private university law schools, not those sponsored by the state universities.

Universities like Yale, Columbia and Johns Hopkins provided a more congenial environment for the development of the reform impulse because they were not, like the University of Wisconsin College of Law, subject to such direct and intense pressures from the business community to concentrate on the traditional curriculum. Significantly, William R. Vance of Yale gave classic expression to the belief that law professors ought to be reformers in his 1911 address to delegates at the AALS convention. Although he recognized that the "primary function" of the law teacher would remain the "technical training" of students, he proposed that the "ultimate function" of the professor of law should "be to serve as an efficient agency in bringing about the wise, comprehensive and prompt adaptation of our law and procedure to new and changing needs of society." [22] The AALS conventions during this period often witnessed such declarations. But not all members agreed that the ultimate function of the law professor was to be a social engineer. Wisconsin's Richards was one member of the AALS who disagreed with Vance's argument. Richards acknowledged that the law teacher had a twofold function: first, as a teacher and second, as a legal expert. But while the professor should acquire an "expert knowledge of his subject, which in time should result in treatises or monographs that are authoritative," Richards did not believe that the majority of law professors were equipped to lead movements for social reform. "Unfortunately," Richards argued, "the present agitation for law reform centers in questions of public law and procedure." Because three fourths of the course in the law school was occupied with courses in private law, "it is absurd to expect that men whose whole study and experience has been with questions of private law can properly be regarded as experts in public law." Richards believed that "their opinions would be of little value in solving public law questions." [23]

The faculty of the University of Wisconsin Law School, reflecting not only Richards' personal stance but also responding to anti-reform sentiment in the legislature and in the business community, generally did not agree that the law professor ought to be in the vanguard of reform movements. Faculty members did not publish extensively and when they did the result was usually a traditional collection of cases or a treatise on aspects of private law. Howard L. Smith published a volume of cases on bills and notes, Eugene A. Gilmore wrote a treatise on the law of partnership and Richards published a case book on corporations. Richards also wrote, in addition to a few articles in law journals, a study of legal education in Great Britain which was published in 1915. In fact, Richards' professional reputation was based upon his interest in legal education, expressed through extensive service in the AALS and the Wisconsin State Bar Association. Richards, at least, acknowledged that the law professor also might be a social reformer, but other members of the faculty were totally uncomfortable in the garment of the reformer. Howard L. Smith, who in 1910 was on leave at the Stanford University Law School, wrote Richards marvelling over the great contrast between Stanford and the University of Wisconsin. At Stanford there was "no excitement, no hysterics, no press bureau, no service of the state, no new sensations over night, . . . no nothing except just work,— teaching and investigation and the pursuit of quiet scholarship." [24]

Smith's complaint to the contrary, the Wisconsin Idea, that close association between the university and the state in the interest of social reform, did not penetrate very deeply into the University of Wisconsin Law School during the first two decades of the twentieth century. John R. Commons, when challenged by businessmen as to why the University always "promoted the 'labor' side against the 'capitalist's' side," always replied "that the university had a great majority of its faculty in several colleges—engineering, law, commerce, the college of liberal arts, the economics department—mainly devoted to training students to serve the interests of business and employers." [25] Some university law faculty were involved in a limited way in reform but those most interested in public issues, like Walter Wheeler Cook and William Underhill Moore, both of whom would become important figures in the legal realist movement, quickly left Wisconsin for positions at Chicago, then Yale (Cook) and Chicago, then Columbia (Moore). Of the faculty who remained only Eugene A. Gilmore and, to a lesser extent, Richards, involved themselves in questions of public policy and legal reform.

Members of a state university law faculty were vulnerable to outside pressure when they tackled questions of broad public policy. The reaction to the activities of Gilmore makes that vulnerability clear. Regent G. D. Jones, who had criticized the law school for not having practitioners on its staff and for not giving students adequate preparation in the practical work of the lawyer, was the most vociferous and influential critic of the professor as reformer. He was critical of the University in general (one of his first acts as Regent was to write to President Van Hise complaining that Van Hise allowed himself to be "unduly influenced" by the socialists in the legislature) but he held a particular animosity toward Gilmore. Regent Jones had been among a group of promoters interested in constructing a power dam on the Wisconsin River. After acquiring the necessary franchises from the state and investing a considerable sum of money in the project, the men found that their plans ran counter to the conception of public interest held by the Wisconsin Conservation Commission. It did not help that President Van Hise was a member of that Commission, nor was Jones pleased when he discovered that Gilmore had written a report on riparian law that threatened the entire undertaking. Although the project eventually proceeded, Jones still believed that the University had meddled too deeply in the private affairs of businessmen.[26] That experience led him to view any research activity conducted by the law school faculty with suspicion. When in 1910 Richards vigorously supported a proposal that the University Regents establish a professorship "for the comparative and critical study of the results of remedial law," the Regents, led by Jones, turned the proposal down. Instead of the three thousand dollars that Richards had asked to support a research professor, the Regents appropriated only five hundred dollars for the project and gave faculty members who worked on the investigation credit toward a leave of absence. Jones pointedly told Richards: "You no doubt appreciate the fact that the value of this work will depend almost entirely upon the spirit in which it is undertaken. It should be taken up judicially. It should be done by an experienced man, who has no pre-conceived theory to prove, and by a man free from the itching desire for notoriety. It is the truth and the whole truth that is wanted." [27]

In 1913 Felix Frankfurter told Learned Hand that "I have long thought that juristically, the Wisconsin idea should be nationalized, and that it was up to the Law School to do it." [28] But it remained for a small number of law professors, mainly at private university law schools, to attempt to do that. These men, at Harvard, Yale, Chicago, Columbia and Johns Hopkins, viewed legal science in a much broader manner than did the stricter followers of Langdell. Associated in its early stages with the writings of Oliver Wendell Holmes, Jr. and Roscoe Pound, this alternative centered upon a concept of sociological jurisprudence. For Roscoe Pound that meant a switch in the focus of juristic analysis from mere doctrine to a study of the social effects of legal rules and practice. That, in turn, implied a much greater sensitivity to the insights of the newly emerging social sciences, like sociology, political science, economics, and psychology. Pound criticized the reduction of legal decisions into a mechanical process of deducing principles from preordained rules and previously decided cases. Instead, Pound wrote in 1912, advocates of sociological jurisprudence "conceive of the legal rule as a general guide to the judge, leading him toward the just result, but insist that within wide limits he should be free to deal with the individual case, so as to meet the demands of justice between the parties and accord with the general reason of ordinary men." [29]

Although it has often been asserted that the legal realism of the 1930s was the "lineal descendent" of Holmes' skepticism and Pound's social engineering approach,[30] it has not been enough noticed that Holmes and Pound echoed in spirit, if not always in method, the view of the professional lawyer and judge that men like Dean Edwin E. Bryant had held. Bryant would have been quite comfortable with Pound's conception of the legal rule as a "general guide to the judge" and with his emphasis upon meeting the "demands of justice" in individual cases with rules that accorded "with the general reason of ordinary men." There was, however, one crucial difference. Where Bryant believed that reason ought to be guided by "immutable principles of justice," Pound sought guidance in the methods of social sciences. Under the influence of Pound and others, many American law schools (again, mainly private institutions) began to engage in what Robert Stevens has termed a "flirtation" with the "soft" sciences of economics, political science, history and psychology. At Yale, for example, an ambitious program, never implemented, was set forth as early as 1916 to expand the law school into a "School of Law and Jurisprudence." During the 1920s Columbia took the lead in integrating the social sciences into the law curriculum; and the trend continued into the 1930s with the leading innovations introduced at Yale, the Johns Hopkins Institute for the Study of Law, and then at the University of Chicago.[31] By that time faculty at the University of Wisconsin Law School also were actively engaged in exploring those frontiers of legal science and legal education.

Despite the excitement such experiments generated, there was an underlying sense of disarray, even chaos, as the search for the science of law eluded men. In the early stages of the movement, Pound's attempt to seek the principles of law in the methods of the social sciences was not an unqualified success. Dean Harlan Stone of the Columbia Law School wrote in 1923 that if what was meant by sociological jurisprudence was nothing more than that "the life of the law is not logic but experience," then, Stone argued, "it is the method which the wise and competent judge has used from time immemorial in rendering the dynamic decision which makes the law a living force. Holt, Hardwick, Mansfield, Marshall and Shaw employed it long before the phrase sociological jurisprudence was thought of." The problem, according to Stone, was that one could not "in any proper sense speak of the application of this principle as a 'method.' " Stone asked: "Has sociological jurisprudence any methodology, any formulae, or any principles which can be taught or expounded so as to make it a guide either to the student of law or to the judge? History and logic are guides but has sociological engineering been reduced to a science and does it embody such formulae or principles that will enable the judge to render a just decision except by the application of that practical wisdom which characterizes the decision of the great judge and distinguishes him from those who are not so great?" Yet the "other resources" which Stone argued were necessary "to make of the common law [. . . a] great and abiding system" became even more elusive under that amorphous movement known as "legal realism." [32]

The legal realists rejected the narrow historicism of the case method. Like Pound, the realists wanted a closer integration of the law and the social sciences. But sociological jurisprudence, they insisted, did not go far enough. The main complaint of realists who criticized Pound was not that his ideas were wrong, but that their detailed implications had not been worked through thoroughly and in sufficient detail for sociological jurisprudence to be more than a set of vague aspirations. Legal realists, most notably at Columbia between 1919 and 1933, proposed to investigate in detail the social purposes of rules of law and to make clear the links between substantive law and procedure. Although any succinct definition of legal realism must vastly oversimplify its complexity, it was, at heart, an attempt to discover through empirical research "the practical effects of rules of law upon life" and then to use those discoveries to better understand how "to regulate human conduct and to promote those types of it which are regarded as desirable." [33]

According to Stevens, the realist movement "finally killed the idea of law as an exact science. Legal rules could no longer be assumed to be value-free. Their predictive value was seriously questioned. The emphasis of legal observation was finally established as being process rather than substance." [34] The emphasis upon process rather than substance constituted the chief distinction between the view of law adopted by Edwin E. Bryant at Wisconsin in the 1890s and that adopted by the legal realists. Both viewed law as an instrument that men could use to order the affairs of society. But the legal instrumentalism of the 1920s and 1930s, unlike that of Bryant, was not supported by "immutable principles of justice," whether defined in moral, social, or scientific terms. Legal realism, in fact, appeared to abandon even the search for agreed upon principles of justice and fairness. It is understandable, then, that Robert Stevens has characterized the postrealist era as "Schizophrenia Triumphant." [35]

The Emergence of a Private Profession

Practitioners began to accept the schoolmen's argument that more stringent standards were necessary to guard the entrance to the legal profession only when they accepted the image, to some extent also promulgated by schoolmen, of an over-crowded bar. But the perception of practitioners that the bar was overcrowded did not reflect economic reality; instead it signified the emergence of a new professional consciousness. The alliance between professors and practitioners meant that practitioners accepted the vision of the "professional" lawyer developed in the law schools. And as law became identified in the minds of practitioners as a science, they also came to view law as a private profession. It was private not only or even primarily in the sense of an economic enclave but more importantly in the sense that lawyers believed that law was too specialized and too complicated for the layman to understand, much less master.

A detailed survey of the Wisconsin bar done under the direction of Dean Lloyd K. Garrison of the Wisconsin Law School and published in 1935 challenged the practitioners' belief that the bar was overcrowded. Garrison concluded that "in Wisconsin since 1880 the volume of legal business and the opportunities for lawyers have increased much more rapidly than the increase either of the lawyers or of the population." Garrison found, in fact, that there were fewer lawyers relative to the population in 1920 (1:1145) and in 1930 (1:982) than there had been in 1880 (1:948) or 1900 (1:945). These figures corresponded roughly to the figures that were then available on the national level. Although the depression certainly heightened the perception that the bar was over-crowded, Garrison argued that the economic "contraction" depressed incomes but not legal business.[36] In any event complaints about over-crowding had preceded the depression by at least a decade. By bringing economic factors to the foreground, one effect of the depression was to conceal the important shifts in professional consciousness that were occurring.

When practitioners in the Wisconsin State Bar Association com-plained in 1932 about the "encroachment" of laymen into legal practice, again they were incorrect. The move to integrate the bar and thus define the limits of professional practice more precisely as well as the effort to define in the statutes those activities that constituted the practice of law all reflected a quite new attitude among leaders of the profession. Lawyers, in fact, were encroaching into areas that in the nineteenth century, particularly on the local level, had not been viewed as the exclusive province of the legal profession. Lawyers then specialized in dispute settlement, but they did not expect to monopolize that practice. Practice in the lower courts often required no formal legal training, and judges frequently were laymen. Lawyers were called in when they were available, when laymen were unable to solve a problem satisfactorily or when the consequences of defeat were especially serious.

A ladder can represent the means through which disputes either were settled or prevented in the nineteenth century. The rungs on that ladder represent a hierarchy of legal sophistication. At the lower levels of the legal process the talents of the courtroom advocate who appealed to common sense notions of justice were most important. At the higher levels the technical skills of the legal counselor, the office lawyer, were of greater importance. The legal counselor used his skills to arrange clients' affairs in such a way that court challenge would not occur in the future; therefore his task was to keep clients off the ladder rungs below. At the lowest end of the ladder the "professional" lawyer disappeared altogether. Here men submitted their disputes to a village patriarch for his advice and judgment. One way to understand the shift in profes-sional consciousness that occurred in the twentieth century is to imag-ine lawyers working their way gradually down that ladder bringing their baggage of legal technicality with them. As they did so they dis-placed those persons, like bankers, notary publics and real estate agents, who previously had engaged in aspects of legal business. Be-cause lawyers now argued that a minimum level of technical legal skill was necessary to hold a place on any rung of the ladder, the men they displaced were charged with "encroaching" on areas of legal practice.

The industrial and commercial expansion of the nineteenth and early twentieth centuries obviously contributed to this shift in professional consciousness. Because the sums of money involved in business transactions often were enormous, entrepreneurs needed certainty and security established by law in order to minimize risks. Those needs encouraged a greater dependence upon the careful legal technician. Both lawyers and judges became more conscious that a departure from precedent created an environment of uncertainty. Although the demands of an expanding economic order may explain satisfactorily why portions of the American legal process developed fairly formalistic procedures in the years 1870 to 1930, the question is not simply one of a growing formalism and technical sophistication at the higher levels of legal practice where most was at stake. The question concerns why lawyers in the first three decades of the twentieth century began to insist that almost all attempts to deal with the settlement of disputes or the arrangement of affairs required technical legal training. That trend was not necessarily an inevitable response to the more complex conditions of modern life, a favorite explanation among lawyers at the time.

The belief that law was a private profession formed part of a much larger shift in the public's perception of the professional. In the twentieth century the test of a true professional was whether or not he approached his calling in a scientific way. Career law professors, of course, had developed a notion of legal science in their effort to establish law as a proper part of the American university curriculum. One largely unnoticed effect of the eventual alliance between professors and practitioners on behalf of higher bar admission standards, however, was that practitioners began to accept the vision of the scientific lawyer articulated by law professors. The practitioners did not, indeed could not, adopt the ideas of legal realism or sociological jurisprudence in their practice if only because professors could not agree among themselves about what constituted a scientific legal practice. There was, then, no compelling single scientific model for practitioners to adopt. Moreover, it is doubtful that the conceptions of science set forth by professors would have affected much, if at all, what lawyers did wholly inside their offices or around business bargaining tables. Indeed, legal realists proposed to study what lawyers actually did rather than to provide scientific guidelines for action. Nevertheless, lawyers did begin to accept, more through osmosis than through conscious decision, the view that law was a science; and if they often confused science with technique, the belief that law was scientific provided practitioners with a rationale to make the legal profession a more private profession.

To view law as a science carried potentially important social and economic benefits. Practitioners would experience an increase in both prestige and financial rewards if they made law the exclusive province of highly trained people. And lawyers did not have to imagine that these social and economic benefits would accrue if they adopted the rhetoric of the scientist. The lures of scientism, in fact, were not easily resisted when the legal profession saw the success with which the medical profession drove marginal medical schools out of business and curbed economic competition within the profession. Doctors did so by defining professionalism in such a way as to exclude "unscientific" quacks from the field. And it was the doctor who in the twentieth century began to represent for the public the ideal model of the professional.

The emergence of the doctor as the exemplar of the professional evidenced a profound shift in American intellectual and social life. In the seventeenth and eighteenth centuries the minister had been the ideal model of the professional. In fact, the very term "professional" carries with it religious overtones still since it initially was used to identify those who "professed" a certain faith and who attempted to lead an exemplary life. By the nineteenth century the lawyer began to challenge the minister as the prime example of the professional. Equally important, lawyers also began to replace the minister in some areas of American life in a functional way. Ministers had been the group most deeply concerned with the definition of social and moral values in the colonial period. As American life became more secularized, however, the setting for the definition and expression of values, particularly in the economic and political realms, tended to shift from the pulpit to the courtroom.[37]

Significantly, because it offers such a striking contrast to the twentieth-century view of law, judges in the early nineteenth century openly and deliberately made law on the basis of their perceptions of the moral and social principles involved. During the years between 1780 and 1820, according to Morton Horowitz, many American judges and lawyers abandoned the concept of the common law as a "fixed, customary standard" and the reliance upon a "strict conception of precedent." What emerged instead was a kind of "instrumentalism" in which the common law was conceived as an instrument of the judge's will, in which substance became more important than form, and in which the significance of technicalities in deciding the outcome of cases declined markedly. "While no judge of the period acknowledged himself to be free from the restraints of 'reason' and 'principle' in formulating legal doctrine," judges did begin "to conceive of common law adjudication as a process of making and not merely discovering legal rules." This led them consciously to "use law in order to encourage social change" and as an "instrument of policy." [38]

This early nineteenth-century "instrumentalism," unlike the instrumentalism associated with the twentieth-century legal realists, remained profoundly moral. If judges could define law according to what they perceived the needs of the citizenry to be, those laws still were reflections of universal moral principles. Far from being a stance that justified a relativity of values, this theory of judicial power only asserted that the universal moral laws might be reflected somewhat differently under varying historical or social circumstances.

The early nineteenth-century instrumentalism, Horowitz implies, laid the groundwork for what Roscoe Pound termed the "formative era" of American law and what others have termed the "golden age" of American law.[39] It was an age dominated by the "grand style," that judicial approach which was impatient with narrow legal logic and acknowledged precedent only as a guideline. Law, of course, was intended to protect property and the established order "but beyond that, to further the interests of the middle-class mass, to foster growth, to release and harness the energy latent in the commonwealth." In Willard Hurst's phrase, the theme of American law prior to 1850 was the "release of energy." Judges contributed to that release of energy through judicial decisions that eschewed technicality. According to Karl Llewellyn:

> Their opinions were often little treatises, moving from elegant premise to elaborate conclusion, ranging far and wide over subject matter boldly defined. They were, at their best, far-sighted men, impatient with narrow legal logic . . . They did not choose to base their decisions on precedent alone; law had to be chiseled out of basic principle; the traditions of the past were merely evidence of principle and rebuttable.

By 1900 the theme of American law no longer was the release of energy; now, according to Lawrence Friedman, the theme was "hold the line." Moreover , legal practice had become increasingly formal and technical. In contrast to the "grand style," legal practice now leaned toward what Llewellyn termed the "formal style." [40] Roscoe Pound characterized the changed attitude as "record worship." Judges exhibited "an excessive regard for the formal record at the expense of the case," and they emphasized a "strict scrutiny of that record for 'errors at law' at the expense of scrutiny of the case to insure consonance of the result to the demands of the substantive law." [41] The "grand style" or the "formal style," a creative view of precedent or record worship, of course, form central tensions in the life of the law; and both attitudes existed side by side during the nineteenth century. Indeed, the early nineteenth-century instrumentalism quickly came under attack by those who, suspicious of the potentially arbitrary power of judicial prerogative, wanted a government of laws, not men. For example, William Cranch, the second reporter of the United States Supreme Court, argued in 1804 that reported cases were essential "to a government of laws." The "least possible range ought to be left to the discretion of the Judge. Whatever tends to render the laws certain, equally tends to limit that discretion; and perhaps nothing conduces more to that object than the publication of reports. Every case decided is a check upon the judge." [42] The irony is that the publication of reports in an effort to preserve the power of the people by curbing the discretion of judges eventually contributed to a more technical spirit which made the law less accessible to laymen.

Although political theory combined with the demands of a corporate economy, then, to contribute to a growing technical emphasis in the law, the transformation in the nation's ideal of the professional contributed most to the trend toward formalism at all levels of the legal process. By the end of the nineteenth century the professional no longer was viewed as one primarily concerned with the articulation, clarification, and definition of basic social and moral values. Instead, he came to be identified by an objective, neutral stance toward the world. Although lawyers would continue to define values in their work, as the scientific model of professionalism gained strength they increasingly masked and even denied that function under the guise of scientific objectivity. Judges in the late nineteenth century, for example, stressed very strongly that they did not make law. "Precedent, the Constitution, principles of common law—these were the rulers; the judge was only an instrument, a vessel." This theory of judicial power, Lawrence Friedman has argued, contributed to the "flight into technicality." But that was only on the surface a flight "toward a more humble, self-effacing role." In reality, it was an attempt to conform to the standards of professionalism defined by the medical doctor. "A doctor does not humble himself when he claims that the principles of medicine determine what he does. The judges claimed that they were professionals; their job was too difficult for the layman, too pure for the politician." They insisted that what they did, "like all experts' work, was value free." [43] Thus, the legal profession, which in the nineteenth century had been primarily and often openly concerned with articulating values, now in the twentieth century began to deny that they dealt in the realm of values at all.

The transition from the "grand style" to the "formal style" of legal reasoning did not proceed at the same pace in all regions of the country. It should be obvious that the development of the law and the legal profession are intimately tied to economic, social and political factors and that the impact these factors have on the law vary enormously over time from state to state and from region to region. But the absence of a regional perspective has constituted the major barrier to construction of a comprehensive framework for understanding legal history. Here the analysis of legal education and the legal profession in Wisconsin can begin to provide a needed corrective to the historiography of law now dominated by an eastern perspective. The Wisconsin experience suggests that the years between 1890 and 1930 were especially critical in the development of the modern American legal profession.

The tension between the "grand style" and the "formal style" began to shift in favor of the latter in the eastern United States by about 1830. After that date, Roscoe Pound argued, "record worship" became the characteristic legal style. That was visible not only at the federal level but at the state level as well. Of the generation of state judges in the last third of the nineteenth century, Pound believed that only one, Charles Doe, Chief Justice of New Hampshire, stood out as a builder of law. Doe was a man who, in the words of his biographer, believed that "judicial power was grounded upon the logic of necessity and the function of the court [was] to furnish a remedy for every right." In a number of significant cases, according to Friedman, "Doe disregarded formalities, ignored the niceties of pleading, and shrugged off the burden of precedent. He believed judges should sometimes make the law and make it openly.[44]

That description of Charles Doe is strikingly similar to the descriptions of prominent judges and lawyers in Wisconsin during the last half of the nineteenth century. Those judges who were admired had no "idolatry for mere precedents" that "violated correct principles," or they were men who were "exceptionally free from the trammels of mere legal technicalities." The admiration for such men, as well as the men themselves, lived on well into the twentieth century. John B. Winslow, who served as Chief Justice of the Wisconsin Supreme Court until 1920, was admired at least by the older generation of lawyers because he "followed principles rather than authorities. A rule of law became such on account of its intrinsic reason and justice, rather than because it had been announced by a court in New York or Kansas." Dean Edwin E. Bryant had tried to maintain a similiar attitude in the Wisconsin Department of Law during the 1890s. He resisted the case method because that "rigid and prescribed system" threatened the "skilled judgment" of the law professor and the lawyer. Lawyers of Bryant's generation in Wisconsin thus had much in common with the early nineteenth-century instrumentalists. "Law had to be chiseled out of basic principle;" and the sculptor was the lawyer.

The battle over the case method in the years between 1890 and 1920 was especially bitter because it represented a fundamental struggle over the image of the professional lawyer. Mistakenly, historians have assumed that the early nineteenth-century law school produced the "black-letter" lawyer because its curriculum was organized around lectures, treatises and textbooks. Given the emphasis on definitional statements of the law in that curriculum, the students in the school must have been trained to take the law literally as it was found in the black letters of the textbooks. But that was not necessarily the case. The early law schools were designed to complement apprenticeship; therefore their curricular emphases cannot be an accurate gauge of the type of lawyer they sought to produce. Instead, one must look at the way that the early law schools fit into the surrounding professional culture.

Here a regional perspective is important because it highlights the clash of professional cultures. In the eastern United States that professional culture moved toward legal formalism after the 1830s. Legal formalism, however, did not begin to characterize the professional culture of most western states until much later in the century; in some respects the "grand style," the rejection of the technicalities of pleading and the burdens of precedent, persisted in a state like Wisconsin even into the twentieth century. When Christopher Langdell introduced the case method at Harvard in 1870, then, he merely was codifying in the law school curriculum a movement already well under way in the eastern states toward "record worship." As the case method moved west it represented much more than an innovation in legal education. It also represented the invasion of a markedly different sense of professionalism. Men like Dean Bryant of Wisconsin in the 1890s and Deans Jenkins and Schoetz at Marquette prior to 1917, even as they presided over a curriculum that stated the law abstractly and definitionally, attempted to preserve the "'skilled judgment" of the lawyer. In their view, the scientific lawyer, trained according to the mechanistic principles of the case method, was simply a careful legal technician. Christopher Columbus Langdell of Harvard was the true "black-letter" lawyer.

The Legacy of Reform

Although many law professors in the twentieth century rejected Langdell's version of science as too narrow and too cloistered, they did not question Langdell's assumption that the study of law could be made scientific. And as the scientific spirit spread from the universities into the consciousness of practitioners, for whom it provided the rationale for a private profession of legal experts, it was ironic that the basic weakness within the bar now were defined in moral terms. The character and ethics, not the technical abilities, of some lawyers preoccupied leaders of the bar. However, in order to establish more formal educational standards regulating entry into the profession, schoolmen and practitioners discredited and obliterated the methods of regulation characteristic of the nineteenth century. The irony lay in the fact that the strength of those highly personalistic methods of training and regulation had been the ability to advance men of proven or at least known character into the profession. One legacy of the period of progressive reform, then, was that the golden age of American law, the formative era, lingered on in the literature of the law but the social and professional circumstances that had nurtured that age receded from memory.

There is a danger, of course, in romanticizing the nineteenth-century professional culture. If professional life was convivial, it also was emotional, volatile and unstable. If judges pronounced law according to prevailing community standards of justice or according to their own notions of "immutable moral principles," the law set forth often was arbitrary, local and ephemeral. And if apprenticeship arrangements worked so that practitioners themselves selected and sponsored worthy men, those admission procedures also surely excluded other worthy men and women capriciously and on the basis of personal whim and prejudices. The problem, as it is so often, was one of balance between the older personalistic arrangements for recruitment and training, where character and talent could be assessed subjectively, and the more formal methods for regulating entrance to the profession that were dependent on rules, where objective measures of talent reigned.

Nor should an appreciation of the strengths of nineteenth-century professional culture be allowed to mask its other shortcomings. Because members of the profession were selected largely on the basis of character and background, admission procedures tended to reinforce existing class and social perspectives. Members of the bar may have articulated social values openly and consciously, but they held, after all, a rather narrow set of values. It should not be assumed, then, that the bar of the nineteenth century was always a conspicuous force for desirable social criticism. Indeed, they usually paid little attention to broader questions of the public interest in their often heedless support of the expansion of the country's economy.

In the twentieth century judges and lawyers who were better and more broadly educated were needed in order to lead the profession beyond a narrow focus on private interests and toward a consideration of the role that law played in shaping social development. Law professors were among the first to grapple with that problem. They attempted to broaden legal study beyond traditional doctrinal concerns by integrating the social sciences into the law school curriculum. And out of the intellectual turbulence of the legal realist movement, especially, came an awareness during the 1930s and beyond that the law played an important functional role in molding society. Professors attempted, not always with great success, to reveal the social effects of law in action and to make explicit the values that legal rules supported. Yet even as law professors rejected the scientism of Langdell, they did not find in their own versions of science a substitute for the "immutable moral principles" that had provided the guidelines for the lawyer in the nineteenth century. The most certain guideline for practitioners in the twentieth century remained the technique of legal reasoning taught through the analysis of leading cases. Langdell's case method remained at the heart of the law school curriculum; and the ability to "think like a lawyer" rather than the ability to articulate values, choices, and problems for the society remained at the center of the professional ethos.

Perhaps the most disturbing legacy of the age of progressive reform was the tendency to isolate law and the legal profession from the larger society. By the 1930s the emergence of the law school as the dominant institution in legal training meant that legal knowledge was sequestered in such institutions. But it has not been stressed enough that an earlier conception of law, dating in America from at least the late eighteenth century, assumed that any liberally educated person ought to have some fundamental understanding of law and how it affected the social order. That this belief that law was part of a liberal education was honored more in principle than in practice is undeniable, yet even the principle appeared lost by the 1930s, not only among the legal profession but also among the proponents of the liberal arts. Law now was too technical, even too scientific, to be within the grasp of laymen. In the twentieth century, then, law became "professional" knowledge in a quite narrow sense. What A. Z. Reed had termed America's public profession now became, as it entered the second quarter of the twentieth century, an increasingly private profession. Even as lawyers sought ways to broaden their perspective by reaching out to the social sciences, they did so within an increasingly private and professional framework.

Bibliographic Notes

Despite the voluminous and ever-expanding literature on the law, the history of legal education remains a rather narrow and parochial field. There are only three general histories of American legal education: Alfred Z. Reed, *Training for the Public Profession of the Law* (1921); Albert J. Harno, *Legal Education in the United States* (1953); and Robert Stevens, "Two Cheers for 1870: The American Law School," *Perspectives in American History* (1971), pp. 403–548. Reed's work, followed by his equally monumental *Present-Day Law Schools in the United States and Canada* (1928), remains the most comprehensive study of legal education and the legal profession. As a source of basic information, his work is not likely to be superseded and my own indebtedness to Reed I hope is given ample expression in the footnotes to this book. Harno's book brings Reed's interpretation forward three decades. Stevens' long article adds an important new dimension to the history of legal education through a fine analysis of the intellectual and ideological patterns of legal thought that were cultivated in the university law schools. To this list of general histories should be added the three articles by Brainerd Currie in the *Journal of Legal Education*, "The Materials of Law Study" (Parts I and II, Vol. 3, 1951, pp. 331–383; and Part II, Vol. 8, 1955, pp. 1–78). Currie's articles, while ostensibly concerned with curriculum development, actually constitute a broad-ranging and perceptive discussion of American legal education and its English roots.

There have been surprisingly few recent full-length histories of individual law schools: Frederick C. Hicks, *Yale Law School: The Founders and the Founders' Collection* (1935); Julius J. Goebel, *A History of the School of Law: Columbia University* (1955); Elizabeth G. Brown, *Legal*

Education at Michigan: 1859–1959 (1959); and finally, to exhaust the list, Arthur E. Sutherland, *The Law at Harvard* (1967). Charles Warren, *History of the Harvard Law School; and of Early Legal Conditions in America* (1908) remains valuable and for the years it covers provides a broader perspective on the links between the law school and professional development than does the Sutherland volume. Of the recent histories, the Goebel study is the best by far. All of the recent studies of law schools, however, focus rather narrowly on internal institutional development and growth. .

The literature on the history of professions also is both voluminous and narrow. The classic study is A. M. Carr-Saunders and P. A. Wilson, *The Professions* (1933). Almost all sociological investigation has followed the lead of that volume and treats the concept of the professional as a static entity. The task is to "measure" in any given historical period how existing professional development corresponded to some ideal notion of the professional. For a discussion of the need to view the idea of the professional as a concept that changes over time rather than as a timeless ideal, see my essay review, "Professions in Process: Doctors and Teachers in American Culture," *History of Education Quarterly* (Summer, 1975), pp. 185–199. Recent studies of the legal profession not only have tended to adopt a static view of the professional developed by sociologists, they also have accepted A. Z. Reed's argument that the most distinctive feature of the American legal profession has been its differentiation along class lines. Studies of the legal profession therefore generally analyze in greater depth and in different historical periods the existing class dimensions within the bar and they explore the links between professional stratification and legal education. Among the best of these studies are Jerome Carlin, *Lawyers on Their Own* (1962); Erwin O. Smigel, *The Wall Street Lawyer* (1964); and, most recently, Jerold S. Auerbach, *unEqual Justice* (1976). The Auerbach study, however, while it does assume that stratification within the profession is the key to understanding its impact on American life, also offers a superb analysis of the shifting meaning attached to the concept of the professional in various historical periods. Two other studies are remarkable for the insights they provide into the process of professional development: James Willard Hurst, *The Growth of American Law: The Law Makers* (1950); and Daniel Calhoun, *Professional Lives in America: Structure and Aspiration, 1750–1850* (1965). Readers familiar with those two works will recognize the profound impact they have had on this study.

'The footnotes to this book provide a detailed guide to the additional secondary sources that I have used but the manuscript sources upon which much of my interpretation rests should be described briefly. The papers and correspondence of Wisconsin lawyers proved to be of much less help than I had expected. They more often shed light on personal and family matters than on professional life. The following, all located in the State Historical Society of Wisconsin, Madison, were the most helpful collections: Levi H. Bancroft, Correspondence, 1879–1897; Moses B. Butterfield, Correspondence, 1842, 1850–53; Alfred A. Jackson Papers, 1876, 1893–1912; Burr W. Jones Papers, 1873–1933; John M. Olin Papers, 1879–1916; Charles B. Rogers, Correspondence and Diaries, 1889–1895; Howard L. Smith Papers, 1826–1940; and William F. Vilas, Correspondence and Papers, 1827–1919. It should be noted that the Alfred A. Jackson Papers contain some of the original records of the Wisconsin State Bar Association. No additional manuscript records of that Association have been located.

The records of the University of Wisconsin Law School, located in the University of Wisconsin Memorial Library Archives, constituted the major source of information for this study, particularly for the years after 1894 when the Law School administration first began to keep systematic records. There is an adequate general index to these records on file in the archives. The most significant series in this collection were the following: Law School General Correspondence, consisting of five letter-press volumes and forty boxes, 1894–1930; Law School General Subject Files, eighteen boxes, covering the years 1895–1954; and Law Faculty Minutes, six volumes spanning the years 1894–1953.

The University of Wisconsin Board of Regents records, also located in the University Memorial Library Archives, were the major source of information on law school development prior to the mid-1890s. Three major divisions of the records were of greatest help: University Board of Regents Minutes, 1848–1930; University Board of Regents Proceedings, 1866–1907, consisting of reports submitted to the Regents at each meeting of the Board; and the University Board of Regents Papers, 1848–1930, also comprising the reports submitted at each meeting along with miscellaneous papers, letters, and financial information. Reports of the Law School Dean can often be found in the Papers of the Regents and usually, though not invariably, recorded in the volumes of Proceedings.

The sources for reconstructing the history of the Marquette Law School are much more limited for the period which this study covers. The Marquette University archives contains little material on the law school prior to 1915: An early account of the founding of the law school is found in Scrapbook #18, p. 41; and miscellaneous early papers from the period 1910–1912 are found in file D-2/Series 4/Box 11. The amount of material, mainly correspondence and committee reports, increases somewhat after 1915 but not until the 1930s does one begin to find fuller primary source material. Consequently, the major source of information for the history of the Marquette Law School has been the printed catalogs and announcements.

Notes

Chapter One

1. *University of Wisconsin Board of Regents' Annual Report,* 1857, pp. 24–25 (hereafter cited as *Regents' Annual Report).*

2. Ibid., pp. 26–27.

3. Ibid., p. 27.

4. A. M. Carr-Saunders and P. A. Wilson, *The Professions* (Oxford, 1933), pp. 30–31. The four Inns of Court—Lincoln's Inn, the Inner Temple, the Middle Temple and Gray's Inn—were, and to an extent still are, the most important institutions for training persons in the elements of the English common law. The Inns reached their height of prosperity in the fifteenth and sixteenth centuries. Thereafter they began to decline in importance as teaching institutions and by the eighteenth century had fallen into a "condition of torpor and lethargy" from which they never fully recovered. Barristers, who eventually gained the exclusive right to act as pleaders or advocates in the common law courts, received their training in the Inns of Court. Solicitors, who could not argue directly before judges but who were responsible for initiating legal proceedings in the courts, were trained in the Inns of Chancery. The Inns of Chancery, numbering at the peak of their development about ten, never gained the importance or the independence that characterized the Inns of Court. Ibid., pp. 29–38. See also Sir William Holdsworth, *A History of English Law* (11 volumes; 4th Edition; London, 1936), Vol. 2, pp. 492–512; and Robert R. Pearce, *A Guide to the Inns of Court and Chancery* (London, 1855).

5. William Blackstone, *Commentaries on the Laws of England,* ed., Thomas M. Cooley (2 volumes; 2nd Edition; Chicago, 1849), Vol. 1, p. 4. The standard biography of Blackstone is David A. Lockmiller, *Sir William Blackstone* (Chapel Hill, North Carolina, 1938). For an analysis of the intellectual and social underpinnings of Blackstone's thought, see Daniel J. Boorstin, *The Mysterious Science of the Law* (Boston, Beacon paperback edition, 1958).

6. Stiles' plan is reproduced in full in Charles Warren, *A History of the American Bar* (Boston, 1911), pp. 563–566.

7. Quoted in Francis R. Aumann, *The Changing American Legal System: Some Selected Phases* (Columbus, Ohio, 1940), pp. 107, 104. Aumann notes an attempt to establish a law professorship at Columbia in 1773 which apparently failed for financial reasons.

8. James Kent, *Commentaries on American Law*, ed., William Kent (4 volumes; 7th edition: New York, 1851), Vol. 1, pp. ix–x.

9. Carr-Saunders and Wilson, p. 29. See also Alfred Zantzinger Reed, *Training for the Public Profession of the Law*, The Carnegie Foundation for the Advancement of Teaching, Bulletin Number 15 (Boston, 1921), pp. 11–14. The difference between the English and European traditions of legal education can be overstated. Brainerd Currie points out that "an undue emphasis . . . has been placed on the role of law faculties in European education. The theoretical study of law in the university, although it is a necessary step toward a professional career, is regarded as non-professional." The practical work is furnished by "an elaborate system of apprenticeship." Brainerd Currie, "The Materials of Law Study," Parts One and Two, *The Journal of Legal Education*, 3 (1951), p. 342 and ibid., footnote 2. The important point is that in Europe there did exist a close intellectual and institutional connection between legal study and the universities. In England, and in nineteenth-century America, law, viewed either as a professional or a nonprofessional (i.e., liberal) study, had no such close ties with the colleges or universities.

10. Reed, pp. 116–117.

11. Jefferson often heatedly expressed his opposition to the doctrines espoused in Blackstone's *Commentaries*. Blackstone's "wily sophistries" and "honied Mansfieldism," Jefferson complained, were making Tories of young American lawyers. See Julius S. Waterman, "Thomas Jefferson and Blackstone's Commentaries," *Illinois Law Review*, 27 (1932–33), pp. 629–659. A good discussion of the origins of the early law professorships is found in Currie, pp. 346–359.

12. Reed, pp. 116–117; Aumann, pp. 110–112; Warren, pp. 343ff.

13. Currie, pp. 350–351; Reed, p. 137. See also Arthur E. Sutherland, *The Law at Harvard: A History of Ideas and Men, 1817–1967* (Cambridge, Massachusetts, 1967), pp. 62–91.

14. Reed, p. 124.

15. Noah Webster, *Dissertations on the English Language* (Boston, 1789), reprinted in part in Daniel Calhoun, *The Educating of Americans: A Documentary History* (Boston, 1969), pp. 89–96. See also Noah Webster, "On the Education of Youth in America" (Boston, 1790), reprinted in Frederick Rudolph, ed., *Essays on Education in the Early Republic* (Cambridge, Massachusetts, 1965), pp. 43–77; Benjamin Rush, "Thoughts upon the Mode of Education Proper in a Republic," ibid., pp. 9–23. The reference to "republican machines" is on p. 17. For excerpts from Washington's address to Congress in 1796 in which he proposed a national university, see Edgar W. Knight and Clifton L. Hall, eds., *Readings in Educational History* (New York, 1951), pp. 103–104.

16. On the growth of courses in government, see Anna Haddow, *Political Science in American Colleges and Universities, 1636–1900* (New York, 1939).

17. James Willard Hurst, *The Growth of American Law: The Law Makers* (Boston, 1950), p. 275; Aumann, pp. 94–119; Reed, pp. 117, 121, 124.

18. Currie, p. 360.

19. Reed, pp. 120–124, 137–143; Aumann, pp. 106–107; Warren, pp. 340–352.

20. Quoted in Reed, p. 124.

21. Joseph Story, "Discourse Pronounced Upon the Inauguration of the Author, As Dane Professor of Law in Harvard University, August 25th, 1829," in Perry Miller, ed., *The Legal Mind in America* (Ithaca, New York, Cornell University Press paper edition, 1969), pp. 182, 184–185.

22. Aumann, p. 97.

23. Reed, p. 131.

24. For more detailed accounts of the Litchfield Law School, see Samuel H. Fisher, *The Litchfield Law School, 1774–1883* (New Haven, Connecticut, 1946); and Dwight C. Kilbourn, *The Bench and Bar of Litchfield County, Connecticut, 1709–1909* (Litchfield, Connecticut, 1909).

25. A list, admittedly incomplete, of private law schools in the United States is found in Reed, pp. 431–433. Evidence for the Wisconsin school is found in *Wisconsin Laws*, 1858, pp. 174–178: "An Act to Authorize the Incorporation of Law Schools and Law Library Associations."

26. Philip Alexander Bruce, *History of the University of Virginia* (5 volumes; New York, 1920), Vol. 1, pp. 102–103.

27. Frederic C. Hicks, Yale Law School: *The Founders and the Founders' Collection* (New Haven, Connecticut, 1935).

28. Wisconsin *Session Laws*, 1848, p. 38. The original draft of the law, titled "A Bill to Establish the University of Wisconsin," is located in the State Historical Society of Wisconsin. The University itself was organized in accordance with a provision contained in the 1848 Wisconsin constitution. Article X stated: "Provision shall be made by law for the establishment of a State University, at or near the seat of Government." An earlier constitution, rejected by the voters in 1847, made no mention of a state university. For attempts during the territorial period to establish a university, all of which failed, see Merle Curti and Vernon Carstensen, *The University of Wisconsin: A History* (2 volumes; Madison, Wisconsin, 1949), Vol. 1, pp. 37–45. For the text of the Michigan charter, see Edward C. Elliott and M. M. Chambers, *Charters and Basic Laws of Selected American Universities and Colleges* (New York, 1934), pp. 340–342. The Michigan Law School was not opened until 1859.

29. "Ordinance Providing for the Organization of the Department of Law," *Papers of the University of Wisconsin Board of Regents* (1848–1864), file marked "Proceedings, 1857" (hereafter cited as *Regents' Papers*).

30. Reed, pp. 145–146, especially footnote 1, p. 145.

31. Ibid., pp. 164–169.

32. Wisconsin *Session Laws*, 1848, p. 38.

33. Biographical information on Lathrop has been gathered from the following sources: C. W. Butterfield, *History of the University of Wisconsin, From Its First Organization to 1879; With Biographical Sketches . . .* (Madison, Wisconsin, 1879), pp. 2–4; Dumas Malone, ed., *The Dictionary of American Biography*, Vol. 11, pp. 16–17 (New York, 1933); Curti and Carstensen, Vol. 1, p. 60. "John H. Lathrop, Tutor," is listed as a student in the Staples law school in 1823. Hicks, p. 13.

34. *The Dictionary of American Biography*, Vol. 15, pp. 421–422. See also Butterfield, pp. 23–24.

35. *Regents' Annual Report*, January 16, 1850, pp. 6–12.

36. Ibid.

37. Curti and Carstensen, Vol. 1, p. 129; Irvin G. Wylie, "Land and Learning," *Wisconsin Magazine of History*, 30 (December, 1946), pp. 163–164.

38. The details of this controversy are found in Curti and Carstensen, Vol. 1, pp. 88–111. Also valuable is an older history of the University: J. F. A. Pyre, *Wisconsin* (New York, 1920), especially pp. 103–110.

39. *Minutes of the University of Wisconsin Board of Regents*, January 29, 1857, Vol. 2, pp. 110–111 (hereafter cited as *Regents' Minutes*). The Report was not adopted.

40. *Regents' Annual Report*, 1857, pp. 24–25.

41. Ibid., 1850, p. 12.

42. Some members of the state medical profession did show substantial interest in a university medical school. See the *Regents' Minutes*, January 17, 1850, Vol. 2, p. 27; Re-

gents' Annual Report, 1851, p. 11. For information on the role of the Wisconsin State Medical Society in early efforts to organize a university medical school, see William Snow Miller, "Medical Schools in Wisconsin: Past and Present," *Wisconsin Medical Journal,* 34 (June 1935), p. 478. The contrasting attitudes of the medical and legal professions toward professional schools are analyzed at length in Chapter Two, below.

43. *Regents' Annual Report,* 1851, p. 11.

44. Ibid., 1855, p. 21.

45. "Ordinance Providing for the Organization of the Department of Law," *Regents' Papers* (1848–1864), file marked "Proceedings, 1857." A good brief discussion of the Bashford-Barstow controversy is found in E. Bruce Thompson, *Matthew Hale Carpenter: Webster of the West* (Madison, Wisconsin, 1954), pp. 40–45.

46. "The Origin of the Law College of the State University of Iowa—Two Communications from John P. Irish," *Iowa Journal of History and Politics,* 8 (October 1910), pp. 553–554. A short biographical sketch of Irish can be found in Edward H. Stiles, ed., *Recollections and Sketches of Notable Lawyers and Public Men of Early Iowa* (Des Moines, Iowa, 1916), pp. 784–789.

47. *Regents' Minutes,* March 24, 1857, Vol. 2, pp. 114–115; ibid., April 1, 1857, p. 116.

48. Report of Daniel Read, *Regents' Minutes,* June 23, 1863, Vol. 2, p. 347.

49. Ibid., January 17, 1866, Vol. 2, p. 405. Sterling's remarks are in the "Faculty Report" dated January 15, 1866.

50. Ibid., p. 395.

51. See, for example, Elizabeth G. Brown, *Legal Education at Michigan, 1859–1959* (Ann Arbor, Michigan, 1959), especially the opening chapter. There an 1837 legislative act which provided for a law school and a medical school in the state university is viewed as "an early recognition of a state's responsibility to provide higher education in the professions of law and medicine for its citizens" (p. 3). This was not the first such recognition of that principle in Michigan. Earlier, Augustus Woodward proposed university instruction in law "of a type that the law schools of the mid-twentieth century were only beginning to appreciate and in some instances achieve" (p. 5). Given this kind of presentist perspective, the development of the Michigan Law School becomes the story of a long battle between perceptive "dreamers" (p. 16), like Woodward, and the majority of citizens who were "unable to appreciate Woodward's foresight in providing an integrated educational system for the territory" (p. 6). A similar perspective pervades Arthur E. Sutherland, *The Law at Harvard* (Cambridge, Massachusetts, 1967), as it does a broader legal history by Anton-Hermann Chroust, *The Rise of the Legal Profession in America* (2 volumes; Norman, Oklahoma, 1965). In the latter, see Volume 2, Chapter 4, "Training for the Practice of Law," where the major theme is the difficult struggle of the early law schools against the "too solidly entrenched" apprenticeship method (p. 220). Except that members of the bar were themselves trained under apprenticeship and therefore could not easily perceive the advantages of the new law school system, Chroust offers no reasons for the persistence of apprenticeship. This is all the more surprising since most of his discussion of apprenticeship consists of its disadvantages. More recently, Robert Stevens, in "Two Cheers for 1870: The American Law School," *Perspectives in American History,* 5 (1971), pp. 403–548, has begun to move beyond this narrow professional perspective by at least asking the question: Why were universities interested in law schools? He provides, however, no answer, except to assert that the American colleges were "more willing to innovate in the sciences, literature and history" than European universities and in other areas were more receptive to curricular innovations (see pp. 414–415). For a more extended discussion of the shortcomings in histories written from a professional's perspective, see my essay review, "Professions in Process: Doctors and Teachers in American Culture," *History of Education Quarterly,* 15 (Summer 1975), pp. 185–199.

52. A significant exception is the study by Brainerd Currie, "The Materials of Law Study," Parts One and Two, *Journal of Legal Education,* 3 (1951), pp. 331–383; and Part Three, ibid., 8 (1955), pp. 1–78.

53. George W. Swasey, "Boston University Law School," *Green Bag,* 1 (1889), p. 54.

54. Reed, p. 183, footnote 1.

55. Ibid., p. 153,

56. David B. Potts, "American Colleges in the Nineteenth Century: From Localism to Denominationalism," *History of Education Quarterly,* 11 (Winter 1971), pp. 363–380.

57. Curti and Carstensen, Vol. 1, pp. 207–217, 296–307.

Chapter Two

1. Abraham Flexner, *Medical Education in the United States and Canada,* The Carnegie Foundation for the Advancement of Teaching, Bulletin Number 4 (Boston, 1910),p. 6; Alfred Zantzinger Reed, *Training for the Public Profession of the Law,* The Carnegie Foundation for the Advancement of Teaching, Bulletin Number 15 (Boston, 1921), pp. 444–443. Morris Fishbein has noted that "the multiplication of medical schools was such that, by the end of the nineteenth century there were about as many medical schools in the United States as there were in all the world." Morris Fishbein, *A History of the American Medical Association, 1847–1947* (Philadelphia, 1947), pp. 888–889.

2. James Willard Hurst, *The Growth of American Law: The Law Makers* (Boston, 1950), p. 277.

3. The first law governing admission to the bar in the Wisconsin territory was passed in 1838 and required that the applicant to the bar be a three-month resident of the territory, a citizen of the United States, twenty-one years of age and of good moral character. The applicant also had to convince one of the judges of the Territorial Supreme Court that he had studied law for at least two years. *Acts Passed at the First Session of the Legislative Assembly of the Territory of Wisconsin, 1836,* Chapter 24, pp. 80–81. These standards were relaxed somewhat in 1839 under terms of a new law that did away with the requirement of two years of study and insisted only upon a "requisite knowledge of the science and practice of law." *Statutes of Wisconsin Territory, 1838–39,* p. 346. This law governed the territory of Wisconsin until 1848 when Wisconsin was admitted to the union and the state legislature repealed all territorial legislation. In place of the old law regulating admission to the bar, the state legislature in 1849 passed a law that required only that the applicant be a resident of the state and of good moral character. No examination of legal knowledge was mandated. *The Revised Statutes of the State of Wisconsin, 1849,* p. 441. This law remained in effect until 1861 when there began a gradual strengthening of the bar admission standards.

4. James G. Jenkins, "Address," *Wisconsin State Bar Association Reports,* 7 (1906), p. 82 (hereafter cited as *WSBA Reports*). See also Nils P. Haugen, *Pioneer and Political Reminiscences* (Evansville, Wisconsin [1930?]), pp. 194–195.

5. Moses M. Hooper to A. A. Jackson, June 8, 1903, in the A. A. Jackson *Papers,* Box 2, Folder 1 (1903–1905), State Historical Society of Wisconsin.

6. A large bulk of this reminiscence can be found in the following works: S. U. Pinney, "Preface," *Wisconsin Reports* (Chicago, 1872), Vol. 1, pp. 9–56; Parker McCobb Reed, *The Bench and Bar of Wisconsin* (Milwaukee, Wisconsin, 1882); John R. Berryman, ed., *History of the Bench and Bar of Wisconsin* (2 volumes; Chicago, 1898); John B. Winslow, *The Story of a Great Court* (Chicago, 1912); Gilson G. Glasier, ed., *Autobiography of Roujet D. Marshall* (2 volumes; Madison, Wisconsin, 1923); *Reminiscences of the Bench and Bar of Dane County* (Madison, Wisconsin, n.d.); James Sibree Anderson, *Pioneer Courts and Lawyers of*

Manitowoc County, Wisconsin: Collections and Recollections (Manitowoc County Bar, 1921); *Wisconsin State Bar Association Reports,* especially volumes 1 through 4 (1878–1901).

7. Moses M. Strong, "Presidential Address," *WSBA Reports,* 1 (1878–1885), p. 53. For an excellent discussion of the lawyer on the Tennessee frontier, see Daniel H. Calhoun, *Professional Lives in America: Structure and Aspiration, 1750–1850* (Cambridge, Massachusetts, 1965), Chapter 3.

8. Moses B. Butterfield to his wife, December 16, 1852, in the Moses B. Butterfield *Papers,* State Historical Society of Wisconsin.

9. Pinney, p. 49; Berryman, Vol. 1, p. 78; E. E. Bryant, "The Supreme Court of Wisconsin," *The Green Bag,* 9 (1897), p. 27.

10. Glasier, *Autobiography of Roujet D. Marshall,* Vol. 1, pp. 256–257.

11. W. H. Seaman, "Address" (1898), *WSBA Reports,* 2 (1886–1899), pp. 174–175.

12. Romanzo Bunn, "Remarks" (March 1, 1905), ibid., 6 (1904–05), p. 114.

13. Ibid.

14. Burr W. Jones, "Tendencies of Half a Century in Wisconsin Courts," ibid., 5 (1902–03), p. 156.

15. Nels Wheeler, *Old Thunderbolt in Justice Court* (Baraboo, Wisconsin, 1883), p. 53.

16. Jones, p. 157.

17. Ibid.

18. Ibid., pp. 157–158.

19. James G. Jenkins, "Remarks," *WSBA Reports,* 7 (1906), pp. 78–79.

20. Ryan's address to the jury on that occasion can be found in Edward G. Ryan, *Speeches and Arguments of Chief Justice Ryan While at the Bar* (Madison, Wisconsin, 1909).

21. Elisha W. Keyes, "Wisconsin Bar in the Territorial Period," *WSBA Reports,* 2 (1886–1899), p. 342.

22. Berryman, Vol. 1, p. 72.

23. Ibid.

24. Hurst, p. 206. Berryman recounts how Judge Gale, challenged in court by John R. Bennett, later apologized to Bennett "at the supper table." Berryman, Vol. 1, p. 278. Wisconsin lawyers simply were following practices common throughout the United States. For examples of conviviality and informal professional sanctions in other areas of the country, see Charles Warren, *A History of the American Bar* (Boston, 1911), pp. 204–208.

25. Jones, p. 159.

26. Dr. John Reeve, "A Physician in Pioneer Wisconsin," *Wisconsin Magazine of History,* 3 (1919–1920), p. 313.

27. Alexander Meggett, "Experiences and Humorous Reminiscences . . . ," *WSBA Reports,* 2 (1886–1899), p. 172.

28. For information on the nineteenth-century American hospital, see William F. Norwood, *Medical Education in the United States Before the Civil War* (Philadelphia, 1944), pp. 44–47. One of the most helpful and suggestive analyses of the hospital's function is Michael Crichton, *Five Patients: The Hospital Examined* (New York, 1970).

29. Calhoun, pp. 6–7.

30. A good general description of the methods and medicines used by the regular doctor is in Henry B. Shafer, *The American Medical Profession, 1783 to 1850* (New York, 1936), Chapter 4, especially pp. 96–115. For the irregular doctors' methods, in addition to the relevant sections of Shafer, see Madge Pickard and R. Carlyle Buley, *The Midwest Pioneer: His Ills, Cures, & Doctors* (New York, 1946).

31. The best treatment by far of nineteenth-century medical history is William G. Rothstein, *American Physicians in the 19th Century: From Sects to Science* (Baltimore, Maryland, 1972). Also useful are Richard H. Shryock, *Medicine and Society in America: 1600–1860* (Ithaca, New York, 1960); Shryock, *Medical Licensing in America, 1650–1965* (Baltimore,

Maryland, 1967); and Joseph F. Kett, *The Formation of the American Medical Profession: The Role of Institutions, 1780–1860* (New Haven, Connecticut, 1968).

32. Shryock, *Medical Licensing in America*, pp. 36–37. The importance of social qualifications in distinguishing between orthodoxy and quackery is evident in the complaint of a Boston physician early in the eighteenth century: "In our plantation a practitioner, bold, rash, impudent, a lyar, basely born and uneducated, has much the advantage of an honest, cautious, modest gentleman." Quoted in Norwood, p. 22.

33. Quoted in Alexander Wilder, *History of Medicine* (Augusta, Maine, 1904), p. 315.

34. For a superb analysis of the shifting meaning of orthodoxy in this period, see William G. Rothstein, *American Physicians in the 19th Century*. Rothstein's work stands literally alone in rejecting the categories of analysis first developed in the nineteenth century by orthodox physicians and subsequently used by all other medical historians. The primary categories are a division of the profession in the nineteenth century into "regular" and "irregular" physicians. The difficulty with those terms is that they imply that irregular doctrines were merely intellectual aberrations from obvious scientific practice. The terms were originally used by orthodox practitioners of the nineteenth century to describe and derogate their competitors; and the continued use of the terms by medical historians today reveals their primary concern with the roots and origins of twentieth-century medical theory, not with understanding professional development in the nineteenth century. This preoccupation has tended to obscure the importance (and the reformist role) of the various nineteenth-century medical sects. With the exception of Rothstein, even the most sophisticated medical histories dismiss the sects as momentary deviations from the norm of orthodoxy and explain their proliferation as a part of Jacksonian Democracy and the rise of the common man. Richard Shryock, for example, in *Medical Licensing in America*, notes that increased educational opportunities after 1825 "had made the public literate enough to read attacks on 'regulars' but not sufficiently educated to make discriminating judgments." Given the state of medical science at the time, it is difficult to know what Shryock means by a "discriminating" judgment. Shryock himself undercuts his own point by going on to state that the "superiority of orthodox medicine still lay to some extent in the general education of its leaders rather than in any therapeutic advantage. Indeed, the mild practice of the homeopaths was probably safer than that followed by the regulars—though equally ineffective. Under these circumstances legislators chartered all sorts of medical schools, accepted cheap or even fraudulent diplomas, and left it to laymen to decide which type of practice was most helpful." Once again, the meaning of "cheap" and "fraudulent" in the context as Shryock describes it, is confused, to say the least. See Shryock, *Medical Licensing in America*, pp. 36–37.

35. William Snow Miller, "Dane County Medical Society," *Wisconsin Medical Journal*, 36 (November 1937), pp. 929–940; *Transactions of the Wisconsin State Medical Society for the Year 1868*, pp. 5–23 (hereafter cited as *WSMS Transactions*); Dr. Louis F. Frank, *The Medical History of Milwaukee, 1834–1914* (Milwaukee, Wisconsin, 1915), pp. 108–116.

36. *WSMS Transactions, 1868*, p. 11

37. Frank, pp. 127–138.

38. *Revised Statutes of the State of Wisconsin, 1849*, pp. 231–234.

39. *Revised Statutes of Wisconsin, 1878*, pp. 438–440.

40. *WSMS Transactions, 1880*, p. 46.

41. *Laws of Wisconsin, 1897*, Chapter 264, pp. 505–509.

42. William Snow Miller, "Medical Schools in Wisconsin: Past and Present," *Wisconsin Medical Journal*, 35 (June 1936), pp. 472–486; Frank, pp. 216–227; Paul F. Clark, *The University of Wisconsin Medical School: A Chronicle, 1848–1948* (Madison, Wisconsin, 1967).

43. *WSMS Transactions, 1855*, p. 27.

44. *Papers of the University of Wisconsin Board of Regents*, Box No. 1, File marked "Misc. Papers, 1849–59; Accounts & Warrants, 1857–58," located in the University of Wisconsin Memorial Library Archives, Madison, Wisconsin (hereafter cited as *Regents' Papers*). The letter is undated.

45. William S. Middleton, "The First Medical Faculty of the University of Wisconsin," *Wisconsin Medical Journal*, 54 (1955), pp. 378, 437. Middleton argues that Castleman's "position that this element of the University should be operated by the Medical profession as a separate educational entity was obviously untenable." Ibid., 437. At the time, however, there did exist precedents for the control of a medical school by a medical society in Vermont, Connecticut and New Hampshire. See Shafer, pp. 43–44.

46. *WSMS Transactions, 1868*, p. 77.

47. Quoted in William Snow Miller, "Medical Schools in Wisconsin," p. 481.

48. Ibid.

49. See, generally, Calhoun, pp. 59–87.

50. P. M. Reed, pp. 478–479; Berryman, Vol. 1, p. 337; *Reminiscences of the Bench and Bar of Dane County*, p. 39.

51. For an example of such a fee bill, see *Reminiscences of the Bench and Bar of Dane County*, pp. 39–41.

52. *General Laws of the State of Wisconsin, 1861*, Chapter 189, pp. 218–219.

53. Berryman, Vol. 1, pp. 329–330.

54. M. A. Hurley, "The Mission of the State Bar Association of Wisconsin," *WSBA Reports*, 9 (1911), p. 292.

Chapter Three

1. Chadbourne to Vilas, October 31, 1867, in the William F. Vilas *Papers*, State Historical Society of Wisconsin.

2. The only full-length biography of Vilas is Horace S. Merrill, *William Freeman Vilas: Doctrinaire Democrat* (Madison, Wisconsin, 1954).

3. Merrill, pp. 9–12; Burr W. Jones, "Colonel Vilas and the Law School," in *Memorial Service in Honor of William Freeman Vilas at the University of Wisconsin* (Madison, Wisconsin, 1908), p. 18.

4. Jones, p. 18; Merrill, pp. 14–21.

5. Jones, pp. 17–18; Merle Curti and Vernon Carstensen, *The University of Wisconsin: A History* (2 volumes; Madison, Wisconsin, 1949), Vol. 1, pp. 110–111.

6. *Minutes of the University of Wisconsin Board of Regents*, February 14, 1868, Vol. 3, pp. 94–95 (hereafter cited as *Regents' Minutes*); *Proceedings of the University of Wisconsin Board of Regents*, Vol. 1, p. 19 (hereafter cited as *Regents' Proceedings*).

7. Edward F. Grose, *Centennial History of the Village of Ballston Spa* (Ballston, New York, 1907), pp. 69–96. Although Cameron and Barron may have known each other before they became members of the University Board of Regents, it is unlikely that they met at Fowler's law school. Barron graduated from the school prior to 1851. In that year he moved to Wisconsin, settling first in Waukesha, then in Pepin, before finally making his permanent home in St. Croix Falls. Cameron, who was seven years older than Barron, graduated from the school in 1853, two years after Barron had left for Wisconsin. Before entering Fowler's school, Cameron had studied law in an attorney's office in Buffalo, New York, far to the west of Ballston Spa. Cameron moved to Wisconsin in 1857 and opened a law office in LaCrosse.

Biographical information on Barron can be found in Reuben G. Thwaites, *The University of Wisconsin* (Madison, Wisconsin, 1900), p. 272; John R. Berryman, *History of the Bench and Bar of Wisconsin* (2 volumes; Chicago, 1898), Vol. 1, p. 446; and Samuel S.

Lifield, Wisconsin Historical Society *Collections*, 9 (1880–82), pp. 405–409. For information on Angus Cameron, see the *Dictionary of Wisconsin Biography*, pp. 64–65; *Wisconsin Necrology*, Vol. 6, pp. 83a–84. Thwaites gives the date of Cameron's graduation from Fowler's law school as 1849—in which case he could have met Barron—but all other sources set the date in 1853.

8. "Report of the Committee on the Law Department," June 15, 1875, *Regents' Proceedings*, Vol. 2, p. 276. The Regents reported their reliance upon the example of the Albany Law School with "some satisfaction" because the Wisconsin Law Department had recently been under attack by the University president for its low admission and graduation standards.

9. *Regents' Proceedings*, Vol. 2, p. 36.

10. Ibid., pp. 57–60. The only reference to the Law Department in the Regents' minutes is the following: "The Report of the Committee on the Law Department was taken up and read and on motion adopted. Said report will be found recorded in the volume of 'Reports.' " *Regents' Minutes*, June 25, 1868, Vol. 3, p. 100.

11. "Report of the Executive Committee," *Regents' Proceedings*, June 22, 1880, Vol. 2, pp. 367–368. Not only was this proposal defeated but the Regents in the following year, when a two-year course formally was approved, raised the annual appropriation to forty-five hundred dollars plus all fees. *Regents' Minutes*, June 22, 1881, Vol. 3, pp. 366–367.

12. Burr W. Jones, "Colonel Vilas and the Law School," p. 18. A brief sketch of Carpenter's career is found in *History of Dane County: Biographical and Genealogical* (Madison, Wisconsin, 1906), pp. 151–152. Carpenter's salary of two thousand dollars was the same as that received by full-time professors in other departments of the University.

13. *Regents' Proceedings*, Vol. 2, pp. 57–60.

14. Jones, p. 18.

15. Alfred Zantzinger Reed, *Training for the Public Profession of the Law*, The Carnegie Foundation for the Advancement of Teaching, Bulletin Number 15 (Boston, 1921), p. 142.

16. G. G. Wright, *The Western Jurist*, 1 (1867), p. 10.

17. E. E. Bryant, Vilas' law partner, would become dean of the Wisconsin Law School in 1889. Vilas described him as having "a natural aptitude for literature. . . . In my estimation, Bryant's gifts were more addressed by nature to this pursuit even than his profession." *Madison Democrat*, May 31, 1904, newspaper clipping in *Wisconsin Necrology*, Vol. 7, pp. 137–138. Similarly, Charles N. Gregory, who became associate dean of the Law School in 1894, was in his younger years regarded (locally) as one of the rising poets of the time and was frequently styled in reviews as "The Bryant of the West." *Wisconsin Necrology*, Vol. 31, pp. 94–96.

18. Frederick A. Pike, *A Student at Wisconsin Fifty Years Ago: Reminiscences and Records of the Eighties* (Madison, Wisconsin, 1935), p. 81. A much more detailed account of the locations of the law department during the 1870s and 1880s can be found in William R. Johnson, "The University of Wisconsin, Law School: 1868–1930" (Ph.D. Dissertation, University of Wisconsin, 1972), pp. 140–145, 212–216. The same is true of all traditional categories of institutional growth: attendance, admission requirements, financing, etc.

19. University of Wisconsin *Catalog*, 1868–69, p. 17. The number of graduates is found in the *Regents' Minutes*, June 22, 1869, Vol. 3, pp. 111–112.

20. University of Wisconsin *Catalog*, 1868, p. 60.

21. Gilson G. Glasier, ed., *Autobiography of Roujet D. Marshall* (2 volumes; Madison, Wisconsin, 1923), Vol. 1, pp. 145–146.

22. Ibid., pp. 200–201.

23. Ibid,. pp. 218–219.

24. Ibid., pp. 245–254.

25. Ibid., pp. 225–226.

26. Ibid.

27. Ibid., p. 235.

28. Ibid., pp. 236–239. Marshall's rigorous examination given in open court, he later recalled, "was quite an unusual proceeding, one which had not occurred before and naturally attracted many persons to attend."

29. This is based on an examination of biographies containing information on the careers of lawyers who practiced in Wisconsin between 1840 and 1890. The bulk of these sketches, over five hundred in number, are found in John R. Berryman, *History of the Bench and Bar of Wisconsin;* and Parker McCobb Reed, *The Bench and Bar of Wisconsin* (Milwaukee, Wisconsin, 1882). Data from the biographies in the Berryman history have been codified and tabulated and is used to provide the basic statistical benchmarks for assessing the experience of Wisconsin lawyers and law students.

30. University of Wisconsin *Catalog*, 1871–72, p. 59.

31. Levi Bancroft to his mother, September 7, 1882, in the Levi Bancroft *Papers*, State Historical Society of Wisconsin.

32. Burr W. Jones, *Reminiscences of Nine Decades* (Evansville, Wisconsin, n.d.).

33. John M. Olin to C. C. Olin, October 18, 1892, in the John M. Olin *Papers*, State Historical Society of Wisconsin, Correspondence, Box 1, Folder 2.

34. Robert M. LaFollette, *LaFollette's Autobiography: A Personal Narrative of Political Experiences* (Madison, Wisconsin, 1913), pp. 3–5.

35. Berryman, Vol. 1, p. 246.

36. There existed some reason to make the transfer from a law school in another state. A student who wanted to practice in Wisconsin could complete the senior year at Madison and, under terms of the diploma privilege which automatically admitted to the bar, avoid the bar examination. As the discussion of the diploma privilege later in this chapter suggests, however, that may not have been a major attraction because admission through examination appears to have been a mere formality.

37. There is confusion over when the Wisconsin Law Department actually began a two-year course. From the catalogs it is clear that the students were divided into junior and senior classes beginning in 1878 but the Regents took no formal action to institute a two-year program until June, 1881. See *Regents' Minutes*, June 21, 1881, Vol. C., p. 360. What happened in the interim is not clear, though the faculty was apparently experimenting with a two-year course in which the junior and senior classes were offered in alternate years. They then tried a plan where the classes were offered simultaneously but first- and second-year students were so designated according to the year in which they had entered the law school, not by the courses they had taken. This absence of a clear sense of hierarchy among the legal studies is discussed at greater length in the next chapter.

38. See "Report of the Dean of the Law School Accompanying the Report of the President, June 24, 1890," *Regents' Papers*, Box 10; and "Report . . . [June 16, 1891]," ibid., for lists of students who entered the school after considerable office study. In 1898 the student newspaper reported that "it has been the practice for some law students to obtain situations in law offices and there to assist in the preparation of briefs and in the practice of law and still keep up their work in the law school." *The Daily Cardinal*, February 3, 1898, p. 1. As the phrasing suggests, this was no longer the normal practice.

39. "A Bill to provide for the admission to the bar of the graduates of the law department of the Wisconsin University," *Journal . . . Wisconsin Legislature, In Senate*, 1870, pp. 190, 218, 244, 246, 323–24, 348, 355, 360, 496, 513, 528, 550, 574. See also the *Assembly Journal*, 1870, pp. 664–700, 731–32, 867–69, 878, 919–20. The bill was introduced into the state Senate on February 12, 1870 by Senator William T. Price and was approved on March 15, 1870. No debate was recorded on the bill in either the Senate or the Assembly. For the text of the bill, see *Laws of Wisconsin*, 1870, Chapter 79, p. 135.

Presumably William F. Vilas and Harlow S. Orton, the latter then the dean of the Law Department, had a hand in the legislation although no definite links can be established between them and Senator Price. Orton and Vilas were Democrats. Price, a Republican and also a lawyer, was noted mainly for his activities in various transportation schemes, especially the promotion of railroads. For a biographical sketch of Price, see the *Dictionary of Wisconsin Biography*, p. 292.

40. Of the one hundred twenty-four lawyers with law school backgrounds identified through the analysis of the Berryman biographies, twenty-three attended the Albany Law School.

41. A. Z. Reed, pp. 250–251.

42. University of Wisconsin catalogs, 1868–1887. Until the late 1880s when more accurate records were kept, it is impossible to tell how much the law school actually received in fees. The tuition fee in the period between 1868 and 1876 averaged about fifty dollars. Therefore, the school would have had to attract at least forty fee-paying students to even equal the initial 1868 annual appropriation of two thousand dollars. But the total attendance did not rise above forty until 1878 and by that time the annual appropriation had been raised to three thousand dollars. It is clear, too, that not all students in attendance actually paid fees. Law School Dean Harlow Orton reported in 1871 that many of the students are poor and "None who could pay for their board and support in the City have been turned away on account of their inability to pay for their instruction." "Report of the Law School Dean," *Regents' Proceedings*, June 20, 1871, Vol. 2, p. 154. For evidence in the records that this practice continued, see *Regents' Minutes*, June 16, 1875, Vol. 3, pp. 229–230; ibid., June 20, 1882, Vol. 3, pp. 380–381; and *Regents' Proceedings*, June 18, 1888, Vol. 2, pp. 573–578.

43. *General Laws of the State of Wisconsin*, 1861, Chapter 189, pp. 218–219.

44. *The Laws of Wisconsin*, 1881, Chapter 144, pp. 152–153.

45. *The Laws of Wisconsin*, 1885, Chapter 63, pp. 50–52.

46. *Regents' Minutes*, January 17, 1872, Vol. 3, p. 165; *Regents' Proceedings*, Vol. 1, p. 42.

47. *Regents' Proceedings*, June 24, 1868, p. 58.

Chapter Four

1. Levi Bancroft to his mother, September 7, 1882, in the Levi Bancroft *Papers*, State Historical Society of Wisconsin.

2. *Dane County Census* (Mss.), 1860, 1870.

3. C. W. Butterfield, *History of Dane County, Wisconsin* (Chicago, 1880), p. 760.

4. *Madison City Directory, 1858–59* (Milwaukee, Wisconsin, 1858), pp. 86–87; *Madison City Directory, 1871–72*, A. Brainerd, comp. (Madison, Wisconsin, 1870), pp. 121–122; *Madison City Directory, 1880–81* (Madison, Wisconsin, 1880), p. 160.

5. *Dane County Census* (Mss.), 1870, pp. 498, 643, 644, 655.

6. *Madison City Directory, 1880–81*, pp. 66, 67, 71, 86, 100, 106, 125, 128, 136, 144, 145, 147, 153, 154, 156.

7. *University of Wisconsin Catalogs*, 1878–1885.

8. *The Aegis*, November 16, 1888, p. 10.

9. James Willard Hurst, *The Growth of American Law: The Law Makers* (Boston, 1950), p. 302.

10. Burr W. Jones, "Tendencies of Half a Century in Wisconsin Courts," *Wisconsin State Bar Association Reports*, Vol. 5 (1902–03), p. 161 (hereafter cited as *WSBA reports*).

11. Gilson G. Glasier, ed., *Autobiography of Roujet D. Marshall* (2 volumes; Madison, Wisconsin, 1923), Vol. 1, pp. 218–219, 225–226.

12. Hurst, p. 302.

13. Brown v. Swineford, *Wisconsin Reports*, Vol. 44, pp. 282–295.

14. On college literary societies generally, see Frederick Rudolph, *The American College*

and University: A History (New York: Vintage paper edition, 1965), pp. 137–146, 451–452. For information on literary societies at the University of Wisconsin, see Vincent H. Knauf, "The History of the Literary Societies at the University of Wisconsin" (Master's Thesis, University of Wisconsin, Madison, 1948).

15. See the history of the Society in the student yearbook, *The Trochos* (1887), p. 119. The constitution of the Society can be found in the *Minutes* of the E. G. Ryan Society on deposit in the University of Wisconsin Archives. The pages which contained the original constitution are torn from the minutes but a printed copy (of uncertain date) is in the file.

16. E. G. Ryan Society *Minutes*, March 1884, pp. 30–33. Almost a decade later the nature of the topics assigned for debate had not changed. In November, 1892, these questions were discussed: "Resolved, that the world's fair should be open on Sunday;" and "that ten percent tax on State Banks ought to be repealed." Ibid., Vol. 2, pp. 18–20.

17. Professor of Law William F. Vilas was one of the founders of the Hesperian Society in 1853 when he was an undergraduate at the University of Wisconsin. Burr W. Jones, also a professor in the Law School, was active in the Hesperian literary society during his undergraduate days.

18. E. G. Ryan Society *Minutes*, April 19, 1884, p. 36.

19. Ibid., February 20, 1885, p. 61.

20. *The Aegis*, October 1, 1886, p. 10.

21. Ibid.

22. In 1886, for example, one writer reported that the program committee of the E. G. Ryan intended "to introduce into the exercises, orations, theses, with accompanying critiques, music, &c., in fact anything that will raise the character of our entertainments and make them more pleasing." *The University Press*, October 1, 1886, p. 11.

23. *The University Badger* (1891), p. 76.

24. Ibid., p. 77.

25. *The Aegis*, May 17, 1889.

26. *The Daily Cardinal*, January 11, 1898, p. 11. For the founding of the other clubs, see: ibid., November 5, 1901, p. 1; ibid., October 23, 1902, p. 1; and ibid., November 26, 1902, p. 1.

27. *Law School Bulletin*, April, 1903, p. 14.

28. *The Daily Cardinal*, January 11, 1898, p. 1.

29. Ibid., November 5, 1901, p. 1.

30. *Law School Bulletin*, 1906–07, p. 6.

31. Ibid., 1911–12, p. 6.

32. Quoted in Ray A. Brown, "The Making of the Wisconsin Constitution," *Wisconsin Law Review* (July 1949), p. 669.

33. Ibid.

34. *The Revised Statutes of the State of Wisconsin*, 1849, p. 441.

35. *General Laws Passed by the Legislature of Wisconsin*, 1861, Chapter 189, pp. 152–153.

36. *WSBA Reports*, Vol. 1 (1878–1885), p. 8.

37. Ibid., pp. 1–3, 12–13, 16.

38. Ibid., pp. 16, 33.

39. John R. Berryman, ed., *History of the Bench and Bar of Wisconsin* (2 volumes; Chicago, 1898), Vol. 1, pp. 329–330.

40. Francis L. Wellman, "Admission to the Bar," *American Law Review* (May 1881), pp. 295–330.

41. Ibid., pp. 304–318. His recommendations are summarized in a series of eighteen rules on pp. 327–330.

42. Ibid., p. 318.

43. Ibid., p. 309.

44. The Committee silently dropped Wellman's eleventh rule which recommended that prizes be given to students who pass the best examinations in jurisprudence and Roman civil law. *WSBA Reports*, Vol. 1 (1881), p. 89.

45. Ibid.; Wellman, p. 239.

46. *The Laws of Wisconsin*, . . . *Legislature of 1885*, Chapter 63, pp. 50–52.

47. *University Catalogs*, 1885–86, 1887–88.

48. The basis for this statement is my own analysis of State Bar membership as reported in the *Reports* of the Association. The most careful estimate for the total number of lawyers in the state in each decade can be found in Lloyd K. Garrison, "A Survey of the Wisconsin Bar," *Wisconsin Law Review* (1935), pp. 129–169.

49. Elisha W. Keyes, "Wisconsin Bar in the Terrritorial Period," *WSBA Reports*, Vol. 2 (1886–1899), pp. 338–339. For another example of this mechanistic imagery used to describe new admission practices and procedures, see Burton Hanson's description of the career of Judah P. Benjamin, *WSBA Reports*, Vol. 7 (1906), p. 53.

50. *Regents' Proceedings*, June 18, 1872, Vol. 2, pp. 172–173.

51. *Regents' Minutes*, January 17, 1872, Vol. 3, p. 165; *Regents' Proceedings*, Vol. 1, p. 42.

52. *Regents' Proceedings*, January 21, 1873, Vol. 2, pp. 200–201.

53. *Regents' Minutes*, January 17, 1872, Vol. 3, p. 165; *Regents' Proceedings*, Vol. 1, p. 42.

54. Alfred Zantzinger Reed, *Training for the Public Profession of the Law*, The Carnegie Foundation for the Advancement of Teaching, Bulletin Number 15 (Boston, 1921), p. 171.

55. "Communication from the Law Faculty," *Regents' Proceedings*, June 15, 1875, Vol. 2, p. 274; "Report of Committee on Law Department," ibid., pp. 275–276.

56. "Report of Committee on Law Department," ibid., pp. 275–276.

57. *Regents' Minutes*, June 21, 1876, Vol. 3, p. 265.

58. Ibid., May 2, 1877, pp. 281–282.

59. Ibid., June 19, 1878, p. 320.

60. *University Catalog*, 1878–79.

61. A. Z. Reed, p. 172.

62. ["Recommendations of the Law Faculty"], *Regents' Proceedings*, June 17, 1879, Vol. 2, p. 360.

63. *University Catalog*, 1879–80.

64. Ibid., 1885–86, p. 86.

65. "Communication from Dean of Law Faculty," *Regents' Proceedings*, June 21, 1881, Vol. 2, p. 402.

66. *Regents' Minutes*, June 21 and June 22, 1881, Vol. C. pp. 360, 366–367.

67. Merle Curti and Vernon Carstensen, *The University of Wisconsin: A History* (2 volumes; Madison, Wisconsin, 1949), Vol. 1, pp. 307–316.

68. *University Catalog*, 1885–86, p. 86.

69. Ibid., pp. 86–87.

70. *Press and Badger*, December 12, 1885, p. 12.

71. In 1879 the faculty divided the graduating class into three categories according to their accomplishments. *Regents' Proceedings*, June 17, 1879, Vol. 2, p. 360.

72. *Press and Badger*, December 12, 1885, p. 12.

Chapter Five

1. On the changes in American higher education generally during this period, see Laurence R. Veysey, *The Emergence of the American University* (Chicago, 1965). An excellent study of the effects of that transformation on a single university is Robert A.

McCaughey, "The Transformation of American Academic Life: Harvard University, 1821–1892," *Perspectives in American History*, 8 (1974), pp. 239–332.

2. Merle Curti and Vernon Carstensen, *The University of Wisconsin: A History* (2 volumes; Madison, Wisconsin, 1949), Vol. 1, pp. 542, 443–448.

3. "Report of Board of Visitors, 1888," in *Reports of the University of Wisconsin Board of Regents*, 1888 (hereafter cited as *Regents' Reports*).

4. "Report of the Law Committee of the Regents," in *Papers of the University of Wisconsin Board of Regents*, Box 9, folder dated June 19, 1888 (hereafter cited as *Regents' Papers*).

5. "Report of the Law School Dean," in *Proceedings of the University of Wisconsin Board of Regents*, June 20, 1871, Vol. 2, p. 154 (hereafter cited as *Regents' Proceedings*).

6. *Minutes of the University of Wisconsin Board of Regents*, June 16, 1875, Vol. 3, pp. 229–230 (hereafter cited as *Regents' Minutes*).

7. For evidence that the practice continued in 1882, see *Regents' Minutes*, June 20, 1882, Vol. 3, pp. 380–381.

8. "Report of the Law Committee of the Regents," *Regents' Papers*, Box 9, folder dated June 19, 1888. The Committee also noted that "new law schools have been started during the past year and still others are contemplated which will tend to draw from our school unless we move forward in a well defined line of improvement." The University of Minnesota Law School, founded in 1888, was probably one of the schools referred to in the report.

9. *Regents' Papers*, Box 9, folder dated September 4, 1888.

10. *Biennial Report of the Regents*, . . . 1888, p. 45.

11. *Regents' Papers*, Box 9, folder dated June 18, 1889. Chamberlin also considered the establishment of a graduate degree in law: "I would further advise that a graduate course of one year be offered, and that at the conclusion of this the degree of Master of Laws be granted. This plan, essentially, will be presented by the Faculty of the Law School of the University of Michigan to the Board of Regents of that institution with a strong recommendation that it be adopted. This is essentially the course now given at Cornell University. There would come to us great advantages from advancing our course at this time jointly with Michigan and putting ourselves upon the same grade as Cornell. It does not seem to me that we can at the present time wisely insist upon three full years work before granting the first degree, but the proposed plan does not require more for the first degree and for admission to the bar than the demands of public sentiment seem to me now to warrant." Ibid., p. 9. This section of Chamberlin's Report was crossed out in the copy in the Regents' files and was not adopted.

12. The Law Department was renamed the College of Law under terms of the University Reorganization Act of 1889. This act divided the University into the College of Letters and Science, the College of Mechanics and Engineering, the College of Agriculture and the College of Law. It provided the basic structure under which the deans of the various colleges were later named. For most colleges, particularly that of Letters and Science, the act represented a decentralization of authority; for the College of Law, which had never been an integral part of the University, the act represented a consolidation of the school into the University administration. *Laws of Wisconsin*, 1889, Chapter 273, Vol. 1, pp. 301–302.

13. Tribute by William F. Vilas after Bryant's death, reported in the *Madison Democrat*, May 31, 1904, *Wisconsin Necrology*, Vol. 7, pp. 136–137.

14. The information in this and the following paragraphs has been collected from various sources. The University catalogs list the members of the law school faculty and their dates of service while the *Regents' Annual Report to the Legislature* gives the membership of the various Regent Committees. The Regent Committee on the Law Department was established in 1874. Biographical information on the Regents and the law school

faculty, which often includes information on professional and personal ties, can be found in the sketches of prominent lawyers contained in the volumes of the *Wisconsin State Bar Association Reports*, in the *History of Dane County: Biographical and Genealogical* (Madison, Wisconsin, 1906), in the *Wisconsin Necrology*, and in John R. Berryman, ed., *History of the Bench and Bar of Wisconsin* (2 volumes; Chicago, 1898). The William F. Vilas *Papers* were of tangential help in establishing some of the relationships among faculty and Regents. I am indebted to Maurice Leon, Professor of Law at the University of Wisconsin Law School, for initially pointing out the existence of this closely knit group of lawyers.

15. *The Chicago Times*, Saturday, April 2, 1892; clipping in the *Vilas Collection of Newspaper Clippings*, State Historical Society of Wisconsin.

16. Biographical sketches of Bryant can be found in *Wisconsin Necrology*, Vol. 7, pp. 136–139; *Wisconsin Supreme Court Reports*, Vol. 122 (1904), pp. xxxi–xxxviii; and Berryman, Vol. 2, p. 337.

17. *Madison Democrat*, May 31, 1904 newspaper clipping in *Wisconsin Necrology*, Vol. 7, pp. 137–138.

18. *University Catalog*, 1889–90, pp. 171–174; ibid., 1869–70, p. 68; ibid., 1889–90, p. 176.

19. E. E. Bryant, "Legal Education," *WSBA Reports*, Vol. 2 (1886–1899), p. 148.

20. "Communication," Dean of the Law Faculty [Bryant] to President of the University [Chamberlin] . . . , *Regents' Papers*, Box 9, folder dated January 21, 1890. "Each student," Bryant reported, "except for a few who are in law offices will prepare complete papers for [submission] to judgment."

21. "President's Report," *Regents' Proceedings*, September 4, 1888, Vol. 2, pp. 585–586; *Regents' Minutes*, June 19, 1889, Vol. 4, p. 32. The new admission standards were printed in the *University Catalog*, 1888–89, p. 172, even though they were not formally approved by the Regents until the June 1889 annual meeting.

22. Alfred Zantzinger Reed, *Training for the Public Profession of the Law*, The Carnegie Foundation for the Advancement of Teaching, Bulletin Number 15 (Boston, 1921), p. 319. By 1890 the Columbia and Ohio State law schools had entrance requirements substantially the same as those required for admission to the college itself. Columbia required an exam in Latin as did the University of Pennsylvania Law School; Harvard required an examination in a foreign language, English and Blackstone.

23. *University Catalog*, 1892–93, pp. 131–132.

24. "Report of the Board of Visitors," quoted in "Report of the Committee on the Law Department," in *Regents' Minutes*, June 18, 1895, Vol. 4, pp. 346–347.

25. Bryant to R. H. Jesse, November 19, 1895, *Law School General Correspondence*, Letterbook, Vol. 1, p. 324.

26. Ibid.

27. Gregory to Charles E. Williams, November 29, 1895, ibid., pp. 332–333.

28. Woolsey to C. A. Green, July 8, 1896, ibid., p. 601.

29. Bryant to George H. Noyes, September 3, 1897, ibid., Letterbook, Vol. 2, p. 140.

30. *University Catalog*, 1889–90, p. 179.

31. Ibid., 1897–98, p. 264. Special students were required to be twenty-three years of age, an indication that the ruling was designed to meet the needs of students who were unable to afford the expense of a traditional academic education. See also *Regents' Minutes*, June 22, 1897, Vol. 5, pp. 3–4.

32. The story is recounted by William F. Vilas in a tribute paid to Bryant and reported in the *Madison Democrat*, May 31, 1904. See *Wisconsin Necrology*, Vol. 7, pp. 136–137.

33. Associate Dean Gregory wrote a classic letter in this genre. Writing not to a parent but to a student who had informed Gregory of an illness which prevented him from attending classes, Gregory replied: "I am extremely sorry to know that you are laid up, and hope sincerely you are getting better. I missed you from my classes especially because

I counted you one of my best students, and speaking of the matter on Friday night at the faculty meeting, was astonished to have the other gentlemen present say that you were attending their classes regularly. Of course it only shows how difficult it is to keep personal track of classes of one hundred and twenty-five men, and that the other gentlemen were mistaken." Gregory to E. P. McClure, April 25, 1895, *Law School General Correspondence*, Letterbook, Vol. 1, p. 95.

34. Bryant to E. A. Birge, October 20, 1900, *Law School General Correspondence*, Letterbook, Vol. 3, p. 607–612.

35. For details on the various locations of the Department of Law during the 1870s and 1880s, and for examples of the criticism leveled against the school's quarters, see: William R. Johnson, "The University of Wisconsin Law School, 1868–1930" (Ph.D. Dissertation, University of Wisconsin, Madison, 1972), especially pp. 140–144. The reader interested in the details of the construction of the new law building in the 1890s should consult the discussion in that dissertation on pp. 212–215.

36. *Laws of Wisconsin*, 1891, Chapter 29.

37. *Regents' Minutes*, April 8, 1891, Vol. D, pp. 92–93.

38. *The Daily Cardinal*, December 21, 1892, p. 7; and ibid., January 31, 1893, p. 1.

39. The twenty thousand dollars from the Jackson bequest was invested at five per cent interest and during the remainder of the decade one thousand dollars of Professor Jairus H. Carpenter's salary was paid through this outside source. Judge Mortimer Jackson had made it a condition of his will that Carpenter be elected the first Jackson Professor of Law. *Regents' Minutes*, January 21, 1890, Vol. 4, pp. 53–56.

40. *Regents' Minutes*, January 21, 1896, Vol. 4, p. 429. Two years earlier the Regents had voted that "the College of Law be made a separate Department and that its funds and accounts be kept separate from other departments." Ibid., June 20, 1894, Vol. 4, p. 284. This resolution was not put into effect and the measure was again passed at the March 6, 1896 meeting of the Board. Ibid., Vol. 4, p. 436.

41. *Regents' Minutes*, April 21, 1896, Vol. 4, p. 449.

42. *Regents' Minutes*, June 18, 1901, Vol. 5, p. 446; ibid., April 15, 1902, Vol. 5, p. 534.

43. *Regents' Minutes*, April 21, 1896, Vol. 4, pp. 470, 465.

44. *Regents' Minutes*, June 19, 1888, Vol. 3, p. 563. Students taking the two-year course paid two-thirds of one hundred dollars for the first year and one-third for the second year. That was calculated to maximize the income from tuition fees because many students attended only the first year and used the knowledge gained to pass the bar examination. The advance in fees was originally set for the year 1888–89 but at the same meeting it was decided to make the advance effective the following year.

45. *Regents' Minutes*, September 16, 1890, Vol. 4, p. 86; ibid., June 19, 1894, Vol. 4, p. 282; ibid., June 18, 1895, Vol. 4, p. 344.

46. Curti and Carstensen, Vol. 1, p. 581, footnote 3.

47. There had been rumors of the establishment of a three-year course in the 1880s. See *The Aegis*, January 14, 1887, p. 10. From the point of view of the law student, the three-year sequence represented an attempt to enforce a two-year program. A writer in *The Aegis* said that "it looks as if a three years' course will, before many years, be required at every first class law school in the country. This would preclude anyone from completing the law course in one year's study in a law school, and compel the student to devote two whole years to work in a law school before he could obtain his degree as a Bachelor of Laws." *The Aegis*, March 9, 1888, p. 10. The first formal recommendation that a three-year program be created was made by University President Chamberlin in 1892. *Regents' Minutes*, April 19, 1892, Vol. 4, p. 158. The Regents officially approved the action, without discussion, two years later. *Regents' Minutes*, June 19, 1894, Vol. 4, p. 276.

48. Reed, pp. 171, 178.

49. *University Catalogs*, 1888–89 through 1903–04, various paginations.

50. *Catalog of Alumni and Faculty, 1848–1905*.

51. Bryant to Charles Kendall Adams, March 17, 1898, *Law School General Correspondence*, Letterbook, Vol. 2, pp. 367–371.

52. Reed, p. 452.

53. Ibid., p. 442.

54. Gregory to W. T. Kelsey, April 25, 1901, *Law School General Correspondence*, Letterbook, Vol. 2, p. 808.

55. Quoted in *A History of the School of Law, Columbia University*, prepared by the Staff of the Foundation for Research in Legal History under the direction of Julius Goebel, Jr. (New York, 1955), p. 35.

56. Reed, pp. 280–283.

57. Ibid.

58. For a more detailed discussion of the spread of the Harvard influence see Robert Stevens, "Two Cheers for 1870: The American Law School," *Perspectives in American History*, 5 (1971), pp. 435–441.

59. *Record of the Commemoration, November Fifth to Eighth, 1886, on the Two Hundred and Fiftieth Anniversary of the Founding of Harvard College* (1887), pp. 97–98, quoted in Arthur E. Sutherland, *The Law at Harvard* (Cambridge, Massachusetts, 1967), p. 175.

60. Ibid.

61. James Willard Hurst, "Changing Responsibilities of the Law School: 1868–1968," *Wisconsin Law Review* (1968), p. 336.

62. A superb analysis of the emergence of law teaching as a vocation can be found in Jerold S. Auerbach, "Enmity and Amity: Law Teachers and Practitioners, 1900–1922," *Perspectives in American History*, 5 (1971), pp. 551–601.

63. Quoted in ibid., p. 551.

64. In 1901 James Barr Ames, fittingly, delivered an address titled "The Vocation of the Law Professor," which was essentially a call to professionalize the career of law teaching. At the time that Ames spoke only about one-quarter of American law teachers were full-time but, he predicted, "these proportions ought to be, and are likely to be, reversed in the next generation." James Barr Ames, "The Vocation of the Law Professor," in *Lectures on Legal History and Miscellaneous Legal Essays* (Cambridge, Massachusetts, 1913), p. 360. See also Auerbach, "Enmity and Amity," pp. 552–553.

65. *Wisconsin Necrology*, Vol. 31, pp. 94–96.

66. Quoted in Charles Forster Smith, *Charles Kendall Adams: A Life-Sketch* (Madison, Wisconsin, 1924), p. 16. The person who made these remarks was identified only as "one of the leading historical scholars of the country." ibid.

67. For an excellent discussion of the European and especially the German influence on American historical scholarship during this period, see Jurgen Herbst, *The German Historical School in American Scholarship: A Study in the Transfer of Culture* (Ithaca, New York, 1965).

68. Charles Kendall Adams to Moses Coit Tyler, June 9, 1883, quoted in Smith, pp. 15–16.

69. Ibid., p. 44.

70. Ibid. See also Gregory to Stuart MacKibbin, February 27, 1896, *Law School General Correspondence*, Letterbook, Vol. 1, p. 428.

71. Gregory to James Barr Ames, December 4, 1895, ibid., p. 373.

72. Gregory to George H. Noyes, April 30, 1897, ibid., pp. 963–964.

73. Auerbach, p. 552.

74. Edwin E. Bryant, "Legal Education" (1895), *WSBA Reports*, Vol. 2 ([1886–] 1899), p. 141.

75. *The Aegis*, May 31, 1889, p. 10.

76. University *Catalog*, 1896, pp. 216–219; Burr W. Jones, *Reminiscences of Nine Decades* (Evansville, Wisconsin, n.d.), p. 97.

77. Bryant to Adams, March 17, 1898, *Law School General Correspondence*, Letterbook, Vol. 2, pp. 367–371.

78. Bryant to Adams, March 16, 1900, ibid., Vol. 3, pp. 328–330.

79. R. M. Bashford to Bryant, May 19, 1900, *Law School General Correspondence*, Box 1, file A–D. Bashford's letter ran for six pages. Olin's letter was ten pages in length. John M. Olin to Bryant, May 30, 1900, in the John M. Olin *Papers*, Correspondence, Box 1, folder 2 (1896–1900), State Historical Society of Wisconsin.

80. *Regents' Minutes*, August 6, 1895, Vol. 4, p. 372; Reuben G. Thwaites, *The University of Wisconsin: Its History and Alumni, 1836–1900* (Madison, Wisconsin, 1900), p. 586.

81. William L. Drew to C. K. Adams, August 31, 1896, *Regents' Papers*, Box 14, file marked September 15, 1896.

82. James Barr Ames to C. K. Adams, August 26, 1896, ibid.; C. S. Montgomery to C. K. Adams, August 31, 1896, ibid.

83. University *Catalog*, 1896, p. 210; ibid., 1897, p. 259.

84. Warren D. Tarrant, "Andrew A. Bruce," *Wisconsin Alumni Magazine*, 13 (1911–12), pp. 114–117. One of Bruce's enduring legacies to his alma mater was the introduction of football to the campus; he was popularly known as "The Father of Football at Wisconsin." Andrew A. Bruce, "The Beginnings of Football at Wisconsin," ibid., 15 (1913–14), pp. 15–16.

85. *Regents' Minutes*, June 16, 1901, Vol. 5, p. 397.

86. Ibid., June 17, 1902, Vol. 5, p. 539.

87. On Gilmore's election to the faculty, see *Regents' Minutes*, September 16, 1902, Vol. 5, pp. 585–86. A biographical sketch can be found in Association of American Law Schools, *Directory of Teachers in Member Schools* (1928), p. 37. Gilmore, like Smith, would remain on the Wisconsin law faculty until the 1920s, although the last decade of his service was spent on leave as vice-governor and then governor of the Philippines.

88. Bryant died on August 11, 1903, while on a trip to the east coast to attend a meeting of the American Fishery Society and to visit the place of his birth in Vermont. See newspaper clippings from the *Madison Democrat*, August 12, 1903, in *Wisconsin Necrology*, Vol. 7, pp. 136–139. For Richards' background, see William Herbert Page, "Dean Harry Sanger Richards," *Wisconsin Law Review*, 5 (December 1929), pp. 257–264; and Oliver S. Rundell, "Dean H. S. Richards—A Leader," *The Wisconsin Alumni Magazine* (May 1929), pp. 254ff.

89. Edwin E. Bryant, "Legal Education" (1895), *Reports of the Wisconsin State Bar Association*, Vol. 2 ([1886–] 1899), pp. 142–144.

90. Ibid., p. 145.

91. Gilson G. Glasier (ed.), *Autobiography of Roujet D. Marshall: Justice of the Supreme Court, of the State of Wisconsin, 1895–1918* (Madison, Wisconsin, 1923), Vol. 1, p. 224.

92. Berryman, Vol. 1, p. 248.

93. Ibid., p. 152.

94. Ibid., p. 218. Judge Charles Dunn was described in similar terms: He "paid little attention to the reported cases, never troubling with them except when they were thrust upon his consideration by his opponent." Ibid., p. 72.

Chapter Six

1. The prevailing view is that the academically selective university law school was in some sense the creature of the professional and especially corporate elite during the late

nineteenth and early twentieth centuries. It is certainly true that the emphasis upon academic measures of talent meshed nicely with the needs of the corporate law firms. Not only were they able to skim the cream of talent off the surface of the graduating seniors from the most prestigious university schools, they also were able to use the high entrance standards of those law schools as a device to exclude from the top ranks of the profession lower class students and students from ethnic and racial backgrounds other than white, Anglo-Saxon protestant. But there is little direct evidence that the demands of such firms created the essential outlines of the new university law school. The argument for such influence is mainly one of propinquity: powerful and exclusive corporate law firms recruited from those university law schools with the highest academic requirements. The evidence from Wisconsin, however, suggests that the elite practitioners merely used what schoolmen already had invented.

2. *Regents' Minutes*, June 16, 1903, Vol. 6, p. 107. Bryant here is listed as professor of law at a salary for the next year of twenty-five hundred dollars. In the resolution passed by the Regents after Bryant's death, the Board noted that he had asked to be relieved of his administrative duties in order to devote his time to teaching and research. A copy of the resolution is in the *Regents' Papers*, Box 20, September, 1903 meeting file. See also Harry S. Richards, "Dean's Report," 1904, *Regents' Report*, 1902–04, p. 115. Richards was elected dean of the College of Law on June 16, 1903. *Regents' Minutes*, June 16, 1903, Vol. 6, p. 50. Richards remained in Iowa through the summer and arrived in Madison to assume his new duties in early September, 1903.

3. When Dean Richards of the Wisconsin Law School announced in 1903, for example, that two years of college training would thereafter be necessary for admission to the College of Law, the Wisconsin State Bar Association had just succeeded in convincing the state legislature to advance the standard of preliminary training for entry into the legal profession to a high school education or its equivalent. George H. Noyes, chairman of the Association's Committee on Legal Education, found that move "gratifying," and he believed "that no serious defects are apparent calling for correction or changes in the present methods of legal education." *Laws of Wisconsin*, 1903, Chapter 19, pp. 30–32; "Report of the Committee on Legal Education, *WSBA Reports*, Vol. 6 (1904–05), pp. 30–31.

4. William Herbert Page, "Dean Harry Sanger Richards," *Wisconsin Law Review*, 5 (December 1929), pp. 257–264; Oliver S. Rundell, "Dean H. S. Richards—A Leader," *The Wisconsin Alumni Magazine*, 30 (May 1929), pp. 254ff.

5. See the various letters of recommendation filed in the *Regents' Papers*, Box 19, file marked June 19, 1903. Among the people whose judgment was sought were John H. Wigmore of the Northwestern University Law School and Joseph H. Beale and James Barr Ames of the Harvard Law School.

Wigmore informed President Van Hise that "should you care for a person not too deeply infected with modern methods, I name Professor [John R.] Rood of Michigan," a suggestion that was ignored. Rood, however, was rapidly becoming "infected" with case study. In 1902 he began to teach a course in execution, attachment and garnishment using only a case book. Elizabeth G. Brown, *Legal Education at Michigan, 1859–1959* (Ann Arbor, Michigan, 1959), p. 204.

6. Memorandum of interview by Gilmore with Professor Hays of the Iowa law faculty in *Regents' Papers*, Box 19, file marked June 19, 1903.

7. Memorandum of interview with Judge M. M. McClain of the Iowa Supreme Court and former chancellor of the Iowa Law School in ibid. See also the memorandum of the interview with Professor Hays.

8. H. S. Richards to Richard F. Tobias, January 2, 1905, *Law School General Correspondence*, Letterbook, Vol. 4, p. 944.

9. *Law School Announcement*, 1904–05, 1910–11.

10. Richards to Tobias, January 2, 1905, loc. cit.

11. Josef Redlich, *The Common Law and the Case Method in American Law Schools*, A Report to the Carnegie Foundation for the Advancement of Teaching, Bulletin Number Eight (New York, 1914), pp. 49–50. See also Robert Stevens, "The American Law School," *Perspectives in American History*, 5 (1971), pp. 441–449.

12. Willard Hurst, "Changing Responsibilities of the Law School: 1868–1968," *Wisconsin Law Review* (1968) p. 338.

13. "Dean's Report," *Regents' Report*, 1910–12, p. 142.

14. *Law School Announcement*, 1903–04, 1904–05; "Dean's Report," *Regents' Report*, 1904–06, p. 140.

15. Alfred Zantzinger Reed, *Training for the Public Profession of the Law*, The Carnegie Foundation for the Advancement of Teaching, Bulletin Number 15 (Boston, 1921), p. 379; Stevens, "The American Law School," pp. 447ff.

16. Quoted in Martin Mayer, *The Lawyers* (New York: Dell paper edition, 1968), p. 88.

17. Redlich, pp. 49–50.

18. Quoted in Julius Goebel, *A History of the School of Law, Columbia University* (New York, 1955), p. 144. See also Stevens, "The American Law School . . .," p. 443.

19. "Dean's Report," *Regents' Report*, 1904–06, p. 140.

20. "Report of Dean Richards," *Regents' Report*, 1902–04, p. 117. Technically the administration of the examination for admission had been in the hands of the University registrar since 1895. See also, "Dean's Report," *Regents' Report*, 1904–06, p. 143.

21. "Report of Dean Richards," 1902–04, p. 116.

22. "Report of the Sub-committee on College of Law [Board of Visitors]," April 11, 1902, in *Regents' Report*, 1900–1902, p. 67.

23. *Minutes of the Law Faculty*, March 4, 1904, Vol. 1, pp. 105–109; *Regents' Minutes*, April 19, 1904, Vol. 6, pp. 141–142; "Report of Dean Richards," *Regents' Report*, 1902–04, p. 119.

24. "Report of Dean Richards," 1902–04, p. 119.

25. "Report of Dean Richards," *Regents' Report*, 1904–06, p. 119; *Law School Bulletin*, 1905–06, p. 14.

26. The attendance figures are taken from the dean's reports for the various years. See also a "List of graduated special students . . . ," in *Law School General Subject Files*, Box 15. The law school had no hard and fast rule about the level of attainment special students needed to be eligible for the LL.B., but Richards informed one prospective student that "we feel that if a student obtains an average of 85% or in that neighborhood, he is doing a grade of work which entitles us to overlook his deficiencies in preparation." Richards to C. W. Wendlandt, August 1, 1907, *Law School General Correspondence*, Box 15, File W.

27. *Law School Bulletin*, May, 1904, pp. 10–11; *Law School Announcement*, 1907–08, p. 14.

28. Richards to Professor Frederick C. Woodward, January 3, 1911, *Law School General Correspondence*, Box 11, File W–Z; "Report of Dean Richards," *Regents' Report*, 1902–04, pp. 120–121; *Regents' Minutes*, June 1, 1905, Vol. 6, p. 254; "Report of the Law School Dean," *Regents' Report*, 1908–10, p. 185; ibid., 1918–20, p. 116.

29. Howard L. Smith, "Relation of the College of Law to the University," *Wisconsin Alumni Magazine*, 5 (1903–04), pp. 66–67.

30. "Report of Dean Richards," *Regents' Report*, 1902–04, p. 122.

31. Richards to Major C. Mead, May 20, 1905, *Law School General Correspondence*, Letterbook, Vol. 5, pp. 137–138.

32. Richards to members of the Regent Committee on the Law School, April 9, 1909, *Law School General Correspondence*, Box 8, File L. See also Richards to President Van Hise, April 8, 1909, ibid., Box 9, File TUV.

33. Richards to President Van Hise and the Board of Regents, June 13, 1911, *Law School General Correspondence*, Box 13, File TUV. After the Regents raised Gilmore's salary to four thousand dollars, Professor Smith also asked for that amount. The Regents were reluctant

to meet that demand but Smith successfully used a tentative offer from Stanford University as leverage. Richards to Mack, January 8, 1912, *Law School General Correspondence*, Box 12, File M.

34. Eldon R. James resigned after one year of service to accept a position in the University of Minnesota Law School; Ernest G. Lorenzen, after three years of service, also accepted a position at Minnesota; and perhaps the greatest loss, William Underhill Moore, appointed to the Wisconsin faculty in June, 1908, resigned in June, 1914, to accept a position as professor of law in the University of Chicago Law School. "Dean's Report," *Regents' Report*, 1912–14, p. 146.

35. Ibid., 1914–16, pp. 153–154.

36. James Willard Hurst, *The Growth of American Law: The Law Makers* (Boston, 1950), p. 311.

37. Lloyd K. Garrison, "A Survey of the Wisconsin Bar," *Wisconsin Law Review*, 10 (1934–35), p. 150.

38. Richards to Professor Frederick C. Woodward, January 3, 1911, *Law School General Correspondence*, Box 11, File W–Z.

39. Statistics on attendance and graduates have been gathered from the law school catalogs and, when available, from the dean's annual report.

Compared to other law schools during this period, Wisconsin remained of medium size. In 1900 the Michigan Law School enrolled eight hundred eighty-three students; the New York School, seven hundred seventy-five students; New York University Law School, six hundred thirty-four; Harvard, six hundred sixteen; Minnesota, five hundred twenty-eight; and Boston Law School, four hundred nine. In 1910, Harvard led in attendance with eight hundred ten students, followed by Michigan (seven hundred ninety-two), New York Law School (seven hundred fifty-one), Georgetown (seven hundred seventeen), New York University (six hundred seventy-nine) and Chicago Kent (five hundred ninety-one). Reed, *Training for the Public Profession of the Law*, p. 452.

40. *Regents' Minutes*, June 16, 1903, Vol. 6, p. 88; "Report of the Dean of the Law College," *Regents' Report*, 1904–06, p. 138; *Laws of Wisconsin*, 1907, Chapter 105, p. 787. This act was approved May 15, 1907. *Regents' Minutes*, June 18, 1907, Vol. 7, p. 3. For a detailed breakdown of the money expended on the law school compared to the support given other colleges in the University during the years between 1900 and 1903, see Howard L. Smith, "Relation of the College of Law to the University," *Wisconsin Alumni Magazine*, 5 (1903–04), pp. 64–71.

41. Reed, p. 443.

42. Alfred Zantzinger Reed, in *Training for the Public Profession of the Law*, and in his later work, *Present-Day Law Schools in the United States and Canada*, The Carnegie Foundation for the Advancement of Teaching, Bulletin Number 21 (Boston, 1928), recommended that the differentiation among schools, based upon function and class distinctions, be officially recognized by the American Bar Association. That position was rejected by both the ABA and the AALS. Ironically, because Reed adopted the categories of analysis favored by the AALS and because of the thoroughness of his work, his two volumes had the effect of setting the terms in which most present analysis of legal education has been done.

43. Charles N. Gregory, "The Past and Present of the Association of American Law Schools," *Proceedings of the Association of American Law Schools* (1909), pp. 44–45 (hereafter cited as *AALS Proceedings*).

44. Reed, *Training for the Public Profession*, p. 443; Stevens, pp. 459–460.

45. V. W. Dittman, "History of the Marquette Law School," *Marquette Law Review*, 8 (June 1924), pp. 299–300; Ralph N. Hamilton, S.J., *The Story of Marquette University* (Milwaukee, Wisconsin, 1953).

46. "Interview with President Burrowes," unidentified, undated, newspaper clipping, *Scrapbook*, No. 18, p. 16, Marquette University Archives. The position in the scrapbook suggests that the date of the clipping is between May 28 and June 5, 1906.

47. These details are taken from an "Account of the beginning of the Law Department" prepared by Father H. S. Spalding, first Regent of the School, prepared on October 12, 1908 and located in *Scrapbook*, No. 18, p. 41, Marquette University Archives. In an addendum written the following day, Father Spalding noted that Marquette also bought the Milwaukee University School of Law, a proprietary school begun in 1905 by three local lawyers. Marquette paid four hundred eighty-five dollars for the school (forty-five dollars for the advertising costs of the three lawyers and forty dollars for each of the eleven students who then transferred to Marquette). Ibid., October 13, 1908.

48. The early records of the Marquette Law School, if any were systematically kept, have not been located. Miscellaneous correspondence and reports are available after about 1916. The information on the school's early history has been gathered mainly from the catalogs. There is a complete run of such catalogs with the exception of the year 1913. The quote from Dean Schoetz is from a speech prepared sometime in 1924 for delivery at the Wisconsin State Bar Association annual meeting and can be found in the *Law School Miscellaneous Records and Correspondence*, UNIV/C-3/Series 1/Box 1, Marquette University Archives.

49. An announcement prepared by the students in the law school "after consultation with the Trustees of the University and with the approbation of the Dean of the School," undated [approximately 1909–10], in *Scrapbook*, No. 18, p. 45, Marquette University Archives.

50. Richards to Henry M. Bates, March 4, 1911, *Law School General Correspondence*, Box 11, File B.

51. *Law School Bulletin*, 1906–07, p. 6.

52. Richards to Edwin S. Mack, March 31, 1910, *Law School General Correspondence*, Box 10, File M.

53. Richards to Howard L. Smith, April 26, 1910, ibid., Box 11, File S.

54. Richards to G. D. Jones, July 30, 1910, ibid., Box 10, File I–J.

55. Ibid.

56. Richards to Clair B. Bird, November 2, 1914, ibid., Box 17, File B.

57. Abraham Flexner, *Medical Education in the United States and Canada*, The Carnegie Foundation for the Advancement of Teaching, Bulletin Number Four (Boston, 1910). For examples of contemporary fascination with what medical doctors had accomplished, see Harry S. Richards, "Progress in Legal Education," *AALS Proceedings* (1915) pp. 60–76; and E. M. Morgan, "The Legal Clinic," ibid. (1916), pp. 146–155.

58. Preble Stolz, "Clinical Experience in American Legal Education," in *Clinical Education and the Law School of the Future* (University of Chicago Law School, 1970), pp. 54–76. Reprinted as *Research Contributions of the American Bar Foundation* (1970), No. 1.

59. O. L. McCaskill, "Discussion Remarks," *AALS Proceedings* (1916), pp. 43–44.

60. Richards to Edwin S. Mack, March 31, 1910, *Law School General Correspondence*, Box 10, File M.

61. *Law Faculty Minutes*, December 4, 1913, Vol. 2, p. 55. The resolution was introduced by Howard L. Smith at the October 23, 1913 meeting; ibid., p. 52. It was officially accepted by the Regents in 1914. *Regents' Minutes*, January 21, 1914, Vol. 9, p. 68. A circular announcing the program to the bar is filed in the *Law School General Subject File*, Box 5, "Regents' Recommendation on Clerkship."

62. Richards to Van Hise, December 4, 1913, *Law School General Correspondence*, Box 16, File TUV.

63. Richards to Professor George P. Costigan, March 9, 1911, *Law School General Correspondence*, Box 11, File C.

64. *Marquette University Law School Bulletins*, 1907–1917. A convenient summary of the rules governing member schools and the changes made over the years can be found in *AALS Proceedings* (1924), pp. 19–25.

65. "Supplemental Report of [the AALS] Executive Committee," December 28, 1916, in *Law School Miscellaneous Records and Correspondence*, Marquette University Archives.

66. Report by Max Schoetz, Jr., Carl B. Rix, and Erich C. Stern to Rev. H. C. Noonan, S.J., President of Marquette University, December 21, 1916, pp. 2–3, ibid.

67. Dean Schoetz to Walter D. Corrigan, June 17, 1918, ibid.

68. See the letter from E. A. Gilmore, Secretary of the Executive Committee, to Marquette President H. C. Noonan, December 1, 1916, ibid.

69. Reed, *Training for the Public Profession*, pp. 259–270; Francis L. Wellman, "Admission to the Bar," *American Law Review* (May 1881), pp. 318–322.

70. Gregory to unidentified correspondent, March 15, 1898, *Law School General Correspondence*, Letterbook, Vol. 2, p. 362.

71. Richards to W. S. Pattee, September 23, 1907, ibid., Box 5, File P.

72. Bill 1024A was introduced into the Wisconsin Assembly on March 12, 1913. A copy of the bill is filed in the *Law School General Subject Files*, 11/1/2, Box 10, folder marked "Misc. legislation affecting the Law School."

73. A. W. Richter, "Reform in the Requirements for Admission to the Bar in Wisconsin," *The American Law School Review* (Winter 1914), p. 437.

74. "Memorandum of objections to that part of Assembly Bill 1024A which repeals the existing law whereby graduates of the university law school are admitted to the bar upon their diplomas, and require of all such graduates to pass the state bar examinations," in *Law School Administration General Subject Files*, 11/1/2, Box 10, folder marked "Misc. legislation affecting the law school."

75. C. B. Bird to Chairman of Assembly Judiciary Committee, April 15, 1915, copy to Richards in *Law School General Correspondence*, Box 18, File B; Richards to C. B. Bird, March 9, 1915, ibid.

76. Bill No. 840A was introduced into the Assembly on March 5, 1913.

77. Howard L. Smith, "Reform in the Requirements for Admission to the Bar in Wisconsin: A Rejoinder," *The American Law School Review* (May–June, 1914), p. 519. The charges levelled by Marquette's Richter were also answered by Robert L. Henry, dean of the University of North Dakota Law School, "Admission to the Bar on Diploma," ibid., pp. 522–527.

78. See the letter from A. F. Mason, editor of the *Review*, to Richards, May 8, 1914, *Law School General Correspondence*, Box 17, File M. An extended correspondence over the Richter and Smith articles can be found in this same file. Marquette was finally persuaded to drop the dispute, at least in the pages of the *Review*. Mason to Richards, September 18, 1914, ibid.

Incredibly, one year after writing the article that the Wisconsin law faculty found so objectionable, A. W. Richter applied for a position on the University Law School faculty, telling Richards that "other things being equal, I believe there are some reasons which might make it advantageous for your school to have me on its faculty." Richter to Richards, November 9, 1915, *Law School General Correspondence*, Box 19, File R. Richards replied that there were no openings at present. Richards to Richter, November 19, 1915, ibid.

79. Although the letters that passed between the two men were polite, Dean Schoetz clearly thought that he was not accorded the respect that was due him. In a draft of a speech given to the state bar association, Schoetz complained: "I do not know why the secretary of this association in his report of the proceedings always refers to Mr. Richards as Dean and to me as Mr. although I have been a Dean . . . for the past ten years. . . . As for me, it means nothing, but as for the school of law I represent, it does mean some-

thing." See the speech prepared by Schoetz sometime in 1924 located in the *Miscellaneous Records and Correspondence* of the school in the Marquette University Archives. Richards did nothing to allay the Dean's feelings because he always addressed him in letters as "Dear Schoetz." Schoetz, for his part, always addressed Richards as "Dean."

80. Jerold S. Auerbach, "Enmity and Amity: Law Teachers and Practitioners, 1900–1922," *Perspectives in American History*, 5 (1971), pp. 574–575. See also Auerbach's *unEqual Justice: Lawyers and Social Change in Modern America* (New York, 1976), for an elaboration of these themes. The essay, "Enmity and Amity," however, is often more detailed on the relationship between professors and practitioners and remains valuable.

81. Harry S. Richards, "Progress in Legal Education," *AALS Proceedings* (1915), p. 63.

82. Quoted in Auerbach, "Enmity and Amity," pp. 579–580.

83. Ibid., pp. 585–586.

84. *WSBA Reports*, Vol. 10 (1914), p. 106. The lawyer was not identified.

85. Christian Doerfler, "President's Address," *WSBA Reports*, Vol. 11 (1915), pp. 70–71; "Committee on Amendment of the Law," ibid., pp. 21–48.

86. Ibid., pp. 57–58. Smith was either Charles C. of Superior or Charles Foster of Rhinelander.

87. "Report of the Committee on Legal Education," ibid., pp. 11–15. Howard L. Smith of the University Law School proposed a resolution which supported an increase in the "general educational qualifications" of applicants. E. E. Brossard, a Madison lawyer, opposed the resolution. He believed that "a man who is able to pass the [bar] examination" should be admitted to the profession. The resolution was adopted by a vote of eleven to nine, a figure which suggests the low degree of intensity with which practitioners viewed Richards' recommendations. Ibid., p. 48.

88. *WSBA Reports*, Vol. 12 (1916–18), p. 55, and for similar remarks, see p. 63.

89. "Report of Committee on Legal Education," and following discussion, ibid., pp. 17–39; ibid., 1917, pp. 194–206.

Richards not only had to contend with lawyers' suspicion of the University Law School; he also faced general resistance from lawyers who believed that the University itself was an elitist institution. At the 1923 WSBA session a lawyer from Watertown complained that in the past year three hundred sixty-six students were dropped from the University and that an additional eight hundred dropped out. "It is time something was done along that line. I know that the average student from the average high school cannot successfully attend the University the first year. You don't hear it at home. They feel disgraced when they are dropped out, and they have some ailments, one thing or the other." Ibid., Vol. 14 (1922–23), pp. 64–65.

90. *WSBA Reports*, Vol. 12 (1916–18), p. 206, 400–403; ibid., Vol. 13 (1919–21) , pp. 16. 382–386. The Committee on Legal Education submitted no report in 1920. For background on the ABA Report, see: Stevens, "The American Law School," pp. 449–464; and Auerbach, *unEqual Justice*, pp. 102–129.

Chapter Seven

1. *WSBA Reports*, Vol. 14 (1922–23), pp. 24–26, 47–64.

2. Ibid.

3. Alfred Zantzinger Reed, *Training for the Public Profession of the Law*, The Carnegie Foundation for the Advancement of Teaching, Bulletin Number 15 (Boston, 1921), pp. 416–418; Jerold S. Auerbach, *unEqual Justice: Lawyers and Social Change in Modern America* (New York, 1976), p. 118.

4. Auerbach, *unEqual Justice*, p. 118.

5. *WSBA Reports,* Vol. 9 (1910), p. 37.

6. Jerome J. Foley, "Practice of Law by Non-Lawyers," *WSBA Reports,* Vol. 18 (1928), pp. 57–63; Charles L. Aarons, "The Practice of Law by Non-Lawyers: By Ambulance Chasers and Claim Adjusters," ibid., pp. 70–78.

7. Interview with Claude D. Stout, Palmyra, Wisconsin, May 19, 1969; Stout to author, November 11, 1969.

8. See C. B. Bird, "Address," *WSBA Reports,* Vol. 11 (1915) pp. 270–282; "Report of Committee on Unauthorized Practice of the Law," ibid., Vol. 22 (1932), pp. 22–33; Dean Lloyd K. Garrison, "Experience of Other States with Incorporated Bars," ibid., Vol. 23. (1933), pp. 40–51; "Report of Committee on Unauthorized Practice of the Law," ibid., Vol. 24 (1934), pp. 60–67; and "Report of Committee on Unified Bar," ibid., pp. 260–286.

9. "Committee on Qualifications of the Bar," *WSBA Reports,* Vol. 20 (1930), p. 122. Practitioners themselves probably found it easier to conceive and respond to the problem of bar membership in economic rather than ethical terms. The Committee noted that it had in the past year sent fifty letters to prominent lawyers in the state asking about the problems associated with qualifications for the bar, "particularly from the moral or character point of view." Only eleven lawyers replied and only three offered constructive suggestions.

10. *Marquette University Law School Bulletin,* 1916–17, p. 4.

11. Schoetz to Ralph W. Aigler, Secretary/Treasurer, AALS, May, 1923, *Marquette Law School Miscellaneous Records and Correspondence.*

12. "Statement of Marquette Law School's Status in the Council on Legal Education of the American Bar Association," ibid.

13. Ibid. President Fox's letter to John B. Sanborn, Secretary of the Council, can be found on p. 5 of the report together with a brief summary of Sanborn's reply. On plans to reorganize and reopen the night school see, Schoetz to Aigler, May 1923; and Schoetz to A. Z. Reed, Nov. 4, 1925. The latter correspondence is in the minutes of the faculty meeting of November 12, 1925, ibid.

14. Schoetz to Walter D. Corrigan, June 17, 1918, in *Marquette Law School Miscellaneous Records and Correspondence.*

15. Minutes of the faculty meeting, December 10, 1925; President Magee to Francis X. Swietlik, May 29, 1935 and Swietlik's reply, June 5, 1935, ibid. According to Swietlik only one faculty member "was interested in that work" and he was willing to cooperate with the ruling.

16. *Laws of Wisconsin,* 1933, Chapter 60, pp. 231–232. A year by year account of this protracted controversy over the diploma privilege would be repetitious. Those interested in the course of the battle should consult the *Law School Administration General Subject Files,* Box 10, Files marked "Marquette Bill," in the University of Wisconsin Archives; and the clippings folder in the Marquette Law School Records, UNIV/A-11/Box 15, Marquette University Archives.

17. *Milwaukee Journal,* October 19, 1939, in clipping folder, ibid.

18. C. H. Herlache to Oliver S. Rundell, October 17, 1930, *Law School General Correspondence,* Box 30, File H–J.

19. "Report of the Dean of the Law School for the Academic Year, 1932–33," p. 6.

20. Quoted in William Twining, *Karl Llewellyn and the Realist Movement* (London, 1973), p. 17.

21. Jerold S. Auerbach, "Enmity and Amity: Law Teachers and Practitioners, 1900–1922," *Perspectives in American History,* 5 (1971), p. 553.

22. William R. Vance, "The Ultimate Function of the Teacher of Law," *AALS Proceedings* (1911), p. 28.

23. Harry S. Richards, "Response," ibid., pp. 4–6.

24. H. L. Smith to Richards, January 31, 1910, *Law School General Correspondence*, Box 11, File S. The three-line emphasis is in the original.

25. John R. Commons, *Myself* (Madison, Wisconsin: University of Wisconsin Press paper edition, 1964), pp. 110–111.

26. Merle Curti and Vernon Castensen, *The University of Wisconsin: A History* (2 volumes: Madison, Wisconsin, 1949), Vol. 1, pp. 181, 20–21.

27. G. D. Jones to Richards, May 16, 1910, *Law School General Correspondence*, Box 10, File I–J.

28. Quoted in Auerbach, "Enmity and Amity," p. 50.

29. Roscoe Pound, "The Need of a Sociological Jurisprudence," *Green Bag*, 19 (1907), pp. 610–611. See also Pound, "The Scope and Purpose of Sociological Jurisprudence," *Harvard Law Review*, 25 (1912), pp. 140–168, 489–516. My understanding of this view and its links to legal realism has benefited from Wilfred E. Rumble, Jr., *American Legal Realism: Skepticism, Reform, and the Judicial Process* (Ithaca, New York, 1968) and especially from William Twining, *Karl Llewellyn and the Realist Movement* (London, 1973).

30. Robert Stevens "The American Law School," *Perspectives in American History*, 5 (1971), pp. 470–480.

31. Ibid., p. 470. The classic study of these curriculum developments still remains, Brainerd Currie, "The Materials of Law Study," Parts 1 and 2, *Journal of Legal Education*, (1951), pp. 331–383, and Part 3, ibid., 8 (1955), pp. 1–78, especially Part 3.

32. Currie, "The Materials of Law Study," Part 3, pp. 9–10, footnote 25.

33. Twining, pp. 24, 38.

34. Stevens, pp. 480–481, 504–511.

35. Ibid., p. 529.

36. Lloyd K. Garrison, "A Survey of the Wisconsin Bar," *Wisconsin Law Review*, 10 (1934–35), pp. 141, 133–137, 147.

37. For a more extensive discussion of these issues, see my essay review, "Professions in Process: Doctors and Teachers in American Culture," *History of Education Quarterly*, 15 (Summer 1975), pp. 185–199.

38. Morton J. Horwitz, "The Emergence of an Instrumental Conception of American Law, 1780–1820," *Perspectives in American History*, 5 (1971), pp. 316, 320, 288, 326, 287.

39. Roscoe Pound, *The Formative Era of American Law* (Boston, 1938); Charles Haar, ed., *The Golden Age of American Law* (New York, 1965).

40. Lawrence M. Friedman, *A History of American Law* (New York, 1973), pp. 99–100, 118–119, 134. See also James Willard Hurst's elegant little volume, *Law and the Changing Conditions of Freedom in the Nineteenth Century United States* (Madison, Wisconsin, 1967), especially chapter one, "The Release of Energy."

41. Friedman, quoting Pound, pp. 132, 332.

42. Quoted in Friedman, p. 283.

43. Ibid., p. 333.

44. Ibid., p. 332–333.

Index

211

CH